# A Sweet and Hopeful People

## A Story of Abingdon Baptist Church 1649 - 2011

**Revised Edition**

**Michael G. Hambleton**

The earliest known mention of the Baptists of Abingdon
is in a letter written by Thomasine Pendarves,
who refers to them in these words:

**"We have a sweet hopefull people amongst us that wait upon God, and have fellowship one with another".**

'Nourished by past wisdom
that sticks to us still.'

(liturgy broadcast from St. Giles, Edinburgh)

First published: 2000
Revised edition published: August 2011

Published by Trojan Museum Trust Publishing.
5 St Johns Close,
Fyfield,
Oxfordshire,
OX13 5LP, UK.
www.trojanmuseumtrust.org

Printed by Catford Print Centre.

ISBN 978-0-956222-12-1

## Preface to First Edition

As I offer this short history of the Baptist Church in Abingdon I am disconcerted both by the scholarship of those who have already published learned articles on this subject and by the haste in which I have had to do my research and rush into print. Daniel Turner, one of my greatest predecessors in the Abingdon ministry, wrote of the apparent necessity for all authors to apologise for their work - but none more so than myself. The book has had to be both researched and written during a sabbatical of just six weeks. This allowed little or no time for original research, so I am indebted to those historians, ancient and modern, whose work I have scanned and whose names will appear in the references at the end of this booklet. But I will take to heart the admonition contained in a delightful Commonplace Book which resides among the Abingdon archives in the Angus Library of Regents Park College, Oxford. Composed, perhaps, by one of the younger members of the 'audience' of our church sometime in the eighteenth century, whose name might otherwise not have received a mention, and written in a slightly shaky copperplate:

> ‘Rebecca Boyce you write too fast,
> I think you write in such a haste;
> if you would write more slow
> I think you would much better do.’

Nevertheless, this short history is needed. The vast majority of scholarship that has been poured into Abingdon Baptist history has concentrated only on the first twenty five years. The story of the remaining three hundred and twenty five years is worth telling.

Hopefully this book will provide a framework for further research, so that one day, writing ‘more slow’, someone will produce the major History that the Abingdon Church deserves.

Michael G. Hambleton, Abingdon 2000.

## Preface to the Revised Edition

The eleven years which have elapsed since the writing of the short history of Abingdon Baptist Church, of which this is a revision, have been, for me, years of retirement. This has given me time to develop my interest in the history of the town and especially its Baptist Church. Invitations to speak on the subject and involvement in the mounting of a major exhibition by the Ock Street Project Group of the Abingdon and District Archaeological and Historical Society, have stimulated deeper study and introduced me to an ever widening circle of local historians who have shared their expertise with great generosity. With every passing year I have grown less satisfied with the book I had produced in such a rush. My copy had become riddled with marginal corrections and inserted additional pages. There were too many missing references and it lacked an index. Its early pages seemed to assume the emergence of the church fully formed in the shape of what gradually formed decades later. Its later pages failed to mention several aspects of the ministry of the church which should have been recorded.

So, when in 2010, the Church Secretary invited me to produce a revision, which might encourage the church in its current attempt to raise the money to extend its buildings, I was in a mood to accept. The result is not that 'major History' that I called for in the first preface. I am not equipped in mind or health for that. But I offer a fresh look at the life of a church which began, not as a little adult, emerging fully formed and clothed from Abingdon's womb, like those portraits of Elizabethan and Stuart children looking like miniature adults - tiny, but weighted down in small yet adult clothing. Rather, we find a very noisy, and to some people's sensibilities, rather ugly and smelly, new arrival, conceived in the recent wars and born at a moment of political turmoil, who would, one day, as they all do, grow into a perfectly respectable member of society, but for the moment spelt trouble - a cuckoo, perhaps, in St. Helen's Church's nest.

Unlike its predecessor, the present work has no special Abingdon anniversary to celebrate. But I am conscious of two quatercentenaries of great significance. 1611 saw the publication of the King James version of the Bible which eventually proved so central to the reformed churches, and 1611 was very probably the year when that small company of exiles, under the leadership of Thomas Helwys, returned from Holland to establish the first Baptist church in England. In a paper in the *Baptist Quarterly* of October 2009 Henk Bakker makes an inspired connection between the group of Puritans, which included Helwys, setting out from Gainsborough in 1608 to cross the stormy North Sea to Amsterdam, and the launching of the infant Moses in his rush cradle 'floated on providential waters'. In the Sinhala Bible, the word we would translate as 'manger', in the nativity story, is translated 'little boat'. In my lifetime I have experienced two weeks on the stormy North Sea, in November, in a Tall Ship, and two years in a Sri Lankan village at a time of bitter civil war. Such experiences brought me close to those from whom I was otherwise separated by time and culture. This story of Abingdon Baptist Church is not the whole or the one and only story. History is not like that. But I offer *my* story, based upon the experience of ministering among them for nine years and being part of that greater company of all faiths who launch themselves on providential waters.

Michael Hambleton, Abingdon 2011.

**For Stella**

## Acknowledgements

I am again grateful to Abingdon Baptist Church, past and present, for inspiring this book and enabling it to be published. My contribution has been the text. Tony Valente, church archivist, has laid it out, formed the index and prepared it for printing. He has visited me regularly, acted, at times, as an unpaid research assistant and used his expertise to produce or enhance diagrams and illustrations. Further photography and similar enhancement has been supplied by Jon Spiller. My son, David Hambleton, of Trojan Museum Trust Publishing, has advised and taken the book through its printing and binding processes. My thanks to this small but vital team.

Once again I am indebted to the staff of the Angus Research Library of Regent's Park College, Oxford; the College Librarian Emma Walsh and her Library Assistant Emily Burgoyne, and archivist Julian Lock, for freely granting me access to their archive and research facilities. I have benefited greatly from the number of scholars upon whose works I have drawn and who are acknowledged in the text or footnotes. I thank those who have granted permission for extensive quotation or for the use of copyright images, among the latter are Sarah Wearne, archivist to Abingdon School, The British Library, The Abingdon Town Council and Ordnance Survey. I apologise to any I may have missed and would be pleased to hear from such and correct any future edition. I wish to particularly mention those scholars whom I have been able to speak with personally over the years and who have shared their wisdom with me, especially Manfred Brod, Roger Hayden, Paul Fiddes and Larry Kreitzer. Others have loaned photos, responded to correspondence, written reports or allowed me to draw upon their memories.

Judy White and Sella Hambleton have done the proof-reading.

Finally, I am greatly indebted to my wife, Stella, still the only qualified historian of the family, whose interest, strength and care have made this revision possible.

Michael G. Hambleton.

# Contents



# Figures

## Introduction

# A reconstruction of the most exciting day in the life of Abingdon Baptist Church, to date: [1]

It is the year 1656. The day is Thursday the 2nd of October. George Allom had slept late in his room in the Lamb Inn - one of the largest of several coaching inns for which the old county town of Abingdon was famous. It stood facing the sheep market, on the site that was later to be occupied by the Regal Cinema. But in the mid seventeenth century such unthinkable technology lay far into the future. Nevertheless, what was about to happen would have been considered good material for a Hollywood B movie 300 years later. He was woken by the sound of horses being reined to a halt in the cobbled yard beneath his window. Immediately the inn was in uproar. He was pulling on his breeches when the door of his room was flung open and a soldier ordered him against the wall. After a quick examination of his few belongings, the cavalryman threw George's papers and precious copy of the Bible into his hawking bag and told him they were confiscated as evidence. The soldier then demanded to know his name and place of habitation before moving on to search other rooms. Confused, frightened and with an even greater dislike than before for Cromwell's regime, George watched the three troopers gather in the courtyard - his were not the only possessions they had confiscated. He joined his fellows in the inn yard and they demanded of the soldiers by what authority or order they were confiscating their goods. The troopers responded by putting their hands to the hilts of their swords - 'there was their order: to which some of us said, that if they could produce no other order, a highwayman, demanding our purses, could produce as good a commission for his action as they did'. At this point a Lieutenant Barker, who was in charge of the party of troopers, rode into the yard. When they demanded to see his orders, he lost his temper and began riding among the protesters, beating them with his cane.

George had travelled up from Exeter and this was his third day in the

[1] The details of this reconstruction are drawn mainly from three sources: a) *The Complaining Testimony of some....of Sions Children,* 1656. For a transcription of this tract see L J. Kreitzer, *Seditious Sectaryes,* 2006, vol.1. p. 323ff., b) William Hughes, *Munster and Abingdon,* 1657, c) B.R. White, *John Pendarves, the Calvinistic Baptists and the Fifth Monarchy, 1974 (reprint from the Baptist Quarterly, vol. XXV no.6).*

town. He had come to represent his church - their 'messenger' they called him - at the funeral of the young pastor of the Abingdon Baptists. The burial was two days past. That had been a sad day. The Abingdon pastor, John Pendarves, had been well known in the Exeter church and indeed throughout the West Country generally. He had been present at the Western Association meetings of the Baptist churches, in Wells earlier this year, and in Chard this time last year.[2] In fact Pendarves had quite a reputation in the West Country and was emerging as one of the leaders of the Baptist cause nation-wide. He had been Pastor of the thriving Abingdon church; widely respected in Berkshire where he was active in establishing an association of churches and encouraging fellowship among churches as widely scattered as Hertfordshire, Buckinghamshire, Oxfordshire, Berkshire and Wiltshire and building strong links with churches in Somerset, Devon and his native Cornwall, even, it was rumoured, invited by General Fleetwood, no less, Cromwell's son-in-law and Lord Deputy in Ireland, to work in Ireland. They had built such hopes on him. And now, at the age of 34, 'in the dispensation of God', he had been taken from them.

They had buried him in the new burying place at the town's west end in Ock Street His death had left such a hole in their Association life and mission that they needed time together for prayer. And so they had agreed to spend two or three days in prayer and debate - all thirty-three of them who had travelled to Abingdon, from Totnes, Dartmouth, Exeter, Cornwall, Hull, North Walsham, Norwich, London and Oxford, plus of course, many of the leading members of the Abingdon church. That first day they were crammed into brother Mayo's home, Pendarves' widow, Thomasine, and other women of the church busy with the food and ale.

And how they had prayed! And how God had blessed them! For they had gathered from such distances, as it was later to be recorded, not simply to perform, 'the last office of love', but also to entreat earnestly of the Lord, that he would be pleased to own the present meeting, that the light which he hath given in amongst the body of his people inquiring after his minde and will in this day, might be so gathered into one as that we might be able to read his minde and will, together with our duty, on this dark and gloomy day. And that he

[2] *Association Records of the Particular Baptists of England, Wales and Ireland to 1660*, Pt.3 The Abingdon Association. 1971. Edit. B.R.White.

would pour forth a plentiful portion of his Spirit upon the remnant of his faithful ones, whereby they may be enabled to prosecute his minde and will so made known unto them'.[3] And as they had waited on God in this way, so the report continued, they experienced 'such tokens of his presence, by his smiling countenance through our Lord Jesus Christ, such quickenings of his Spirit, such melting and brokenness of heart, such tastes of his peace and joy, such renewings of first love, such endearing of saints to each other, such longings after the glory of God, and groanings for the prosperity of Sion, as some ancient professors affirmed they seldom experienced the like'.[4]

George Allom had returned to his room in the Lamb last night exhausted but spiritually renewed and concerned to rest well before the meeting reconvened on the morrow. He had placed his notes, which must later be written into his report to the Exeter church, beneath his Bible and slept until the three troopers, alerted by a fourth who, in plain clothes, had spent the night in the inn 'as a spy, to take notice and give information of what he could hear and see done among us', broke in upon them.

It was later to emerge that The Lord Protector, Oliver Cromwell, fearing that the gathering in Abingdon for the funeral of Pendarves, might spark off a Fifth Monarchy inspired rebellion, had stationed Major General Bridges with eight troops of cavalry seven miles away in Wallingford to keep an eye on things.

George, outraged by the confiscation of his bag and belongings, made his way along the street to brother Mayo's house, where yesterday's meetings had been held, only to find two soldiers at the door preventing entry. That was when tempers flared and, not for the first or last time, over reaction by the authorities turned a peaceful gathering into violent confrontation. That, at any rate, is how the Baptists saw it and made the basis for their later *Complaining Testimony*.

---

[3] *Complaining Testimony* op. cit. p.1.

[4] ibid. p.2

*Figure 1 Abingdon Market Place - St Nicolas Church*

Barred from the house, the meeting moved to the Market Place where they made use of the Cryer's pulpit. After a prayer, 'our brother Jones of Longworth in Barkshire, an ancient grave Christian, who was formerly persecuted by the bishops, proceeded with a word of exhortation'. But then while a man called Allen from the Oxford church was speaking the soldiers began to break up the meeting. Tempers rose, rash words were shouted. It was claimed that John Tomkins of Abingdon had challenged a soldier to a duel and had made wild boasts that this gathering at Abingdon could count on the support of thirty thousand others. Another was heard to shout, 'we are not for Cromwell's kingdome'. These allegations were made by one W. Hughes, of Hinton, Berks, an old enemy of non-conformity, in a book rushed out three months later entitled *Munster and Abingdon* which compared the 'tumult late at Abingdon' with the excesses of the Anabaptists in Munster a hundred years before. The Baptists had previously published *The Complaining Testimony* putting their side of the incident. In it they described John Tomkins, who was to become virtual pastor of the church, as 'an elder of the church at Abingdon, being well known for his grace, cautious and very sparing of his expressions at all times'.

*Figure 2 Abingdon Market Place - County Hall*

But to return to the 'tumult', at this point more troops, led by Major General Bridges himself galloped over the bridge from Wallingford and, as the visitors dispersed to their inns all that could be found were arrested. After interrogation by the Major General, in the New Inn in the Market Place, all but five were released. The five were imprisoned in Windsor Castle, but were released by the time Hughes wrote his account two months later.

*Figure 3 A 17th Century Troop of Horse*

We have no information as to how this momentous day ended so what follows is entirely conjecture. But four of the thirty-nine who put their names to *The Complaining Testimony* came from the West Country. Let us assume that all four returned home together:

Staying only long enough to approve the draft of *The Complaining Testimony*, so that he could add his signature, George Allom made his way westwards. We can picture him travelling in the company of the three other messengers from the distant West Country. Beneath the high elms of the Vale of the White Horse, did he ride, side by side, with Richard Steed of Dartmouth? The minister of the Dartmouth church was Robert Steed, who was an early Baptist at Abingdon before moving to his present post. Dartmouth was the home town of Thomasine Pendarves, now a young widow. There were other Steeds in the Abingdon church, William and Dorothy, who both lived into the 1690's and a Richard Steed was in membership at Longworth.[5] The Baptist family in the 1650's must have enjoyed many such family ties. Then in the evenings, resting in the inns where they stopped each night after completing another thirty five or so miles, George would have talked with Captain Francis Langden. He was a Cornishman, with the furthest to travel. He had sat as M.P. for Cornwall in the Barebones Parliament of 1653. Described as a firebrand and among the most extreme Fifth Monarchists among those who had attended Pendarves' funeral, he would surely have used every opportunity to impress upon George the need for greater political and even militant, involvement. And then there was the fourth member of the party - Henry Forty of Totnes. He had been a close friend of Pendarves, seven years his senior. As he and George spoke together of the young pastor, they would have encouraged each other to press on with his vision of political and moral reform and establishing closer ties and union among the emerging Baptist churches across the country. Four

[5] John Stanley, *The Church in the Hop Garden* 1934 pp 79, 241.

years later, Henry Forty would begin his twelve year sentence in Exeter gaol - a prisoner of conscience. After his release he would eventually find his way back to Abingdon, to serve the church there as pastor for seventeen years. George may have lost his notes and his precious Bible, but what a story he was taking back to the young church in Exeter.

In a paper by Dr. B. R. White, from which much of the foregoing material is drawn, he offers this conclusion: 'On the whole it seems that the soldiers behaved with some restraint: it is clear that some people were knocked about but no serious injury appears to have been done to anyone present. For the friends of John Pendarves it may be said that there was no suggestion that any of them were armed or equipped for any kind of violence. If the outcome of the deliberations at Abingdon can be judged from what happened, or rather, failed to happen, afterwards those who favoured violence against the Protectorate were a minority which included few if any of the local Baptists'.[6] But if Dr. White concludes that John Pendarves and many of those who came together for his funeral, though having some sympathy with the militant views of the Fifth Monarchists, posed no immediate threat to Cromwell's regime, Stevie Davies, with wit and biting sarcasm, encourages us to beware. She sees evidence that behind the innocence of the *Complaining Testimony* lie trails of conspiracy which justify Cromwell's wisdom in placing his cavalrymen just seven miles down the road.[7]

---

[6] B.R. White, op. cit. p.266.

[7] Stevie Davies. *Unbridled Spirits* 1998 pp 156-157

# Chapter 1
# The Seventeenth Century

Civil war is a time when law and order break down. While it lasts, the organised life of a nation is thrown into confusion. The establishment has been challenged. The rebels will no longer accept its rule. If the rebellion is crushed, then the old order is re-established, though it may never be quite the same again. But if the rebels succeed, then everything is in the melting pot. From the highest courts of the land to the social and moral niceties which govern everyday life, everything is open to question; to re-adjustment; to change.

This was the situation in the British Isles in the fourth decade of the seventeenth century - the decade which gave birth to what today is known as parliamentary democracy and the decade which also gave birth to what today is known as Abingdon Baptist Church. But if we speak of birth, we have to remember that before birth there is the period of gestation during which the foetus only slowly takes the form of the child that is seen and handled at the birth. So it was with the embryonic Baptist church in Abingdon. It drew upon its political and devotional environment; the scriptures; the numerous patterns of worship and church order that were challenging the established ways. It was influenced by religious dissent from the continent of Europe and from its home-grown John Wycliff and others. And from it all emerged, as from the womb, something both recognisable and yet new; the child of the adult yet to be.

**The origins of Abingdon Baptist Church.**

We begin this account in Abingdon in the year 1649. The town, like the nation as a whole, is in a sorry state. Nearly eight years of civil war and a decade of bad harvests, have left its townspeople traumatised, bereaved and impoverished, while its buildings have taken a battering from royalist artillery and from the enthusiasm of puritan iconoclasts. But the war is over. The king, Charles I, has been be-headed. The victorious parliamentary regiments are being disbanded and are leaving the town. Abingdon soldiers are returning from their barracks in Oxford and from further afield. There are still just the two churches. The old feud continues between the Mayott party favouring St. Nicolas' Church, which still clung to the liturgy introduced by Archbishop Laud, and the Tesdales active in St. Helen's, now reformed along Calvinistic, Presbyterian lines.[8]

Yet it is in this year, 1649, that we read the first mention of a new congregation which identifies itself as Baptists. Just as the first witnesses to the resurrection of Jesus were women, so it is two women whose written words have survived the centuries to give us the first mention of the church whose story this book will tell. They appear in a tract written by Elizabeth Poole. Known as 'the Abingdon Prophetess', Elizabeth was a daughter of a poor London family and had joined the church of William Kiffin - one of the most influential of the Baptist ministers of the day. In the late 1640's she began to be recognised for her prophetic gifts - the ability to apply the Scriptures and her own devotional understanding of them to the great affairs of state. Her gifts were acknowledged at the very highest level and she was used as a sort of consultant by the Council of State which met in Whitehall and consisted of the generals and leading divines whose task, after the king's defeat in the Civil Wars, was to decide the fate of King Charles and to work on a constitution by which the nation would be governed after the end of the monarchy. She was obviously greatly valued while her prophesies conformed with the broad views of the Council, but with one issue she found her prophesies increasingly out of step. She believed that God would never sanction the execution of the king. Kings were called and anointed by God and however they failed, their life was sacrosanct. The Council believed she was wrong and should be silenced.[9] Perhaps it was this dispute which decided her to leave London. We do not know why she came to Abingdon. Did she already have a friend in Thomasine Pendarves? But we know that by the winter of 1648/9 she was part of the Baptist community in Abingdon. It appears that William Kiffin, her former pastor, had written to John Pendarves asking him to denounce Elizabeth Poole publicly and to expel her from the church. John did not receive the letter. His wife opened it first and decided not to pass it to her husband. Instead, Thomasine Pendarves added a letter of support to the tract which Elizabeth was about to publish. The title of that tract was *An Alarum of War given to the army, and to the High Court of*

---

[8] For the historical background to this and an excellent revue of the situation in Abingdon in the 1640's, see Manfred Brod, *Religious conflict in seventeenth century Abingdon*, pub. in *Aspects of Abingdon's Past*, 2004. A St. Nicolas Church publication.
[9] The fore-going account of Elizabeth Poole is based on notes of a lecture by Manfred Brod, delivered at Rewley House, Oxford, in 2001.

*Justice...foretelling the judgements of God ready to fall on them, for disobeying the word of the Lord, in taking away the life of the KING.* Its publication date was March 1649. The added letter from Thomasine was headed, *A Friend to truth and of the Authors to the Reader.*[10] It acknowledges Kiffin's letter and justifies her decision to keep it from the Abingdon church with these words:

> For though, blessed be the Father, we have a sweet hopefull people amongst us, who wait upon God and have fellowship one with another, yet whether they may digest such things as you write of, I really question; therefore it would be unfaithfulness in me, if I, apprehending an evil to them, or any other, should not, as much as in me lies, prevent it; and this I shall do, by detaining the letter till further manifestation from God what to do with it.

This not only speaks of the church as 'a sweet and hopefull people' already gathered in March 1649, but also gives an insight of a strong and courageous woman, ready to risk the wrath of the mightiest in the land, as well as that of her husband, for the sake of justice and the peace of her church. Thomasine was the daughter of Thomas Newcomen, a wealthy and devout Baptist of Dartmouth. She was now the wife of twenty-seven year old John Pendarves. John, also from the West-country,[11] had graduated from Exeter College, Oxford, seven years earlier.[12] He had then served as chaplain in the parliamentary naval ship *The Eighth Whelp* [13] and then had come to Abingdon in c. 1644/5 as a chaplain in the New Model Army's 7th Regiment of Foot commanded by Col. Thomas Rainborowe.[14] Finding St. Helen's vacant, he set himself up as vicar there and later

[10] E. Poole, *An Alarum of War.....* British Library 8/m E555(32) London 1649.
[11] Born in Crowan, Cornwall c. 1622.
[12] John, and his elder brother Ralph were students at Exeter College. Both were matriculated 9th Feb. 1638. John graduated BA 3rd March 1642. L.J. Kreitzer, Baptist Quarterly vol. 43 Jan. 2009 p 53.
[13] So Larry Kreitzer in an as yet unpublished monograph - used with permission of the author.
[14] Larry Kreitzer *The Fifth Monarchist John Pendarves Chaplain to Colonel Thomas Rainborowe's Regiment of Foot (1645-7.* BQ Vol 43 April 2009 p 112.

was recognised as such by the church authorities. In 1644 and 1645 the chamberlain's accounts record, 'Mr. Pendarves the minister for his pains £5.'[15] He appears to have been a powerful and popular preacher, sharing the Calvinistic and puritan stance of so many in the army.

*Figure 4 Church of St Helen, Abingdon*

[15] Abingdon Chamberlain's Accounts, Berks Record Office, AF Ac3 1644-5.

*Figure 5 St Helen's Pulpit, 1630.*

From 1648 Pendarves became the beneficiary of a bequest by a Mr. Richard Wrigglesworth, of Marcham. He left £800 to found a lectureship - a weekly lecture to be given at Marcham in the summer and St. Helen's in the winter, with the proviso that, as long as he stayed in the Abingdon area this should be given by Mr. Pendarves. In June 1649 John Pendarves became vicar of the parish church at Wantage and from Christmas Day, John Tickell was vicar of St. Helen's. But the lectureship arrangement would have continued after his move to Wantage. Pendarves and Tickell would have had much in common and probably appreciated each other's ministry, though at a later stage, as Pendarves became disillusioned with Presbyterianism and wrote to that effect in his *Arrowes against Babylon* (1656), John Tickell condemned Pendarves' publication in his answering pamphlet:

*Church-rules proposed to the church in Abingdon* (1656). On Sundays in Wantage and more certainly at his weekly Tuesday lecture, at Marcham in the summer and in St. Helen's in the winter, Pendarves was drawing audiences in their hundreds.[16]

Yet what of that other gathering, which included Elizabeth Poole, Thomasine Pendarves and, presumably John, her husband? It appears to be a proto-Baptist fellowship that was separate from St. Helen's. From evidence that I shall detail later, it appealed to those of a 'spiritual' inclination - less interested in church order than in responding to the Holy Spirit's influence within and upon them. This included an understanding of the Scriptures as individually revealed to each member of the fellowship and often resulting in the gift of prophesy. This was that 'sweet and hopefull people' who had 'fellowship one with another'. They could well have pre-dated, by some years, the arrival in the town of the Pendarves' family. It is fascinating to conjecture what influence this group was having on John and Thomasine, and vice versa. While remaining a distinct group of believers, it was probably caught up in attending John's ministry in St. Helen's and, from 1648, his weekly lectures in Marcham or St. Helen's. Then, around the year 1650, John's personal disappointment with the lack of reform in the Anglican church reached the point that he was considering separation from it. Did he offer his full-time services to that separate fellowship, or did they approach him with the possibility? To become pastor to that fellowship would solve both his need for financial support and his need for an ongoing ministry.

From 1650 John Pendarves was pastor of an increasingly organised Baptist church in Abingdon. In his entry on John and Thomasine Pendarves in *The Dictionary of National Biography*, Dr. Manfred Brod attributes the founding of The Abingdon Association to John Pendarves and Benjamin Cox, and John was certainly active in this and other Associations, especially in the Midlands and the West country, for the remaining four years of his short life. The emphasis of his ministry was upon evangelism and the building up of truly reformed churches according to the understanding of the Calvinistic Baptists as set out in *The Baptist Confession* (1644). His writings suggest disappointment with the Commonwealth, believing its reforms

[16] For above biography of Thomasine and John Pendarves see Brod's entry in *The Dictionary of National Biography.*

of church and state had not been taken far enough. And as disappointment grew, Pendarves courted those radicals, known as fifth-monarchy men, who were calling for its overthrow in favour of direct rule by King Jesus through his saints. Their strange name reflected their millenarian theology, but their danger to the establishment was not purely a *religious* challenge. Fifth monarchy thinking had a challenging political agenda - a programme of social reform which included the abolition of tithes, the purging of the clergy, reform of the law, schools and universities. The taxation system was to be over-hauled and laws enacted to encourage biblical morality in individuals and society.[17] Such views were widely held and Pendarves' writings show sympathy with them, especially in the last year or so of his life. The fear was that they could lead to further civil war. Would Pendarves have encouraged an armed rebellion? Dr. B. White argues[18] that the balance of evidence suggests he would not. I am inclined to the same conclusion.

***The pastor turn'd pope (1654).***

At this point I should like to use a document which throws much light upon the very early Baptist fellowship, both before and after the time John Pendarves became its pastor. It appears that an early member of the embryo church, John Atherton, disagreed with Pendarves on several issues of faith and practice. Finally he absented himself from the fellowship. After some time representatives were appointed by the church to visit him, to hear his grievances and encourage his return. When he still stayed away Pendarves visited him and when this achieved no change in the situation the church informed Mr. Atherton of his excommunication. Atherton saw this as a slight against his good character and demanded an opportunity to debate the issue with Pendarves in a public meeting, with the mayor and the town's burgesses present. On a cold evening in St. Helen's church in February or March 1653 this meeting took place. Atherton followed this up in1654 when he published a pamphlet in London stating his grievances and entitled *The Pastor turn'd Pope.*[19] In it he states that he had 'walked three years or thereabouts, with Mr. Pendarves and his company' before leaving them in August 1652. This is proof enough

---

[17] See Stevie Davies, *Unbridled Spirits* 1998, Women's Press pp. 158-9.

[18] B.W.White, *John Pendarves, The Calvinistic Baptists and the Fifth Monarchy, op. cit. pp. 266-7.*

[19] J. Atherton, *The Pastor turn'd Pope,* London 1654.

that the Baptist congregation, with John Pendarves as their pastor, had been in existence from 1650. But another remark in this pamphlet suggests an even earlier date for the church. Atherton claims that Pendarves denies any responsibility for the practice of his congregation of anointing the sick with oil, on the grounds that this happened 'before he was pastor and he did not approve of it'. This suggests that the congregation was in existence before Pendarves became its pastor, and possibly before he joined it as a member.

Most of this information was available to me in the writings of several authors when the book of which this is a revision was written in the year 2000. But since then I have had access to the full text and from this has come fascinating detail of these early Baptists including their first separate place of worship.

From the text of *The Pastor turn'd Pope,* the basic argument between the two Johns, Atherton and Pendarves, is one of authority, order and discipline within the life of a local church. Pendarves was moving from Presbyterianism, believing that it was not sufficiently reformed, to that model of the church found in the pages of the New Testament. Yet he retained its Calvinist doctrine and its belief in strong leadership. He appears to have been a good administrator and would have brought order into that Baptist fellowship which for years may have enjoyed a less structured existence. Atherton, in contrast, though he has a knowledge of the Scriptures which he regards as being as good as any man's, understands the *true* biblical church as a much simpler affair. He has no time for an organised church and believes that the Church has failed God in this way for the past fourteen hundred years. Therefore no pastors, teachers or other church officers are required. He argues for a spiritual relationship with God and with similarly minded people, in which God deals directly with one's soul; Spirit to spirit. I am left with the impression that at the heart of Atherton's dispute with Pendarves lay a personality clash. As Pendarves began to exercise his pastoral authority within the Baptist fellowship, and to bring order into what had been a fairly informal gathering, Atherton found his position impossible and absented himself. But when, four months later, he was publicly excommunicated, the fight was on and he would seek to exonerate himself equally publicly.

Yet something must have drawn him to this fellowship, back in 1649. Perhaps he had found several of its people of similar outlook to his own, including the minister of St. Helen's wife. In Dr. Manfred Brod's writings on the Bradfield group, near Reading, he refers to their faith as 'spiritualist'.[20] This is to be understood not in the sense of the later Spiritualism of the 19th century onwards, but as a mystical spirituality which seeks fellowship with like-minded people though without the structure of an institutionalised church. He links this with Familists and early Quakerism. And he shows that Thomasine Pendarves, wife of John, had correspondence with and possible fellowship with the leaders of this Bradfield group.[21] She was drawn to their use of prophesy, as perhaps her friend Elizabeth Poole may have been and others in the Abingdon fellowship including John Atherton. So are we to see the early Baptists of Abingdon as part of that 'primordial soup' of ideas which was slowly separating into the denominations of later English Christianity? And could Thomasine have been something of an embarrassment to her husband?

To return to the text of *The Pastor turn'd Pope,* a picture of what happened when these Baptists came together emerges:

- They have appointed a Pastor, other Church Officers and Teachers.
- 'They call themselves saints, as opposed to people of the world'
- The saints are said to be 'within', while others are 'without'.
- They refer to each other as brothers and sisters and also as believers,
- They say they obey Christ by being baptised and by baptising others,
- They break bread often, but will not share in communion with other Christians not baptised in their way,
- Some say they raise the dead, cleanse lepers and cast out devils etc,
- In these ways they seek to imitate the primitive churches;
- They occasionally anointed the sick with oil (but not after Pendarves became Pastor).
- Worship included confession and penance.

---

[20] M. Brod, *The Case of Reading,* 2006. p.106.

[21] These views expressed by M. Brod in a lecture delivered on 4 Feb. 2004.

- There was 'visiting'.
- There was a 'Stool of Repentance'.
- They were not against wearing rings and necklaces.
- They were 'more than' a hundred strong.

This information is scattered throughout the text but, brought together, gives an impression of the corporate life of the young church.

Also scattered about this somewhat convoluted document appear names of Atherton's contemporaries in the Baptist fellowship, Three men deputed to inform Atherton of his excommunication, late in September 1652, were J. Combes, Capt. Fox and John Tomkins. Later in the document Mr. Thomas Tisdale is mentioned, as the Baptist Atherton chose to communicate to Pendarves his wish for the public meeting to be in daylight, as he could no longer refer to his Bible in candle-light. He seems to have respect for this Mr. Tisdale - but then he was a chief Burgess of the town. He has less respect when he refers to Robert Steed and Henry Tomkins. Robert Steed was another preacher. He was a young man and soon to leave Abingdon to be pastor of the Baptist church in Dartmouth.

Henry Tomkins - a glover and preacher, was laughed at when he gave evidence to support Pendarves at the public meeting. Also mentioned are Richard Tyrol the linen draper, Lawrence Ambrose, Richard Lyvord, Widow Lathe and Francis White. The first membership roll of the church is dated 1748. But this trickle of names from the early 1650's will soon become a strong stream as other names are picked out of several other sources contemporary with the 17$^{th}$ century church. Their names form the early part of lists 1 and 2 in Appendix A.

John Atherton's *The Pastor turn'd Pope* is also the valued source of information concerning some of the very first meeting places of the Abingdon Baptists. Atherton reads to the public meeting a letter which he had sent to Pendarves in 1653. It seeks to answer, point by point, the accusations that Pendarves has brought against him. Then comes this passage:

> You charge me further with saying, I heard lyes in publike, and at the School-house: which is true enough; but all by you and your company. If you speak it to the end (as I conceive you do) that somewhat might reflect

> upon Mr. Tickle, Mr. Hanson knows that I told him at his house, that I never heard Mr. Tickle deliver anything but what I could close with him in it.

It is clear that this quotation speaks of three meeting places. He had heard lies 'in public and in the School-house'. 'In public' is in St. Helen's in this context, where he has often heard Pendarves preach and deliver lectures. But 'in the School-house' is somewhere quite different. From this and other places Atherton speaks of Pendarves ministry as being in the *public* setting of the parish church or in the *private* setting of the School-house. He doesn't use the word 'private' but implies this contrast when the School-house is mentioned. What and where is this School-house? It is the meeting place of Pendarves' company; his more than 100 strong Baptist fellowship. They meet in St. Helen's, with many others, for the Tuesday lectures in the winter months, but, one assumes, on Sundays they meet in private in the School-house. In 17$^{th}$ century Abingdon there were only four, or possibly five, likely places large enough to house a congregation of one hundred plus: the two churches, the Market House (County Hall), the School-room (what is known today as the Roysse Room) in Butchers Row (today's Bridge Street) and possibly the Old School in Stert Street. Of these five, the choice must be between the two school premises. Little is known of the Old School; not even if it was still standing in 1653. The local historian A.E. Preston, writing in the 1920's, locates what he calls 'Old Grammar School' next door but one north of St. Nicolas' Church.[22] I have not found any other reference to this in Preston's book. But the earliest school premises are treated in some detail in Abingdon School's illustrated history *The Martlet and the Griffen.*[23] There are various fourteenth century references to school boarding houses and the authors of this school history conclude that by the time of the dissolution of the Abbey in 1538 the school premises formed 'an establishment of some substance' in Stert Street. The school moved to its new premises in 1563, partly funded by John Roysse. What then became of the old school room and whether it was still available for the Baptists to hire nearly a century later, I have not been able to discover. The other schoolroom, the Roysse Room, was certainly there in John Pendarves' day. In 1440 this was the common

---

[22] A.E. Preston, *St. Nicholas, Abingdon and Other Papers* 1929. Plan 2 and Plan 3, folded inside back cover.

[23] T. Hinde and M. St. John Parker, *The Martlet and the Griffen* 1997. pp 19ff.

room of St. John's Hospital; in 1563 it was purchased by John Roysse, a wealthy mercer of Mincing Lane, London for the re-founding of the Grammar School. Abingdon School still refers to this as the (Old) Schoolroom.[24] When the local political and religious background is taken into consideration the availability to Dissenters of both these school premises raises problems,[25] but I am inclined to the conclusion that this room was 'the School-house' referred to in Atherton's letter as the first meeting place of the separated congregation under their pastor John Pendarves.

*Figure 6 Abingdon School in 1793.*
*The Roysse Room is lit by the three windows above the benches.*[26]

[24] T.Hinde & M.St John Parker, ibid. pp 48, 58, 77.

[25] Ibid. See pp 47f. During the Civil Wars and into the Commonwealth period Anthony Huish was Headmaster of the school assisted by Robert Payne as Usher (not to be confused with his contemporary Robert Payne the prominent Baptist). Both Headmaster and Usher worshipped in St. Nicolas Church, where much later Payne would be Rector, known for its Laudian practices and so disliked by the Parliamentarians that they made a determined effort to have the church building physically demolished. If the school allowed the Baptists to use its school-house on Sundays, it may have been an attempt to appease the enemy.

[26] This and the following image are in the Abingdon School archive and are used with their kind permission.

*Figure 7 Interior of the Roysse Room before 1868*

The third place mentioned in the letter is the house of Mr. Hanson. Later in the century the homes of Katharine Peck and Captain Consolation Fox are licensed as places of Baptist worship. Katharine's continued to be so used into the next century even after the building of the 1700 Meeting House. It is interesting to note that Katharine was the daughter of the Mr. Hanson referred to in Atherton's letter, whose house, in St. Edmond's Lane, she inherited on his death in 1668. Although Katharine was a Baptist, her father may have been a Presbyterian, though in the above quotation Atherton's speaking to Hanson when 'in his house' could indicate that the house was already a weekday meeting place of the Baptists.[27]

Before we leave this fascinating document, may I offer you three choice quotations from it:
Atherton's most *damning* words, comparing the true, New Testament Church with the Abingdon Baptists - 'They had the Spirit, and you the Carcase'

[27] See M. Cox, *Peace and War, the story of Abingdon part three,* 1993 p. 154ff and end-note p. 231.

His most *amusing* words, as he plays on the idea behind his title, that by exercising authority over his church Pendarves is behaving like a Pope - 'The old Pope, when he delivered anyone to Satan… it is said did it with Bell, Book and Candle… But you being but a young Pope, have not yet brought in your Ceremonies'
And the most *evocative*, as he thinks back to candle-lit St. Helen's on a mid-winter night in 1653 - 'I being ancient, felt myself weary with long standing: and being about the middle of winter, and the weather cold, found my head cold, standing without a hat; I said my spirits grew weak and low.'

**Evidence of earlier Baptists in Abingdon.**
John Atherton's *The Pastor turn'd Pope* and Elizabeth Poole's *Alarum of War* both give us the year 1649 as the earliest mention of a Baptist church in Abingdon. But there is evidence which suggests some form of Baptist fellowship as early as 1642.

In his two volume work *Seditious Sectaryes,* Dr. Larry Kreitzer extracts from the Oxford city records and many other sources the biographies of five early Oxford Baptists. Among them is Roger Hatchman,[28] a stonemason and later a soldier who rose to the rank of major in Cromwell's New Model Army. He was one of many anti-royalists who fled the city after the arrival of the king in September 1642. Many of these refugees fled to Abingdon; one of Dr. Kreitzer's sources gives the figure 'above 100 families'. In a personal letter to the writer, Manfred Brod urges caution with such figures when drawn from propaganda tracts and atrocity literature. But it would be reasonable to conclude that a number of families of Baptist inclination chose to escape to Abingdon after the king's arrival with his army in Oxford. In her book *The English Civil War,* Dr. Diane Purkis refers to a 1644 list of inhabitants in Oxford, which shows how over-crowded the city had become, and she writes: 'Another source of housing was the residences of those who had fled to the cosy embraces of godly Abingdon; their houses were soon stripped and crammed with lodgers'. Just how cosy Abingdon would have been, equally over-crowded and impoverished, is debatable, but from September 1642 to June 1646 Roger Hatchman, the Oxford Baptist, lived with his family in Abingdon. It is surely highly likely that he either joined, or gathered about himself, a fellowship of like-minded believers. Thomasine Pendarves may have been one of several Abingdon

---

[28] Kreitzer, *Seditious Sectaryes,* Vol.1 pp.166ff.

residents who continued this fellowship after Hatchman's return to Oxford (she was married to John 'before 1647').[29]

**Early Organisation.**

Lacking a church minute book of our own, perhaps we may gain some idea of how the church ordered its life in the second half of the seventeenth century from the records of Broadmead church in Bristol, which have survived intact. I quote from Dr. Roger Hayden's *English Baptist History and Heritage*[30]*:*

> The worship was public, with lengthy prayers by the elders, the reading and the exposition of the Scriptures, and Psalm-singing. In the seventeenth century, on account of illiteracy, a person would usually give out the first line of a Psalm and then the congregation would join in singing it. [A pitch pipe used to give the note.][31] There was a regular mid-week meeting called a Conference, at which there were sessions for guidance in which the interpretation of the Scriptures played a vital part. All members could participate in free discussion. Usually held on Tuesdays, the meeting was maintained, even at the height of the persecutions, from 1672 onwards.
>
> The church meeting was held after public worship. Applications for membership were received and members would be subjected to discipline. Only the members would remain for this purpose. Admission to the church was usually by profession of faith made before all the church members, who would then vote for or against admitting the applicant. The church withdrew its fellowship from those who 'walked disorderly'. .....The church observed the two ordinances: baptism and the Lord's Supper. .........The Lord's Supper was a monthly service, and there was usually a day of preparation in the week preceding it. Only the pastor could preside at the Lord's Table.

---

[29] Brod, *Dictionary of National Biography -J. & T. Pendarves.*

[30] R. Hayden, *English Baptist History and Heritage,* 1990 B.U. p 61

[31] This phrase appears as a caption in R. Hayden's text.

Although these details come from Bristol, they probably give a fair picture of the Abingdon church. Echoes of this structure are still heard well into the eighteenth century. But you will remember that we do have some details of the organised life of the early Abingdon fellowship that can be extracted from Atherton's *The Pastor turn'd Pope*. I quote again:

> You have built you a Church, you have made you a Pastor, and other Church Officers, and you have Teachers; you say you shew obedience to Christ by being baptized, and by baptizing believers: you break bread often, and some of you said you raise the dead, you cleanse lepers, and cast out devils, etc. and thus you imitate the primitive Churches.

Elsewhere Atherton says their worship included confession and penance and mentions a 'stool of repentance' on which, presumably, members disciplined by the church must sit until forgiven. He also says that there was 'visiting'. This may refer to pastoral care, or have a more disciplinary nature. The claim, 'You have built you a Church' is unlikely to refer to a church building but rather a separated, gathered community which, as we have seen, at this time (1653) was meeting in the School-house. However, we can hold the phrase in mind when a little later, I come to consider the possibility of a seventeenth century chapel.

**The missing archives.**

Mention has already been made of documents which are contemporary with the early Baptists of Abingdon. But the archives of the church do not include an early Church Book with minutes of church affairs or an account book. Nothing of this sort survives before 1721. The story goes that they were lost in the great flood of 1894. Ken Read, a former Treasurer of the church, recalls talking to a Mr. Sidney Cullen in 1939. Sidney was the second generation of grocers who owned three shops in Stert Street. He remembered his father, Edward Cullen telling him how, when he was church secretary in the 1890's, he stored the church books in the cellar of his shop because there was no space for them at the church. After the flood the older records, presumably at the bottom of the pile, were beyond salvaging. This account must indicate that there was some loss in that flood, and at least one of our books shows evidence of water damage.

But this was not the time when the older records were lost. In an informative letter from the church to the Berks Association in 1850 it is stated 'we have in our possession the records of the Church regularly kept from the year 1721'. The church's archives still begin with the 1721 Church Book.[32] However, from documents such as The Abingdon Association Records and the Longworth Church Book, and other contemporary records, names begin to emerge of at least the leaders of the church during and immediately after Pendarves' ministry, while the St. Helen's Burial Registers,[33] which had to record all deaths in the parish, wherever the actual burial took place, give us some names of humbler members, or their infant children.

**How others saw us.**

There is evidence that the move of John Pendarves from the state church to a largely despised congregation of dissenters made him unpopular among his former colleagues and those of the established church. The Oxford antiquarian, Antony Wood, wrote that Pendarves had 'sided with the rout and by a voluble tongue having obtained the way of canting went up and down, unsent for, preaching in houses, barns, under trees, hedges etc.'.[34] He goes on to say that he became minister of an Anabaptist conventicle in Abingdon where he had 'a numerous multitude of disciples, made himself head of them and defied all authority'.[35] In another place Wood writes of an occasion when Pendarves travelled to Watlington parish church for a debate with the vicar of that church, Jasper Mayne. A number from the Baptist congregation went with their pastor and Wood describes them as 'a great party of Anabaptists and the scum of the people who behaved themselves very rude and insolently'.[36]

**The Death and Burial of John Pendarves.**

In his short ministry as pastor of the Abingdon Baptists, Pendarves established and organised a separated church, dissenting from the town's two Anglican churches. As pastor he led a fellowship of perhaps two hundred members under the care of church officers and the tuition of church teachers, or preachers. As mentioned in my

---

[32] The Abingdon Baptist Church archive is housed in th Angus Library of Regent's Park College, Oxford, where it is on long-term loan.

[33] St. Helen's Church, Abingdon.

[34] Anthony Wood, *Athenae Oxonienses* iii pp 419-421.

[35] Ibid.

[36] Ibid.

reconstruction of the events surrounding his funeral, the church was linked to like-minded fellowships at first in the immediate vicinity, the Abingdon Association, but soon drawn from neighbouring counties also and forging links with similar Associations in England, Wales and Ireland. It was in these Association meetings that the doctrines and organisation of these Calvinistic Baptist churches were decided upon and recommended to the churches for their acceptance. He kept in regular contact with the Baptist churches in London and it was while he was away from Abingdon, in London, that he died, at about 34 years of age. The cause of his death is first given in a brief anonymous note, dating from 1673 or thereabouts, which reads:

> About ye beginning of September 1656 the famous preacher mr Pendarvis of Abington died at London of ye plague in ye gutts and likewise John Price died suddenly and our Hutchins died suddenly in Abinton. Ye new Church yard or Cimitary for his church then was made and goodman Tomkins children was first there buried.[37]

This is quoted in a paper by Larry Kreitzer,[38] devoted to the question of Pendarves' fatal illness, in which he tracks down a publication by the celebrated physician Gideon Harvey in which Harvey writes of having performed or attended a dissection of 'one Pendarves, an incomparable hard Student, and Minister of that Town, who being dissected, his Lungs were found to be withered and dried up'. The diagnosis was that Pendarves suffered from studious bastard consumption (or pneumoconiosis) probably brought on by his five years of unrelenting study at Exeter College. This may not have been the direct cause of death, but if we are to think of John Pendarves as having to struggle with the debilitating effects of lung disease throughout the fourteen years between leaving college and his death, it makes his achievements all the more remarkable.

---

[37] Ms among the Baskerville family papers in the Bodleian Library, Oxford. Quoted by L. Kreitzer in his paper *The Fifth Monarchist John Pendarves (d.1656): A Victim of Studious Bastard Consumption'?* Chap.11 of *Recycling the Past or Researching History? p221.*

[38] Ibid.

Added to the question, of what did he die? is the question, where was he buried? After the delay probably caused by the dissection, the body was brought by river to Abingdon. Anthony Wood supplies the details:

> Whose Body thereupon being embowelled and wrap'd up in Sear-cloth by care of the Brethren, and afterwards Preparations made for his Funeral, the body was some weeks after conveyed by water to *Abendon* in *Berks*'.[39] [Then, on the 30th September, the corpse was laid] 'in a new burying place, before a Garden (for such a one of late hath beene procured at the Town's West end, in the Oxestreete...)[40]

The St. Helen's burial records take up the story:

> 1656 13 Sept. Tomkins, Grace and Benjamin, son and daughter of John Tomkins and Martha, in the Ock Street as it is reported.
> 30 Sept. Pendarvis, John, in ye garden in ye Ock street.

One can almost hear the tetchy disapproval as the clerk records for the first time this new burial place, for which St. Helen's would have received no burial fee! But there were to be many more entries, running through the centuries to 1809 (when at last the Baptists were permitted to record their own burials). We may also surmise that there would have been little time between the death of Pendarves and his burial to go through the formalities of purchasing this plot. And where was it? Obviously in Ock Street. But not necessarily in the garden of what is today number 35. It is surprising that no tombstone commemorating their first minister survives in the chapel burial ground and no tradition as to where his body was placed. Stella Hambleton has researched into the Quaker burial ground even nearer the west end of the town. This occupied the site of what is now the Juniper Court flats. She has made a case for the hypothesis that this plot was the burial place referred to by Wood and others. Having

---

[39] Anthony Wood, *Athenae Oxonienses 1692 pp 127-28.*
[40] Ibid

looked at Quaker records in the County Record Office[41] and the Town Council offices, she concludes 'John Tomkins senr. came to an arrangement with John Thatcher, the owner of the two acre site, to have a corner of his land fenced off for the burial of his two children and Pendarves etc. Quakers may have been given space in this plot as well. This arrangement stood until Mr. Thatcher died in 1679. A John Tomkins, not senr., possibly even a Quaker, then agreed to purchase the burial ground but when he died in 1696 no purchase money had yet been received. The land reverted to John Thatcher's heirs who offered it for sale. The Baptists by this time had their more convenient burial ground in the garden of 35 Ock Street, so the Quakers bought the two acres and built their first Meeting House next to the burial plot'.

The alternative is, of course, that Pendarves was buried somewhere in the grounds of 35 Ock Street, even under the present chapel. But if a burial place was given to the church for this purpose, who was living in or owned the house of which this was part of the garden? As we shall see when we come, in the 1730's, to the Will of Benjamin Tomkins, a strong case can be made for this property being in the ownership of the Tomkins family from the beginning of the church's connection with the site. But this will remain surmise unless documentary evidence comes to light.

**The first meeting places.**

But where did this congregation of perhaps over two hundred meet? After the early use of the Schoolhouse we begin to hear of houses being registered as meeting places. Certainly more than one house would be required. As we come to look at the phases of persecution and the short periods of toleration between the years 1650 to 1689, these 'meeting houses' (a name which would still be attached to places of dissenting worship long after church buildings were allowed to be built, so that even in the year 2011 the official name entered on each certificate of marriage is 'The Baptist Meeting House, Abingdon') come to light either as the homes of people who were fined for allowing unlawful 'conventicles' to take place in their home, or as houses licensed for public worship. The home of Katherine Peck appears to have been used throughout the second half of the century and even into the first decade of the 1700's. Oral tradition in the church claims that the church met in a barn in her orchard behind the

---

41 Oxon. County Record Office, BOQM IV/1/1; XVIII/I; XVIII/I/2; XVIII/1/1.

large house in St. Edmund's Lane. But other houses were also used including that of Captain Consolation Fox, a maltster, who may have remained in Abingdon following his military service in Cromwell's army.[42]

**A seventeenth century chapel?**

In the first half of the nineteenth century Joseph Ivimey produced a history of the Baptists in four volumes. In the first volume he describes how, after a period of persecution in which any worship had to be conducted in secret, it suddenly became lawful for the Abingdon church to use its meeting house again. The date is the 10th July 1686. He then records, 'The very same evening they prepared and cleaned their old meeting house, and the next day, both in the morning and afternoon, many hundreds assembled very quietly and without any disturbance'. [43]

At face value this suggests the existence of a purpose built meeting house - needing cleaning after a period of disuse and large enough to pack hundreds in. The problem is that Ivimey gives no source for this statement. Some years later, in volume four, he wrote: 'The present meeting house was built in the year 1700. There had been a place of worship on the same site before, the garden and the minister's house having been purchased prior to 1670'. [44] Again he gives no source. Can we accept his word for it? In 1895, Thomas H. Pumphrey, a deacon of the church, gave a lecture on the history of the church which was later published. He used Ivimey as one of his sources and he quoted the passage about the cleaning of the old meeting house almost verbatim. But when he comes to the second passage he adds details which appear to come from his imagination and a misunderstanding of a receipt which he has found among the church papers. He writes, 'Many of Cromwell's Soldiers worshipped in the old Meeting House when in the District. The Minister's House and Garden were purchased in 1660 and we have among our old papers a receipt for £20 paid for the transfer of the premises'.[45] This receipt is almost certainly that glued onto the last page of the 1766-98 Church Book. But the receipt is folded and on the outside is written 'Combes

---

42 *Baptist Quarterly*, XXXVI No.2 p 98.

43 J. Ivimey, *A History of the English Baptists 1811-1830* vol 1 p 463.

44 Ivimey (op cit) vol IV p 420.

45 T.H. Pumphrey, *History of the Baptist Church, Abingdon.* (1895) p 10. Orig. copy in Angus Library, Regent's Park College, Oxford.

receipt for 20L for premises conveyed'. The receipt itself simply acknowledges that John Combes has received £20 from six named representatives of the church. This relates exactly to an indenture of 1678 now in the archives of the Baptist Union Corporation, which concerns the sale of a 'plot of ground' only, which John Combes is selling to the same six named representatives of the church, on the same date, for the sum of £20. This leads me to feel that Pumphrey's publication has little to offer on the question of the possibility of a 17th century chapel. He merely quotes Ivimey's unsourced statements and misrepresents the one piece of original material he has found. But what had he found? Not evidence of the purchase of the minister's House and garden in 1660, which, though used by the minister beforehand, will not be owned by the church until the death of Benjamin Tomkins in 1736. But he has handled and read the earliest manuscript document that was available to him among the Abingdon church archives. A receipt which is now enlarged upon by the full indenture. And this could well point to a 17th century chapel, or at least to the intention to build one. For the indenture gives us the details that this plot of land will have access from Ock Street (which access will in no way prevent existing access to the properties and their gardens either side of it). The plot is 60 feet N to S and 44 feet E to W. Interestingly this is almost exactly the size of the present (1841) chapel (excluding its rear hall). The entry to the plot will run north between houses and their gardens from a door on Ock Street, between stone walls to the plot of ground. The garden of the house to the east will run behind the plot to its N. This plot has been owned by John Combes, cordwainer, and, on 17th March 1678 is sold to Philip Lockton, mercer, Arthur Hearn, ironmonger, Edward Roberts, linen draper, John Tyrold, maltster, John Tomkins, maltster and Henry Tomkins, glover. These six will be the first trustees of the church plot. There can be no doubt that this is the plot on which the 1700 and then the 1841 chapels were built. But was Pumphrey right when he concludes: 'In 1700 the old Chapel was built on the site of the old meeting house'?[46] You will remember we have been holding in mind Atherton's words, 'You have built you a Church'. But these words were written twenty five years before the plot was bought. Of course, John Combes, cordwainer and preacher, who in 1656 left to become pastor of the Longworth church, *could* have bought this Ock Street plot and sold it on to the six trustees twenty two years later, with a meeting house already erected. At the time of writing, the floor of the

46 Ibid p 14.

present chapel is still in need of extensive repair. When the boards are removed evidence may come to light not only of the dimensions of the 1700 chapel, but just possibly of a still older place of worship.

**Baptisms.**

Where the baptisms were done is a mystery. The rivers of the town, Thames or Ock, would have been the obvious places, but tradition links baptisms at a later date with a spring and pond in the field behind the present church site. At some point in its story, but before 1838, the church bought, or was given, a field which is now part of the lower playing field of Abingdon School (sold to the school in 1908).[47] In a short, typed, history of the church, Brian Orland writes of the mid 18th century:

> The cause at Oxford had sunk to a very low level during this period and several people came from Oxford to be baptised in the baptismal spring in Lower Field. Abingdon helped Oxford to pull through.

The large scale O.S. map of Abingdon (1874) shows this spring/pool as a walled rectangular pool, ca. 15 feet by 5 feet, with a narrow channel from the SE corner into a walled and roughly oval shaped pool of about the same size. The site is about 80 feet SW of the Abingdon School entrance gate; about 20 feet south of the stone wall separating the field from the pavement of Park Road. The rectangular pool is now the site of a stone barn but a slight oval depression can be discerned running from the SE corner of the barn. The barn is not on the 1874 map. All this adds up to a strong case that this was a baptising pool which the church could have constructed for use in the 17th century and perhaps continued to use into the next century even if, as seems probable, the 18th century Meeting House offered an indoor baptistery. The 1874 O.S. map shows two other possible sites. There is a very large and secluded fish pond in the garden of Stratton House, the home of Benjamin Tomkins senr. And there is a walled

[47] See St. Helen's Church map and accompanying notes, 1838. It numbers the present 35 Ock Street as '227, occupier John Kershaw, house, gardens and meadow est. extent 2 acres 16 perches. Est. rental £32.14.0. Rateable value £23.0.0'. For the date of the sale of the meadow see *Abingdon Baptist Church, Statement of Accounts* 1908, 'The Meadow behind the Chapel (agreed to be sold to the Grammar School Governors)'. £1,000 appears to have been the sale price which, invested in Consols, gave an interest of £25.13s. In 1908 towards 'The Support of the Minister'.

pool roughly 15 feet square abutting the south wall of the Stratton House garden. Neither of these structures may have existed a century or more earlier, but since a round tower which I am told was the Workhouse water tower was and is sited between them, the area was obviously rich in springs.

*Figure 8 Aerial view of 'Lower Field'.*
*The barns are at the centre of photograph*

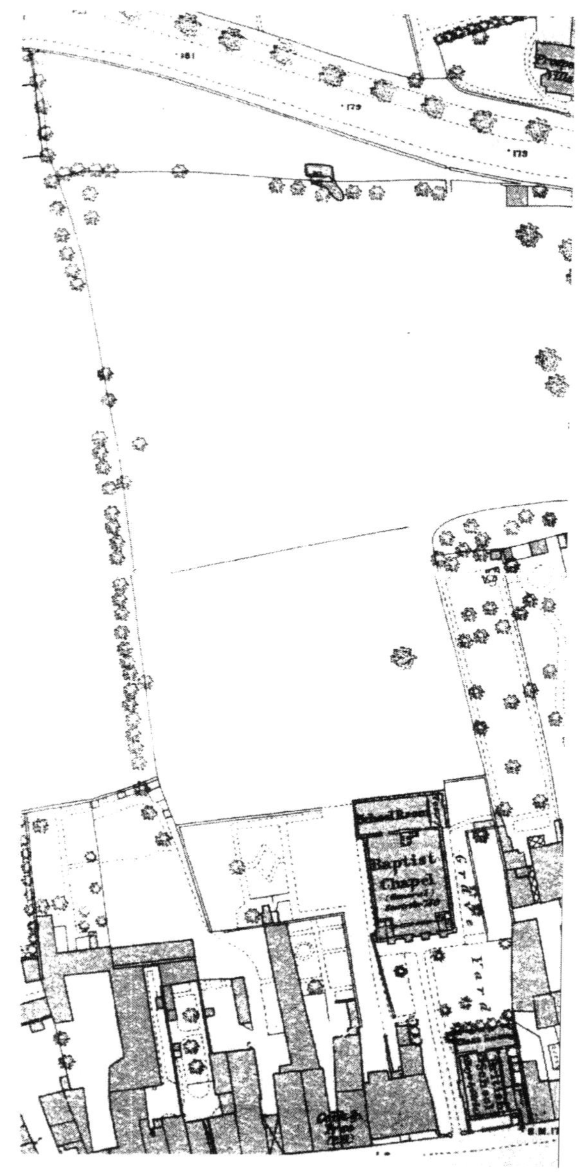


*Figure 9 Ordinance Survey Map, 1874*

**Leadership after John Pendarves.**
Following the death of Pendarves the church continued for nineteen years without calling a minister. Pendarves had not worked alone. He had often been absent from Abingdon, engaged in evangelism and Association work in the Midlands, West-country and in London. Meanwhile a number of very capable men were overseeing and furthering the work in Abingdon and its surrounding districts. These continued to offer leadership after his death.

John Belcher, of fifth monarchist and seventh-day Baptist views, ministered in Abingdon before he left under a cloud to become the elder of the Seventh-Day Baptist church in Bell Lane, London. Captain Consolation Fox ministered in Abingdon and for a while in Wallingford. Edward Stennett was also to play a leading role in Abingdon before becoming minister of the Wallingford church. But three names come to the fore: John Tomkins, John Coombes and John Jones. Tomkins' and Coombes' names appear in the Association records along with John Pendarves as the Abingdon 'messengers', as does John Jones a little later. All three were present at Pendarves' funeral and provided the necessary leadership afterwards. John Tomkins would exercise leadership in the Abingdon church until his death in 1708. He was 35 years of age in 1656. The son of a yeoman farmer, John entered the Malting business and prospered. His malting house still stands beside the slip-way where East St. Helen's Street meets the Thames.[48]

In the December following Pendarves' death, with the full agreement of the Abingdon church, the new Baptist congregation at Longworth 'did first stand upp as a church of Christ distinct from Abingdon church'.[49] Ninety-nine men and women were sent from the Abingdon membership to form the new church, including John Coombes, a shoe-maker and one of the Abingdon leaders, to be their minister - 'to see how the Lord will own his labour amongst us'.[50] And just a year later, at a meeting in Longworth at which representatives of Abingdon, Wantage and Oxford were present, twenty-three Longworth members

[48] See L.G.R. Naylor, *The Malthouse of Joseph Tomkins.* Angus Library, Regent's Park College, Oxford.
[49] Longworth Church Book, quoted by John Stanley *The Church in the Hop Garden p 67.*
[50] See Appendix A list 1

who lived in or near Faringdon were 'solemnly given up to walke as a particular congregation of Jesus Christ' in Faringdon. And John Coombes was to minister there two Sundays in every three.[51]

That the Abingdon church could send nearly one hundred of its members to form a new church is some indication of its size in these early days. It also indicates how its people were not only drawn from a wide area, but had a wide and fluid concern to plant churches and reach new areas with the gospel. It seems that no sooner do we try to examine the life of the Abingdon church than we are led away by the story to the wider picture.

The third John, John Jones, has been researched by Manfred Brod. He is first mentioned in 1638 as 'the minister' who is in Abingdon negotiating with Major Brown concerning a prisoner. In 1646 he is put forward to be minister of Stanton Harcourt parish church. He then becomes minister of Charney Bassett. In 1650 Lydford and Charney Bassett were formed into a new parish. Brod, in a lecture delivered in 35 Ock Street on 3 February 2004, went on to suggest that Jones, this Anglican minister of puritan sympathies, would be concerned for the financial well-being of his ministerial friend John Pendarves, since his income now depended on the size and giving of his separated congregation. His solution was to dispatch some 100 of his Charney Bassett congregation to the Abingdon Baptist Church, perhaps once every six weeks, to receive communion from Pendarves. After Pendarves' death in 1656, the need ceased for these to travel to Abingdon and they formed the nucleus of a church in Longworth. Jones attended Pendarves' funeral when he preached in the market place and is described as being of Longworth, an ancient Christian and 'formerly persecuted by the bishops'. A few weeks later it is his name that heads the list of those forming the church at Longworth.

This interesting theory may throw further light upon the fluid leadership situation throughout the 1660's as a group of men ministered in Abingdon and its daughter churches in Longworth and Faringdon. In an article entitled 'Abingdon Revisited' in the *Baptist Quarterly,* Geoffrey Nuttall writes of the three prominent leaders, John Tomkins, John Combes and John Jones, but concludes: 'It would probably in fact be a misreading to regard any individual as

[51] Ibid. p 69

pastor at Abingdon in the 1660's; but if one member more than any other deserves the title it is John Tomkins'.[52]

**Seventh-Day Baptists.**

In a short contribution to a public meeting of the Abingdon Area Archaeological and Historical Society in 2008, Manfred Brod read a paper entitled *Some Amateur Theology in Seventeenth-Century Abingdon.* He spoke of a series of events in 1657 or 8 which were triggered when a number of Baptists began to preach in the Market Place claiming that Saturday, the seventh day of the week, and not Sunday was the day for rest and worship. In the light of this, they argued, all the laws relating to Sunday, backed up with heavy fines for those who disregarded them, were null and void. To make the point, some of them were opening their shops for business on Sundays and defying the magistrates to fine them. The authorities apparently sought to resolve the issue in a congenial manner, calling a meeting to hear the arguments on both sides. Other meetings may have followed. Edward Stennett, who was a brazier, with John Belcher and a few other companions represented the Baptists, while John Hanson, several times mayor during the recent wars, represented the Corporation. By argument or authority the Corporation won the day. But the Baptist church seems to have been divided on this issue. They later excluded John Belcher. Edward Stennett remained in Abingdon until 1671,[53] when he became pastor of the Wallingford church which became known for its Seventh-Day views. Edward Stennett was progenitor of four generations of Seventh Day Baptist ministers.

**The state of the church in 1659.**

The 21st meeting of the Abingdon Association in 1659 gives us a brief report of the Abingdon church. John Tomkins read the Abingdon letter:

> The church of Abington acknowledgeth God's goodnes in keeping them under diverse tryalls. As to the enemies endeavour they have had great shakings but have bene hitherto kept by the good hand of God. They have had of late small increase as to number and

[52] *Baptist Quarterly* XXXVI No 2 p 100.

[53] For this date see G. Nuttall, *Baptist Quarterly* vol XXXVI No 2, p 98 and end-note 19, quoting B.W. Ball, *The Seventh-Day Men,* Clarendon Press 1994, p 168, with n.19, and p 178, n.71 (correcting Clapinson).

> one of their members is now under admonition. They blesse God that they are (for the moste part) in a lively condition and none of them do now appear to be under shaking save the one that is under admonition. They are kept unanimous and in much love and union and do mind the work of the Lord although they are ensible of their falling short as to measure etc. ........ One of the brethren hath lately experienced and acknowledged the great goodnes of God which hath appeared in the alteration of the ill frame of his wife. Also several remarkable answers of prayer have been received and observed amongst them.[54]

The 'shakings' refer to trouble with the authorities for non-attendance at the parish church and for meeting illegally for worship. The brother under admonition would have been disciplined by the church for some misdemeanour and refused admission to communion for a period. But their shakings were to increase after the death of Cromwell in 1658 and the restoration of the Stuart dynasty in 1660.

**Henry Forty.**

In 1675 the church called Henry Forty as pastor. He was fifty years old and had been freed from Exeter gaol just three years previously. Those three years were spent ministering in London and it would be good to know what considerations caused him to move from there after so short a time and what moved the Abingdon church to call him. An old friend of John Pendarves, was he still weakened by his twelve years in prison? Did the church see him working in tandem with John Tomkins? Pumphrey, who appears confused regarding the date of Forty's death, claims that John Tomkins was 'assistant-pastor' to Mr. Forty for some time and continued for a year after the end of Forty's ministry:

| | | |
|---|---|---|
| Henry Forty, | pastor from | 1675-1687 |
| John Tomkins | pastor | 1688 |
| Tom Tomkins | pastor from | 1688-1700 |
| - Keen | Co-pastor | - 1700'[55] |

[54] Association Records (ed. B.R. White) Part 3 p 129.

[55] T.H. Pumphrey, *History of the Baptist Church, Abingdon* 1895, p 21.

But Joseph Ivimey, who, it will be remembered, wrote a history of the English Baptists and was used by Pumphrey as a source for his lecture, knows nothing of Tom Tomkins, and no Thomas appears in this generation in the Tomkins family tree. Ivimey writes: 'After the Revolution in 1688 Mr. John Tomkins was the pastor and Mr. Keen assistant. They were contemporary and were men of solid judgement and great piety, who had suffered in the cause of Christ and his truth'.[56]

Further clear evidence that Pumphrey was mistaken comes from the minutes of two gatherings of Baptists in London in 1689 and 1692 in which the Abingdon representatives were listed as:

'1689 - Henry Forty, pastor. John Tomkins, Philip Hockton.
1692 - John Tomkins, minister.'[57]

Ivimey also states that Forty 'settled in Abingdon in 1675 and continued till his death in 1692.' [58]

Little is known of these ministries except that the Abingdon Association which ceased to hold its General meetings in 1659, though it continued to encourage active fellowship between many of the churches, began its meetings again in 1678 and Henry Forty is credited with this. We know that Forty held the view that only those who had been baptised as believers might receive communion in his church. This was a keenly debated matter throughout this period. A hundred years later one of Forty's successors at Abingdon, Daniel Turner, will powerfully argue that all Christians, however baptised must be welcomed at the Table - a view that has persisted in the Abingdon church to this day. Ivimey concludes his short biography of Forty: 'In 1692 he finished his course in the 67th year of his age. His funeral sermon was preached by Mr. Benjamin Keach and printed with an Elegy on his death entitled *The Everlasting Covenant*.'[59]

Thomas Crosby, a Baptist historian in the eighteenth century, writes of Henry Forty: 'He subscribed to the Baptist confession of 1651 and was pastor of the church at Abingdon... he was a man of great piety, one who long and faithfully served Jesus Christ under many

56 Ivimey (op cit) vol IV p 420.
57 Ibid. I p 503.
58 Ibid. II p 66.
59 Ivimey ibid. II p 68.

afflictions, great trials and sufferings. He was an instrument in God's hand for the conversion of his own father and mother and many others. He lay twelve years in the prison at Exeter for the testimony of a good conscience, lived an unspotted life and died at Abingdon.'[60]

Of John Tomkins there is a legend, that a large, carved oak chest in the possession of his descendants was used by him to hide from those who sought to arrest him. In 1980 the Revd. Basil L. Stock, of Tarsona, Tasmania provided a sketch of this chest then in his possession. I have been unable to trace the chest since.[61]

*Figure 10 The Tomkins' chest*

**The years of persecution.**

It is time to look at the series of various Acts of Parliament and their effects on the church during these early years. This will throw up many names of the church's first members.[62]

---

[60] T. Crosby, *The History of the English Baptists, from the Reformation to the beginning of the Reign of King George I.* 1740. vol III p 100

[61] For further details of this and Tomkins' family see Correspondence between B. Stock and B.R. White 1980 Angus Lib. ref 41 e3 ®

[62] The names and figures in this and the following section are drawn from Mieneke Cox *The Story of Abingdon Part III*, whose source was A.E. Preston, *St. Nicholas, Abingdon and other Papers* Oxford Hist. Soc., 1935.

From the reign of Queen Elizabeth fines could be imposed for absenting oneself from the sacraments of the Church of England. The Church Wardens kept a record of those attending, especially on Easter Day when it might be expected all would wish to receive the Eucharist. As the influence of independency grew, bishops increasingly sought to bring pressure on the parish priest and his church wardens to make returns or 'presentments' so that fines could be imposed. But whatever difficulties were placed upon the Baptists during Pendarves' ministry, or which, by their behaviour, they brought upon themselves, local persecution of dissenters and Roman Catholics began in earnest in 1662 after the restoration of the monarchy. In August of that year 53 Abingdon people were named for non-attendance and 23 were fined one shilling. Among those named was a Baptist, Edward Mitchell, who had earlier in the year found himself before the magistrates for an incident which may have been typical of the way loose talk and ill feeling between neighbours could be exploited by the authorities. One Joyce Page was encouraged to lodge a complaint stating that Edward Mitchell had said to her: 'All the whores, rogues and gallow's birds in England were of the Church of England'. In his defence Mitchell claims he merely asked her a question: 'Howe many whores and rogues she believed there were of the Church of England which were baptised into that church?' The case was referred to the next session and the outcome is not recorded. A week after the 53 were named, eight, all Baptists, were arrested for not attending St Helen's - Edward Roberts, George Grove, John Allen, William Taylor, Henry Thorneton, John Roberts and two widows, Thomasine Pendarves and Jane Tesdale. The two women paid a fine, the others were imprisoned.

In March 1664 Charles II signed the First Conventicle Act which made it illegal 'for anyone over the age of sixteen to attend any assembly, conventicle or meeting under show or pretence of any exercise of religion in other manner than according to the liturgy and practice of the Church of England'. The penalty was £5 for the first offence; £20 for the second; transportation for the third.

The Second Conventicle Act of 1670 levied fines for persons allowing their homes to be used for illegal meetings - £20 for the owner; £20 for the preacher. And to tighten up the local reporting of such offences, church wardens, or constables or overseers would be fined £5 for not reporting them. Five days after the Act was passed the church wardens and overseers of St. Helen's gave evidence against 32 for assembling 'in the house of Simon Peck, maltster; John Skinner, practitioner in Physick and Henry Tomkins, glover, being preachers'. Peck, Skinner and Tomkins were fined £20 each and the others £5. These were, of course, considerable sums in those days.

Baptist children were among the ten boys expelled from Roysses school in 1671 for non-attendance of the parish church. By this, and the exclusion of the sons of dissenting parents from Pembroke College, Oxford, the Corporation effectively cut off the normal route of education to all but those prepared to conform. Pembroke College was the usual place of further education for Abingdon's young men, especially since Thomas Tesdale, some of whose descendants were Baptists, had established scholarships for thirteen Abingdon-born scholars earlier in the century.

Relief came, though briefly, with the Act of Indulgence in 1672. Passed more for political than religious reasons, this Act nevertheless brought a year's respite from the harassment and fines. The Baptists immediately obtained a license to hold services in Katharine Peck's house (her husband, Simon, had died the year before) and John Mann, schoolmaster, and John Coombe, cordwainer, were licensed to preach there.

But in 1673 these licenses were withdrawn and the Test Act excluded anyone who refused to take the sacrament according to the rites of the Church of England from public office. Continual harassment and the interruption of worship seems to have sometimes provoked strong reaction. In 1682 it is recorded that Robert Payne and three other Baptists were accused of 'riotously assembled arrayed modo guerrimo and with swords and sticks assaulting the constables in the exercise of their office'. The redoubtable Katharine Peck was excommunicated by the parish church in 1686 after being taken to London and imprisoned for a time.

Katharine Peck was the daughter of John Hanson.[63] Her father, described by Mieneke Cox as one of Abingdon's most belligerent characters, was a Presbyterian and churchwarden of St. Helen's before the Civil Wars. He was a brewer and a Principle Burgess of the town for twenty years from 1648. Several times during the wars and in 1654 he served as Mayor. His large house stood in St. Edmund's Lane and this passed to Katharine on his death in 1668. Katharine had married Simon Peck a year or so before her father's death. Simon was a widower with four children when he married Katharine and the birth of Katharine's first child, Philadelphia, named after Katharine's mother, must have added to the cramped conditions in which they lived. So the inheritance of her family home would have come as a great relief as well as providing a place for the Baptists to meet. But in 1671 Simon died of a sudden illness, leaving Katharine with five children and a sixth yet unborn. This, a son, was to be given his father's name, Simon. Katharine, still a young woman, might have been excused if she had lived quietly and concentrated on raising her family. But she appears to have inherited her father's fighting spirit along with his house. Again and again she was heavily fined and she suffered excommunication and imprisonment for her faith. And her house continued to be used for Baptist meetings until her death in 1709.

**The end of persecution.**

In 1686 King James II took measures to ease the lot of his fellow Roman Catholics and to seek to defuse the growing fear of rebellion in the light of the increasing nonconformist reaction to such persecution. He offered a Dispensation which was obtainable if two judges would sign a certificate of peaceful demeanour for anyone who was a householder, and if the sum of fifty shillings was paid. This led to the incident in Abingdon that same year which Pumphrey records with such glee in his lecture. The pastor, Henry Forty, and seven other members were cited to appear before the spiritual courts for absenting themselves from the sacrament. The case was going against them. The fact that the old pastor had already spent twelve years in Exeter gaol earlier in his life, for his dissenting views, would not help his case. They all expected heavy fines or gaol. Then, in a dramatic

[63] So Mieneke Cox in notes sent to the author, turning round her previous conclusion that Katharine Peck and Katharine Hanson were two individuals. I hope to place her notes, with other of my effects, in the Angus Library of Regent's Park College, Oxford, in due course.

move, their defence lawyer, Mr. Medleycott, whose house still stands in East St. Helen's Street, produced a copy of the royal Dispensation, which he had secured on behalf of the defendants. Pumphrey concludes his story:

> There was but one course open to the Judges, and they discharged the prisoners. This was on Saturday July 10th 1686. There was great rejoicing among their friends, and the old meeting house was cleaned up the same night, and on the next day (Sunday) several hundreds attended both morning and afternoon services. Thus God protected his own.[64]

The end of this persecution must have seemed in sight when, on 11th December 1688 William of Orange and his army rode into Abingdon on his way from Torbay to London. He appears to have been accommodated in Mr. Medleycott's home and it was here that William received news of the king's flight to France. However, the church wardens continued to make their Presentments for at least a further thirty years, the last relating to Abingdon being in 1718 when eleven were named, including at least one Baptist, Abigail Pye.

William and Mary brought to British politics lessons learnt in Protestant Holland where religious toleration was considered an important factor in their country's economic prosperity. The Toleration Act of 1689 gave Dissenters the freedom to meet for worship without fear of interruption or fine. We can imagine the relief, which lingers on in Baptist vestries to this day - the most frequently repeated prayer offered by a deacon before worship is a thanksgiving that we can meet in freedom. This is far more likely a folk memory of our seventeenth century origins than a comparison with contemporary situations where such freedom is still denied.

But throughout the eighteenth century a wary eye would be kept on governments which could so easily remove the freedoms gained. Following the death of William in 1702 a General Baptist preacher gave thanks that 'our liberties are not lost with our prince'.[65] The

[64] Pumphrey (op cit) p 12.
[65] Joseph Jenkins, *A Sermon Preached on the Death of William III* 1702.

coming century would see further threats to limit the influence of the non-conformists, especially in the realm of education. We must remember that it was not until as late as 1870 that non-Anglicans were accepted at English universities. Alternative educational arrangements had to be made for the sons and daughters of all others. But the state church feared that the Dissenting Academies would influence not only the religious but also the political heart of the nation and they bitterly opposed them.

In 1679 the Bristol Academy for the training of Baptist pastors was founded. This would supply ministers and guidance to the Abingdon church, among many others, in the coming centuries.[66]

[66] See N. Moon, *Education for Ministry - Bristol Baptist College 1679-1979.* pub. Bristol Baptist College 1979.

# Chapter 2
# The Eighteenth Century.

The new freedom cleared the agendas of the Baptist and other dissenting churches for doctrinal and other concerns. Not that they waited for this before commencing such debates, but matters of faith and order now became a great feature of denomination life. Rationalism and the conceived clash between faith and reason; the decline of morals; church order - especially for Baptists the question of open or closed communion; election; evangelism; all these and more were to give the impression that the Baptist churches of the eighteenth century were unduly quarrelsome. But in fact this was a feature of all the denominations at this time. Major questions needed to be addressed and people still cared enough to feel hotly about them. Nevertheless there were many who called for peace and unity within and among the churches. And evidence of all these concerns will be found within the minute books and published writings of the Abingdon church.

Two ministers span the eighteenth century. William Fuller was called to serve the church very early in the century and ministered in Abingdon for about forty years, dying in office in 1745. After a short and disturbed interregnum Daniel Turner A.M. filled the years from 1748 to 1795. They were two outstanding ministries which bucked the general trend among the Baptist churches, enabling the church to remain strong in numbers, influence and good order in a century which is so often depicted by Baptist historians as one of toleration and decline.

**The Reverend William Fuller, ca. 1705-1745.**

For the first twenty one years of the new century we are still in that period before the start of the Abingdon Baptist Church records. So, compared with his illustrious successor, Mr. Fuller receives hardly a mention in the general Baptist histories. Ivimey can only state: 'Mr. William Fuller, it is said, settled here [i.e. Abingdon] about 1705 and was pastor upward of forty years; he died November 24th 1745 in the 74th year of his age'.[67] His only other reference is that 'Fuller of

[67] Ivimey (op cit) IV p 420.

Abingdon' prayed at the ordination of Benjamin Beddome at Burton-on-the-Water in September 1743. However, we begin to build a picture of the man as we draw upon evidence of his Berkshire background.

William Fuller was the sixth son of the wealthy John Fuller of Hall Barn, Blewbury.[68] John and his family were the principal landowners and farmers in the Astons. They were dissenters. William would have grown up under the teaching of active local Presbyterians such as Richard Comyns, 1617-1705, a close associate of Stennett of Wallingford (the seventh-day Baptist) and Thomas Cheeseman. Ejected from their livings in 1662, they were influential preachers in the area between Wallingford and Wantage. Encouraged by John Fuller they started a 'society' in Aston Upthorpe. This barn meeting was the forerunner of the chapel in Aston Tyrrold which was built by John's sons Joseph and Richard in 1728 and is now a URC retreat centre. John eventually moved his allegiance from the Anglican Church to this society. Despite his wealth, John was apparently known locally as 'poor Mr. Fuller' as by his death in 1704 he had bestowed one of his six estates on each of his six sons and kept none for himself. His eldest son, John was the first of the family to live in Aston Tirrold and was Lord of the Manor.[69]

So, with a boyhood under the influence of local Presbyterians, William, born c. 1671 into an extensive family of wealthy farmers, had inherited an estate some time before 1704. Did he farm this for some years? Did it give him the wealth to train for the Baptist ministry? In his early thirties he received the call to be pastor of the Abingdon church. We do not yet have details of his marriage, but David Smith's family tree records a son, Ebenezer (m. Sarah) and a daughter, Hannah. To this can certainly be added another son, Benjamin who, as a leader or pastor of the Baptist church in Devizes appears in correspondence in the archives of Bristol Baptist College in the 1740's.[70] Andrew Smith's family tree lists four children: 'Benjamin (of Devizes), Ebenezer, Joseph (a wool-stapler of

---

[68] This connection to the Fullers of Blewbury is claimed in correspondence from two sources: i) by Andrew Smith of Cambridge d. ca. 1998, a descendant of the Blewbury Fullers, ii) by David Smith of St. Leonard's on Sea whose family tree includes the Fullers of Blewbury and Aston Tyrrold.

[69] Frances McDonald, *Monument to Faith - Aston Tyrrold United Reformed Church a History*. 1978.

[70] Foskett Letters. Bristol Baptist College Archive.

Abingdon) and Hannah (who married Joseph Filkes)'. Other Fullers are listed in the earliest Abingdon list of members, c. 1746,[71] but it is at present impossible to place these as relatives of the pastor since what seems to be a second William Fuller, a grocer, was made a trustee of the Nicholas Whitby Trust, an Abingdon Baptist charity, in 1700.[72] This second William was possibly the father of Thomas Fuller, described variously as mercer or mealman, who was a deacon and prominent in the church in the 1740's. However, Andrew Smith claims that a Thomas Fuller, the brother of the pastor of the Abingdon church, owned Fitzharris House in Abingdon and Thomas' sons became famous in the banking world. Arthur Preston, the Abingdon historian, in a paper on Fitzharris Manor writes, 'after the Badcocks came the Fullers of Blewbury, respectable farmer-folk, who quickly advanced themselves in the world, and became also in 1764 lessees from Christ's Hospital of Lacy's Court farm; by 1759 the Fuller tenant of Fitzharris was described as of the City of London esquire'.[73] So we have two William and two Thomas Fullers. Of course, it is just possible that William the grocer and William the pastor are one man, and also that the mealman and the occupant of Fitzharris Manor are one. If this were so it would link William Fuller to the Abingdon church five years earlier than Ivimey tentatively suggests; if not as pastor, at least as an interested partner whose wealth might have had a bearing on the building of the 1700 meeting house. As yet I have not found an example of the grocer's signature to compare with the quite distinctive signature of the pastor. But assuming there were two Williams and two Thomases, it means that in the early 1700's the Blewbury Fullers, and perhaps their wealth, were exerting a strong influence on the Abingdon Baptist church.

---

[71] See flyleaf of Second Abingdon Church Book for undated but pre 1748 list.

[72] No.1 in Index to 38 micro film cards of documents held by the Baptist Union Corporation which relate to Abingdon Baptist Church. Baptist House, Didcot.

[73] A.E. Preston, *St. Nicholas, Abingdon and Other Papers* 1929 Oxford. P 471.

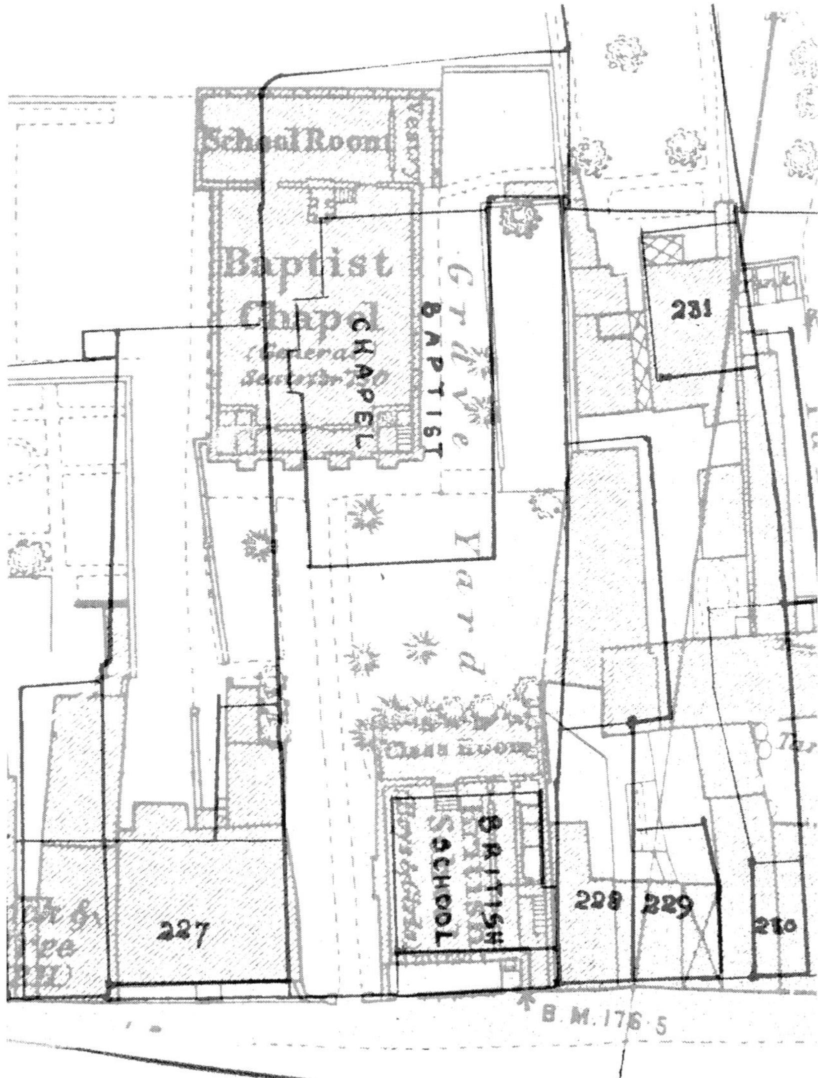


*Figure 11 The two maps (St Helen's 1838 bold, and O.S. 1874 feint) Superimposed to show the relative positions of the two chapels*

**The 1700 Meeting House.**

The new religious freedom also created the climate, both political and legal, in which places of worship could be licensed and built. Both the Baptists and the Congregationalists erected their meeting houses in the first year of the new century[74] - soon to be known in the town as the Upper (Presbyterian/Congregational) and Lower (Baptist) Meeting Houses. The adjectives had nothing to do with social or theological differences, but reflect their geographical relation to the town centre!

In my 2000 history of the Abingdon church I sought to build a picture of the 1700 chapel from the remaining masonry and what might be suggested from structures of the time which have survived in other places. This led to conclusions that at the time seemed reasonable but which have now been challenged by new evidence. This evidence is principally the document of 1678, referred to in the previous chapter, transferring the plot of ground from John Coombes to the six Baptist trustees, and a detailed map of the town made for St. Helen's Church in 1838 which shows a ground site plan of the Baptist chapel as it was three years before its demolition in 1841.

The discovery of the St. Helen's map made it possible to compare it with the large scale and very detailed Ordnance Survey map of Abingdon made in 1874. Tony Valente, Church Secretary at the time and a computer expert, was called in and history unfolded before our eyes as he digitalised the two maps, reconciled their different scales, made both images transparent and then superimposed the one on the other. With minor differences, the details matched well. Using the line of Ock Street, 35 Ock Street and the British School as reference points the 1838 map coincided with the 1874 map. This gave us confidence that the outlines of the old and new chapels were also correctly aligned. If this needed confirmation, it was reassuring that the east wall of the old chapel clearly lined up with that section of wall which the church has always maintained was a wall of the old chapel. But its south wall projected some twenty four feet to the south of the present chapel. So the new, 1841, chapel was not simply built on top of the old. It was sited some fourteen feet to the west of the old chapel - this we had known. But it was also much further north of, and not a lot larger than, the chapel it replaced. The old building was approximately 37 feet wide (W-E) and 76 feet in depth; the new

[74] Ivimey op. cit. vol. IV p 420. But what was his source?

building is approximately 45 feet wide and 82.5 feet in depth. Within these dimensions, each building has a meeting room/vestry at the north end, very roughly a quarter of the size of the adjoining worship area. Another unexpected feature was that protrusions towards the rear of the 1700 west wall look very like the 'covers' or porches which were being contemplated later in the century.[75] If this is so, perhaps the old chapel faced west - not south as I had assumed. And if it faced west, how was the interior oriented? Finally, if the dimensions of the 1700 buildings are compared with the 1678 indenture, there is a remarkable match. The depth of the old chapel (S-N) if we exclude the rear meeting room/vestry, exactly coincides with the depth of the original 'plot of ground' - sixty feet. The width of the plot, 44 feet would allow for a building 37 feet wide plus a forecourt or 'passage pitched with stone'[76] to give access to the chapel from the west.

In the light of the above maps and indenture, and drawing on the evidence of the part of the old wall which stands today but may soon be demolished in the course of twenty-first century extensions, I draw the following conclusions:

The claim that the 32.5 foot stone and brick wall which runs c. 11 feet to the east of the present east wall and parallel with it, was the old (1700) chapel east wall is confirmed. Sufficient of this wall remains for us to conclude that the 1700 chapel was built of random-shaped limestone edged at the corners with red brick quoins. The window and door apertures were probably edged with similar indented brickwork. The bricks were 17$^{th}$/18$^{th}$ century narrow bricks - i.e. 2 inches in height rather than the later 3 inches. From ground level, the walls began with a decorative plinth rising to c. 19 inches. This was formed by four courses of stone then four of brick - the two central courses of which used shaped bricks to form an ogee (a reversed 'S' shaped curve). A near similar plinth can be seen on the mainly brick house on the corner of Checker Walk and Abbey Close, which may be by the same builder. Such detail suggests that the chapel may have enjoyed other decorative features, such as the single course of concave bricks which separates the ground and upper floors of the Abbey Close house. Although both ends of the remaining chapel wall are properly ended with brick, only the rear (northern) end is high enough

[75] See the section 'property matters' later in this chapter

[76] ibid.

to retain the quoins. I believe this was the original NE corner of the chapel, before the meeting room/vestry was added. The wall would have run southwards from this corner for 60 feet, but when the rest of the chapel was demolished in 1841 it was cut short, after 32.5 feet, level with the frontage of the new chapel and sealed off using old bricks from the demolition. The purpose behind the leaving of this wall is recorded in the trustees minutes of 1841[77]: 'That in consequence of the removal of the old chapel' the Tomkins 'Private Burying Ground' shall be extended to form a quadrangle. A photograph of the Independent Meeting House, also said to have been built in 1700 but still visible before a front extension of 1864, has survived. This may indicate something of the architecture of the Baptist chapel - particularly its hipped roof and somewhat ungainly additional porches.

So far my conclusions have been strictly based on the evidence available to me. But there are questions as to how this building worked, with only hints from the pages of the church books. So allow me to reconstruct a possible scenario - if only to imagine a picture which future evidence can either confirm or improve upon.

---

77 ABC archives, Angus Library, Oxford.

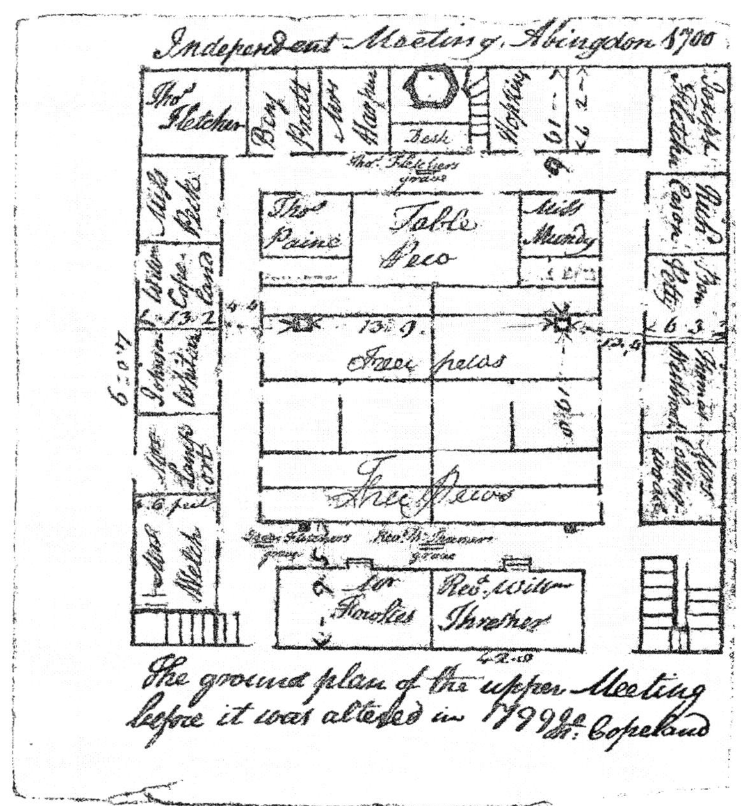


*Figure 12 Plan of interior of the Independent Chapel, The Square, Abingdon. Probably very similar to the Baptist Chapel.*

Let us imagine ourselves in Ock Street on a Sunday morning in the year, shall we say, 1706. We are part of a company of people, in our best clothes, converging on a doorway, set in the wall between the two houses which John Tomkins now owns but which are occupied by John Prince (that's the one to the left of the doorway) and John Watts (to the right). The door is open and a cobbled passageway leads up, between the low garden walls of the two houses, to our new Meeting House, built just six years ago. As we make our way up this main walk to the Meeting, careful not to twist an ankle on the cobbles, we pass the left corner of the sunny south wall of the chapel, with its rows of windows below and above. The cobbled passage leads us straight on across the front of the chapel to the entrance door at the far end. We turn right, into the warm, sun-filled interior. A flight of stairs leads to the north gallery and an aisle runs under this gallery towards the table pew and pulpit. Another aisle, to our right, leads to the south gallery stairs and then left under that gallery. The interior is plain but clean, as we like it -white-washed walls, pine boards, pulpit and pews. We are in good time. Groups of our Christian brothers stand in the aisles greeting each other; talking quietly together. Women have herded their children into the box pews, like lambs in a pen. Mr. Fuller, our young pastor, is near the pulpit talking with Richard Green, John Tyrrell, Edward Roberts and old John Tomkins. There will be a meeting of all the brothers after the service. The women will hear about it afterwards. There is a rumour that old John has bought the two houses at the gate so as to make part of their gardens available to the Fellowship. Of course he won't turn his tenants out, but it's said that Mr. Watts is thinking of giving up the part of his garden that lies just north of the chapel. Anyway, it doesn't grow things as well since the chapel blocked out its sunshine until late afternoon. If we had that piece of land we could build a vestry - even with an upstairs…

This picture may be severely flawed. The gateway between the two houses may have been a cart entrance to a trader's cobbled yard. The Meeting House may have been orientated with its front facing south, with doors that never had the proposed porches built and so did not show on the St. Helen's map. The early galleries may have run south to north, not west to east. But the group of senior members in discussion with William Fuller is drawn from a legal document of 1700 from which they appear to be leading figures in the church.[78] Old John Tomkins, who made his will in 1706, did leave his two houses to his son Benjamin.[79] Benjamin would install the pastor, William Fuller, in the house to the left, probably when John Prince's tenancy ended. In the 1720's the church was building a third gallery 'at the Vacant End of the meeting house'.[80] In the 1730's Benjamin would bequeath both the houses and their gardens to the church.[81] By the 1770's the time had come to consider the expense of improving the 'passage in front of the Meeting House' and 'the main walk to the

---

[78] Appointment of extra trustees for Whitby charity 1700, B.U. Corporation, Didcot. op.cit. footnote 6 of this chapter.

[79] Will of John Tomkins 1706, Public Record Office cat. ref.: prob 11/502.

[80] Church minutes March 6th 1725.

[81] Will of Benjamin Tomkins 1731.

Meeting' by replacing the surface 'which is now pitched with stones' with a smoother surface of brick [82] By 1805 the Sunday Schools were meeting in an 'upper room' of the old chapel.[83] In the 1820's John Watts' descendants were giving up their family's long tenancy and the house would be demolished to be replaced with the British School and the garden become or extend the chapel's burial ground.[84] I have not mentioned a baptistery in my reconstruction. The only 'evidence' for an internal baptistery comes from the church minute books of the 1720's and 30's which record baptisms conducted in winter as well as summer.

We know nothing of the communion plates and chalices at this early date but the church would certainly have had them. The church does still have and uses silver chalices and pewter plates which date from the early days of this building. The earliest are a pair of George I tapering circular communion cups on skirted bases with moulded rims, each with two scroll handles, made by Gabriel Sleath, London, and inscribed 'Ex donis Benjamin Tomkins 1717'. The pewter plates are inscribed 'Abingdon Baptist Church 1749'. These, together with one further chalice, would all have been in use in the old chapel.

**Fuller's early ministry.**

At sometime between 1710 and 1715 a scandal relating to a former Baptist leader of the Oxford church is alleged in the *Post Man,* a local news sheet. The Baptist reaction to this has been preserved in an unpublished manuscript by Benjamin Stinton (1676-1718).[85] This helps to throw some light on the weak state of the Oxford church, which was to persist until Daniel Turner and others' successful reconstitution of that church in 1780. But it also gives us an insight into the character of William Fuller, who is prepared to make the whole matter public and go to law against the scandal-mongers if necessary. Stinton writes:

> Upon this we made all ye enquirey we could into the matter, for it was a story intirley new to all ye Baptist Ministers at London, & we could find no

---

[82] Church minutes June 1772.

[83] Pumfrey op. cit. p 19.

[84] Indenture 1828 at B.U. Corporation, Didcot.

[85] B. Stinton *A Journal of the Affairs of ye Antipaedobaptists beginning with ye Reign of King George whose Accession to the Throne was on the first of August 1714,* pages 35-39, quoted by Larry Kreitzer in B.Q. vol. 42 Jan. 2007.

> manner of foundation for it; the last minister that preached there on ye Lords Days for some time was Mr Jn. Toms, a person of an nblemished character & universally Respected as an honest and sober man, when he removed to London, wch. was some years ago, the few Baptists that were at Oxford join'd themselves to ye church at Abingdon, since wich time they have only had a Lecture at Oxford on the week days, Supplyed one Week by Mr Joseph Collet, elder of a church at Coate, & Mr Fuller elder of ye church at Abingdon. To ye latter of these we sent a letter acquainting him wth. this scandlous Report and desireing him to give us wht. account he could of ye Matter. In his answer we were assured that ye Charge was utterly false, groundless a Malition of ye Post that he supposed it to be invented by Abel (* Ye publisher of ye Post Man) & that he thought it ought to be contradicted in ye most Public Papers, & if it could be, come at to prosecute ye Authors & Publishers of ye Same.

If scandal, deserved or otherwise, could be brought against the dissenters locally, the national government could also still be hostile. There must have been rejoicing in the church when the Tory party's Schism Act came to nothing because of the death of Queen Anne, on 1st August 1714, the day it was to receive the royal assent. This would have prevented dissenters from teaching in the schools and academies which they had opened. Queen Anne was succeeded by George I, the choice of the Whig party, and whose Protestantism commended him to the non-conformists. Reference to the annual sermon which was established in the Abingdon church to give thanks for all this, will be made a little later in this book.

Still in this early part of Fuller's ministry, before the church minute books begin, there is the Abingdon entry in a census of dissenting societies, taken in the reign of George I, which gave the number of 'hearers' in every dissenting congregation: 'Abingdon 400 William Fuller'. [86] And that would be the sum total of my knowledge of Fuller's ministry if it were not for the survival of the church records

[86] *Transactions of the Baptist Historical Soc.* II p 95.

which thankfully begin fifteen years into William's ministry and then continue with hardly a break to the present day.

So I intend to follow Mr. Pumphrey's example from 1895, though in more detail, and allow the church of the time to speak directly to us by quoting extensively from the first church book, to build a picture of the life of the Abingdon Baptists from 1721 to 45. This book, and the two others which take us through the century, are chiefly the record of the church meetings which were called after Sunday morning worship. They deal with matters relating to membership; with matters of discipline sometimes ending with members being excluded for a time from communion, sometimes with their being removed from the membership altogether; the appointment of officers; calls to prayer and occasional practical matters relating to money and premises. They also provide us with lists of church members, though these do not begin until the coming of Fuller's successor in 1748. However, it has been possible, from the first minute book, to compile an incomplete yet sizable list of members during Mr. Fuller's ministry (see appendix A, list 3).

**Baptism, membership, and the Church Covenant.**

Throughout the century in Abingdon the size of the congregation appears to have been far larger than the number of members. The congregation is called the 'auditory' - those who gathered to 'hear' the preacher. We shall see later, from a letter on the state of the church in 1776, that the auditory was then seven times the number of members. But applications for baptism and membership, which were clearly seen as inseparable, came frequently. The process usually took two weeks and began with the person who had requested baptism being asked to speak of their faith before the full congregation. The church meeting immediately after this service would then agree to the baptism. This took place the following Sunday. The baptised would then be received into membership on the next Sunday. An edited but typical sequence of entries reads:

> Dec. 1st 1723. John Clanville, carpenter, and Thomas Fuller, son of Thomas Fuller, requested baptism and having heard 'their experience of the work of grace upon their hearts' the members 'granted their request'.
> 'Dec. 15th 1723. John Clanville and Thomas Fuller jnr ...were baptised by immersion in the sight and presence

> of all the auditory about four o'clock in the afternoon.'
> Dec. 22nd 1723. John Clanville and Thomas Fuller jnr were received into membership.

Four entries reveal an exception to this pattern - Miss Hannah Winsmore, for instance, was permitted to give her testimony privately to three visitors because she 'could not be prevailed upon to make declaration thereof before the whole church'. In 1731 another, Mary Browne, was too 'slow of speech' to make confession before the church and after a satisfactory report from her visitors 'was baptised privately'. A week later she was 'received into the church having first signed the Covenant'. This refers to the *Church Covenant of a Society of Christians baptised upon profession of faith, usually meeting at Abingdon* dated November 16th 1728.[87] (see appendix B). The church book also refers to the practice of new members signing *The Terms of Communion.* It is my conclusion that *Church Covenant* and *The Terms of Communion* are one and the same text.

On 3rd November 1728 the church book states that the 'Terms of Communion' were read and, when approved, were 'engrossed on parchment for all members to sign'. December 22nd: 'The Terms of Communion were read and signed by most of the members'. June 29th 1729: 'It was also proposed that every member that for the future should be received into the Church shall sign the Terms of Communion which are engrossed on parchment'. I am not aware that a document written on parchment and titled *The Terms of Communion* has survived. But the Covenant document, cited above, is dated just thirteen days after *The Terms of Communion* was read and approved and may be the same text - possibly the text from which the fair copy on parchment was made and when it was given the new title *The Terms of Communion.* The Covenant document in the Angus Library is not on parchment and bears no signatures. It sets out, in eleven paragraphs, what is expected of church members and concludes with a thirty-one verse poem or hymn which could have been used as a way for individual members or the whole congregation to respond to the Covenant. A second very similar covenant, written in 1739, also survives in the Abingdon archive. Such covenants become usual among Baptists in the eighteenth century.

---

87 Abingdon B.C. archive, Angus Library, Regent's Park College, Oxford.

**Discipline.**
The church obviously felt great responsibility for both the welfare of its members and the good name of the church. Immorality and intemperate behaviour were not ignored or hidden and occasionally judgement appears to be pre-emptory: 'Bro. John Burham cut off from the Church for disorderly behaviour'. Usually such matters were gone into with great care, consciously following the instructions in Matthew 18: 15ff. Visitors would be appointed to speak to the offender privately. Only if the visit was unsatisfactory would the matter be brought to the church. And even then the church would hesitate to 'cut off' the person concerned.

**The case of Anthony Pisley.**
On October 22nd 1721 William Fuller acquainted the church of the case of Anthony Pisley. He had borrowed money to set up in trade supplying cord. Brother Benjamin Tomkins had taken his goods at a good price, but by carelessness and idleness he had lost the money. Tomkins had helped him again but he had frequented an alehouse and run up debts. The church seems to have tried to help him but he constantly fell back into debt through drinking. Furthermore, he was courting Thomas Emerson's fifteen year old daughter against her parents' wishes. All this had brought dishonour to the church and the minister requested that he be rejected out of the church. This was opposed by a proposition that the church should regularly summon him to come before them, before sentence was passed - which was agreed.

**Trouble at Newbury.**
This sense of responsibility for its members extended to ensuring that they were in safe hands in their church or when they moved to another district. At the meeting on 2nd February 1724 Fuller informed the church that he had been asked by the Newbury church to 'come to their assistance, Mr. Broadmead, the preacher there, to supply his place'. But the meeting objected that Mr. Broadmead 'was of unsound principles'. The matter was deferred until a suitable stand-in for Abingdon could be found. At the next meeting a letter of transfer from Abingdon to Newbury was requested by sister Consdale. This was approved but Mr. Tomkins declined to sign it - 'desired to be excused from recommending S. Consdale to a people that were not capable of taking care of her'. At the following meeting the matter of this letter was re-opened and declined on the grounds that 'the church

at Newbury it being at present much out of order and not under the care of any pastor'.

**Care of the sick.**

On 3rd March 1734 the church decided to pay Mr. Sawyers (surgeon) for expenses run up by Bro. Francis Churwell, a poor member who 'had for a long while been under the Surgeon's hand'. A month later Francis Churwell's wife was baptised.

**Pastoral care.**

Before leaving this subject of the care of its members, it should be noted that an unusual amount of space in this first church book is devoted first to the appointment of a 'Ruling Elder', whose chief responsibility appears to have been the pastoral care of the church, and then to the appointment of a panel of visitors to take over this elder's work. It appears that before the book begins, Benjamin Tomkins has some responsibility for visiting members - perhaps particularly those who are considered to be misbehaving.

Benjamin Tomkins was the son of John who had been such a leading figure and then minister of the church. John had also been a successful businessman and at his death in 1708 had left lands and a malthouse and £6000. Benjamin expanded the malting business in Ock Street and had his own wharf and barges for the shipping of his malt to London.[88] He increased the family fortune and built, or rebuilt, Stratton House in Bath Street in 1722 - his maltings were in the grounds of this house through which a path is said to have led to the Baptist meeting house.[89] He moved to The Clock House in Ock Street which he built in 1728. A memory lingers of Benjamin and his wife Sarah travelling from The Clock House across the street to the chapel by sedan chair. We shall come to Benjamin's Will later, but in the 1720's he was a man in his 50's, who had experienced the persecutions in his youth and obviously now enjoyed the respect of the church even if, at times, he found himself in a minority of one at church meetings.

---

88 Mieneke Cox. *The Story of Abingdon* part IV p 63.

89 Ibid. p 67

*Figure 13 Benjamin Tomkins c. 1706.*
*Oil on canvas 123.5 x 100.5 Property of Abingdon Town Council*

In 1721 he was called to be Ruling Elder by the church - a position he accepted with some reluctance. It invested in him, it would seem, the duty of visiting the members of the church and especially attempting to ensure that the members attended the services regularly and lived in such a way as not to bring dishonour on the church. No doubt Benjamin attempted to keep on top of this difficult task, but felt he was to blame whenever the church expressed concern over the morals of some of its members:

April 5th 1723: The purpose of this meeting was 'to call over the members' and take notice of some misbehaviour: 'a practice of some of the members to frequent alehouses several times a day without any business there and they having been reproved of the same and not convinced of the evil of it.' The meeting agreed that this shouldn't be tolerated. 'Bro. Tomkins then taking notice of the stay of conversions and the decay of godliness among us requested leave to resign his office. This was left to consideration'. Three years pass, and then:

> At a meeting of the Church on first day April 10th 1726 the names of the members were called over, bro. Fuller told the Church the design of it was that the members might better know one another and do their duty towards each other and then took occasion to complain of the neglect of the discipline and though bro. Tomkins with a great deal of reluctance had taken upon him the office of a Ruling Elder yet he was discouraged from acting as such therefore desired that the Church, in which the power of Government doth lodge, to think of some method by which the Society might be preserved in order and unity, it being agreed that without a regular government the Church could not long subsist.

Tomkins then requests again that he may resign, but when it is put to the vote 'whether Bro. Tomkins were thought capable or not', the church affirms him Nem Con. 'The matter was adjourned to the next church meeting and a Committee appointed to consider of what things were proper to be laid before the church'.

The outcome is a carefully thought through 'Scheme of Visiting' devised by the committee and agreed by the church - 'B. Fuller, B. Roberts, B. Hopkins, and B. Benjamin Tomkins Junr. were appointed to perform that work and give an account thereof in five or six weeks.' Benjamin Tomkins Senr.'s resignation is at last accepted. Thirteen weeks later:

> Bro. Fuller then gave an account of the Visitors viz. That all the members were well established in the principles of religion that they make profession of, that most of them were very comfortable and in a thriving condition, some were under compts of deadness but their desire were to be more lively, some were under afflictions, and some were not so orderly in maintaining the worship of God in their families but it was hoped that upon admonition they would reform.

**Deacons.**

The office of Ruling Elder seems to have ended with Benjamin's resignation, but Edward Roberts, whose name is second to the minister in the list of Visitors, does seem to have a leading role, possibly something equivalent to a modern church secretary. The office of Deacon is mentioned first in 1725, though it is not clear if this entry records the appointment of the first Deacons, or assumes their existence already:

> Bro. Roberts acquainted the church that he had a letter and several things to communicate to them, upon which Bro. Fuller moved and the Church agreed that certain of the brethren should be appointed to meet the Deacons and consult about those affairs, accordingly were named Bro. Stibbs, Bro. Winsmore and Bro. Waite and they to call in whoever they pleased to their assistance.

But by 1736 the only Deacon appears to be Benjamin Tomkins Jnr. and he has just died, only four years after his father.

> January 23rd 1736. At a Meeting on the Lord's Day Brother Fuller took notice of the awful Providence of God in removing a valuable member Mr. Benjamin Tomkins and by his Death occasioned the want of a Deacon or Deacons to supply his place, accordingly it was proposed to choose three Deacons the present state of the Church requiring of it. Some objected against it

> seeing no necessity for so many, however it was agreed to by the majority and that these should be chosen by Balloting in order thereto that the Church may be directed to make a right choice, it was agreed to meet at the Vestry to beg direction at the Throne of grace that the lots may fall on such whom the Lord would dispose the hearts of his people to choose.
> February the 6th 1736. At a Meeting on the Lord's Day Bro. Fuller reported that this was the time for the Church to give in the Tiketts in order to choose the three Deacons, accordingly it was desired that Bro. Roberts would collect the same and that Bro. Fuller should assist him in numbering and examining of them.
> The numbers of the three on whom the lot fell were thus:
> For Bro. Hall 55
> For Bro. T Fuller 53
> For Bro. Hopkins 41

There were about 20 votes for B. Winsmore and a few less for some others. The three were given three weeks to decide if they would accept this call to office - they all accepted. It was then decided that they were to 'make their observation what members were absent on the Lord's Day and it was agreed the Deacons should do business of Wednesday next evening exactly at six of the clock at the Vestry'. The church was then asked to appoint a time for the Deacons to be ordained for their task. A Wednesday evening was agreed and the three men were 'set apart by Prayer with hands laid on them, after Bro. Fuller preached from 12 chap. Rom. v7 on Ministers, let us wait on our ministry'. 'Bro. Fuller and Bro. Roberts in a solemn manner begged assistance for them at the Throne of Grace, that they may be every way qualified for their office.'

**Prayer.**

Prayer was obviously a natural part of worship and of meetings, though normally it seems to have been led by the minister. However, special times of prayer are recorded in the church book:

> 'December 1st 1723 Bro. Roberts then proposed that in consideration of the town being visited with the

Smallpox, and his youngest son and two grand-daughters being at the time afflicted with the same distemper, a time of prayer be fixt.' This was held on Dec. 12th at 5.00 p.m. and another on Boxing Day. The following December saw another outbreak of this disease and this time they call for days of prayer to be held frequently and open to the general public and that leadership of these be shared with the Presbyterian minister, Mr. Bensen.

**Worship.**

Testimonies to faith appear to be a normal part of worship and not only by those seeking baptism:

> May 31st 1741 After the ordinance of the Lord's Supper was administered a daughter of Mrs. Keats of Aston declared what God had done for her soul to the universal joy and satisfaction of the Church in a very affecting manner. And what added to the delight in hearing this wonderful account she gave of a work of Grace begun and carried on in her soul was her tender age - she being scarce eleven years old.

But not all children created such delight:

> March 6th 1725 Bro. Fuller also took notice of a disorder that frequently happened in prayer or sermon times by boys getting in the galleries out of sight and playing together to the disturbance of the congregation, to prevent which he proposed the building of a Gallery at the Vacant End of the meeting house for the boys to sit together yet they might be kept in order by being under his eye, a person sitting with them to assist in it. It was accordingly agreed that a Gallery be built for that purpose and that a general contribution be made for it after debate.
>
> March 13th 1725 ... a subscription then was made for the building of a Gallery and Bro. Winsmore and Bro. Waite were desired to go to the absent friends to complete the same and a Gallery was ordered to be built accordingly by Bro. John Clanvill.

Postscript:

> March 1st 1727 Bro. Jonathan Hut then complained that several of the boys had left their places in the Gallery built on purpose for them to sit in, and on debate it was ordered that Bro. John Hut from the Church do desire the Parents to Command their sons to sit there and that Bro. Clanvill be one of them that shall overlook them and keep them from playing and disorder.

Faded ink on paper faded brown with age, but still the impatience and annoyance bristle from this entry!

**The Will of Benjamin Tomkins.**

At his death in 1732 Benjamin Tomkins Snr. was one of the wealthiest men in Abingdon. His son Benjamin inherited 'my dwelling house in the Ock Street wherein I now dwell [i.e. The Clock House] and the malthouse, stables, orchards, gardens and all the edifices and buildings etc.' To his son Joseph 'my new built house in the Boar Street where my son Benjamin now dwells' [Stratton House] 'and the malthouse, granary, orchards and gardens etc.' In addition these and other sons inherited various properties in the town and wide estates in Berkshire. His daughters were to receive the income from other estates, one daughter, Elizabeth Rickards, to receive this 'for her own separate use - her husband not to intermeddle'.

*Figure 14 The Clock House.*
*Final home of Benjamin & Sarah Tomkins and heirs.*

*Figure 15 Stratton House.*
*Home of Benjamin & Sarah Tomkins and heirs.*

The bequest which is best remembered in the town is that which established the almshouses in Ock Street: 'all my dwellinghouse, malthouse and granaries called Steeds in the Ock Street ... my executors shall out of my personal estate within one year of my decease convert ... into eight tenements to be inhabited by four old men and four old women'. He gives detailed instructions as to how these almshouses are to be constructed and the yard and garden laid out. They appear exactly so today.

*Figure 16 The Ock Street frontage of the Almshouses.*

*Figure 17 Almshouses Ca 1900.*
*The courtyard has hardly changed to date.*

Another bequest gives property in trust 'for the use of a Minister of the Congregation of Protestant Dissenters called Baptists or Anabaptists in Abingdon for the time being to dwell in as long as there shall be a Minister'. This is for two houses - the one now known as 35 Ock Street, which was already occupied by the Revd. William Fuller, and the house to the east of this, across the passage which gave access to the meeting house, 'now in the occupation of Walter Watts, the income to be towards the maintenance of the Minister'. As has already been pointed out in the previous chapter when considering the possibility of a $17^{th}$ century chapel this bequest of 35 Ock Street throws into question the claim made by Pumphrey that 'The Minister's House and Garden were purchased in 1660, and we have among our old papers a receipt for £20 paid for the transfer of the premises'. Benjamin had been bequeathed both these houses in the Will of John Tomkins - then referred to as two houses in the occupation of John Watts and John Prince. (Details of these and other bequests appear in appendix D.)

**The Schism Sermon.**

On the 1st August 1714 an act of parliament was passed which made it illegal for any non-conformist to teach the young, in school or college. But that very day, before it could receive the royal assent, Queen Anne died. To this day, on the Sunday nearest to the anniversary of the queen's death, a sermon variously known as the Twelfth of August Sermon or the Schism Sermon is preached in Abingdon Baptist Church. This had its origins in the Will of Benjamin Tomkins jnr. who died in 1736. He left to his daughter, Elizabeth Tomkins, a dwelling house, malt-house and brew-house in Stert Street:

> subject to the payment of 20s. every first day of August to the Baptist minister ... upon his preaching a sermon in the Meeting House on that day in commemoration of the deliverance of the nation from threatened Popery, which was so happily prevented by the accession of King George the First to the Crown of these realms.

So the emphasis was intended to be less upon the timely death of Anne or on the defeat of the Schism Act, but upon the accession of the Protestant Hanoverian George I, rather than the Jacobite 'Pretender'. These days it tends to be of an historical nature. The old name 'The Twelfth of August Sermon', is a hang-over from the old Julian calendar. When the more accurate Gregorian calendar was adopted in England in 1752 eleven days were lost, hence the 1st of the month became the 12th. Each year the preacher is paid twenty shillings (i.e. one pound) for this sermon. In a recent letter from Ken Read, who was Church Treasurer in the 1960's, he writes of his putting together presentation packs containing twenty old shillings at the time when the coinage was being changed. He intended one of these packs to be given to each new minister after his first preaching of the sermon. Altogether, he estimated, there were enough packs for the next 200 years! The past four ministers have all received one of these packs. But in the last year or so another detail has crept into the tradition. On Schism Sermon Sunday 2008 a Queen Anne shilling appeared in the offering bag. No one owned up to placing it there though those who know the congregation have their suspicions, but for two years now the preacher has been given this shilling at the close of the service. He returns it to the Treasurer and it is then placed in the church safe until the following year.

**Fuller's Assistants:**

**John Beasley.**
Sometime around William Fuller's 70th birthday the church called a minister to assist him and 'September 12th 1742 it was agreed that the Reverend John Beasley should be continued as an assistant to the Revd. Will Fuller and that the Deacons with the assistance of Bro. Hopkins and Bro. Rawlings will use their endeavours with the Subscribers to make provision for him'.

**Robert Day.**
It appears that by 1745 John Beasley was no longer at Abingdon and the church was strongly drawn to Robert Day, a final year student at Bristol Academy. Robert had been baptised at Wellington, Somerset, in 1741 and entered Bristol in 1743. Letters in the college archive, from William Fuller and the Abingdon church to the college principal Bernard Foskett show that Day had preached at Abingdon on several occasions, probably with a view to becoming Assistant Minister. He had been well received by members and the auditory and letters were sent urging the principal to recommend he accept a call to Abingdon. This extract from that correspondence throws light upon the state of the church and of its minister, as Fuller's ministry drew to its close:

> ...the Baptist interest formed according to the London Confession did for many years flourish here under the blessings of heaven, and the Church here has not been the least useful in supporting many others far and wide, but for a little time past our tranquillity was unhappily disturbed by the indiscretion (not to say worse) of some who are gone over to the Presbyterians, yet now they seem entirely quiet, and we are persuaded and satisfied that Mr. Day will be... And comfortable in his situation and subsistence here... To establish our unity and confirm our harmony... Our present much esteemed minister is now far advanced in years and attended with many infirmities, and we can't expect his usefulness, or his life, to continue long; and tis fit that he should soon be relieved...[90]

[90] See Roger Hayden, *Bernard Foskett and Abingdon 1743-5,* Baptist Quarterly vol. 43

The church offered to support Mr. Day for the rest of his final year at college if he would agree to the Abingdon invitation. But the invitation was refused and he went back to minister to his home church in Wellington in December 1745.

**Fuller's death.**
William Fuller died on November 24th 1745. It appears to have been a faithful ministry during which he oversaw the care of the members and preached to a full church. Apart from the entries in the church book, his life's work at Abingdon is hardly mentioned, but it should be recorded that the numbers attracted and held by his preaching, and the number brought into membership, compare favourably with those of his great successor. In a letter which is probably the annual report to the Association on the state of the church in 1776, twenty eight years into Daniel Turner's ministry, this comparison is made with the situation at the death of Fuller:

> This society is in tolerably flourishing circumstances; the auditory is between two and three hundred, and has continued much the same these thirty years past. When Mr. Turner first came to Abingdon the church consisted of between sixty and seventy members, but is now reduced to about forty; and though most years some have been added, yet not a proportionate number: the audience has of late been increasing.[91]

We do not know the size of the audience at Fuller's death but are reminded that during the reign of George I (1714-27 ) it was 300-400.

**The inter-regnum.**
John Beasley's assistantship appears to have ended in the same year as Fuller's death since the Wantage church called him in that year.[92] Pumphrey states that 'for three years the church was without a pastor'. But, though aware of his short ministry,[93] he ignores the affair of

---

Apr. 2009 p.68ff.

[91] Ivimey IV pp 421ff

[92] Ernest Payne believed that John Beasley was probably a native of Abingdon - see footnote 9 p 68 of his *The Baptists of Berkshire*.

[93] See facing page of p 48 of the 1721 Church Book where Pumphrey, in his indelible pencil has noted: 'Report of Rev W. Fuller death cont. Rev Thomas Flower for short time'.

Reverend Mr. Thomas Flower, clearly recorded in the church book. We know nothing from the church book of the call of Mr. Flower, but again the historian Joseph Ivimey throws some light on the man's situation, gifts and character. It was becoming the usual practice to invite a potential minister for a probationary year or more, before confirming him in office. Ivimey writes, 'After being pastor of the Unicorn Yard church about eight years, Mr. Flower resigned the office; after which he preached for some time as a probationer at Abingdon, Berks.; but was not invited to settle as pastor'.[94] Thomas Flower went on to hold a fourteen year ministry at Cirencester but then returned to London where he did not seek another ministerial post but preached occasionally. These particulars, writes Ivimey, 'are from the manuscripts of Mr. Joshua Thomas; who adds, 'He was a person of considerable wealth. I have been informed by a good judge that he had certain great talents, and was affectionate in the pulpit, but had not the best utterance." Ivimey, it appears, has little respect for a minister who forsakes his calling and goes back into business, for he concludes, 'It should seem that his true character was that of a tradesman as he was distinguished by the appellation of worldly-minded Flower'.

Perhaps these comments throw some light on the sad situation recorded in the Abingdon church book:

> June 15th 1746 After evening service The Revd. Thos. Flower stayed the Church and after a short Harangue respecting some reports that had been spread against him and as he was going to London desired to know the sense of the Church in regard to his staying here. And after he was desired to withdraw a motion was made and seconded and the question put whether Mr. Flower should be continued or dismissed at Midsummer next. And it was agreed to dismiss him at Midsummer next by a great majority - For his dismission 36; for his continuing 16.

Arrangements were then made 'in order to provide supplies for the time after Midsummer day next'. So began a sequence of events which bitterly divided the church. The minority withdrew from the

[94] Ivimey III p 427 IV pp 121 ff

church. A major attempt to resolve the situation was made on August 26/27. Three ministers, Phillip Jones, Hugh Evans and Joseph Stennett were invited by the majority to Abingdon 'in order to assist in settling the differences that subsist at present in the Church'. Since none of 'the dissatisfied brothers and sisters' were present at the first meeting with these ministers, four members were deputed to call on them and encourage them to meet with the rest of the church at 9.00 a.m. next day. At the appointed time next day it was reported that the invitations had received 'an evasive answer' and then a message was received from Bro. Rawlings Senr. that he had consulted with his fellows who had withdrawn from the church and they chose not to attend the meeting 'unless the Church would agree to grant them the use of the pulpit and other things belonging to the Meeting House once a fortnight or at such times as should be agreed upon'. Two of the ministers then reported that the dissatisfied members had agreed to talk to the three ministers at the house of Mr. Rawlings Jnr. at 11.00 a.m. The Church Meeting agreed to this and arranged to reconvene at 3.00 p.m. at which time the three ministers reported that the dissatisfied members were adamant that as the Majority of the Church had voted against Mr. Flower's continuance, and had not given the reason of their dislike of him, they could not join with them, without, as the first point settled, Mr. Flower should be accepted as their Pastor'. The ministers then urged the church to reconsider their decision since it was likely that if Mr. Flower was not accepted there would be a division 'and the dissatisfied members would, they feared, rend themselves off from the Body'. The church took another vote but, with one against, the original decision was upheld 'most of them saying that they did not think it would be for his comfort, or theirs' if he continued. And here, tantalisingly, the book ends. We don't know the outcome. But in a list of members drawn up in 1748, two years later, three of the five men in the dissatisfied group have their names entered. There were 'seven sisters in the group but, not being named, their continuance with the church or otherwise, cannot be known. But it is clear that Mr. Flower did not remain. This is a sad interlude between two great ministries and perhaps the nearest the church has come in its 360 years to a major division.

**Revd. Daniel Turner A.M.**

'This worthy minister had received an education for the ministry from the Rev. Dr. James of Hemel Hempstead. He settled first at Reading, but in September 1748 he removed to Abingdon, and there continued till his death'.[95] So the historian Joseph Ivimey begins his short biography. To the Baptist world beyond Abingdon Daniel Turner is chiefly known and respected for his publications. These consisted of moral essays, poetry and hymns, a school exercise book on rhetoric, a tract on open communion and his main work *A Compendium of Social Religion* to name but a few. But if it were not for these publications; if, like his predecessor, we had only the church book to draw upon, there would be little to distinguish him from any other good, faithful minister who had devoted his life to the church and died in office. He was born in St. Albans in 1710. He was educated in near-by Hemel Hempstead and continued in his school as an usher (the 18th century equivalent of a classroom assistant). At the age of thirteen he published his first book, *An Abstract of English Grammar and Rhetoric*. Dr. James, his minister in Hemel Hempstead, recognising his potential, gave him theological instruction and prepared him for ministry. Aged 21 he was invited to the Reading Baptist Church to be their pastor. He was at Reading for seventeen years during which time he wrote poetry and published his small book of hymns. He married sometime in the mid 1730's and a son, Daniel, was born. Some years after the birth of their son, Daniel's young wife became seriously ill. From a letter written to a fellow minister early in 1743 we get an insight into his sense of unworthiness yet complete trust in God - the times may have changed, but the piety of the Puritans is still there. He writes of his father's illness and then continues:

> But God has laid his hand also on my dear wife who has not been abroad, unless twice or thrice into the garden, since Christmas and has kept above stairs this fortnight. Her case is a universal weakness, and I am sometimes afraid she will never go abroad again - the Lord knows what He has to do with me but it's a heavy stroke. I hope He has given me (Glory be to His Grace) some good degree of resignation and patience, for the most part sometimes He lets me see I have a heart fearfully rebellious. My poor wife is in a good measure resigned; but has many doubts and fears, but some good hope in the main.
>
> What I desire of you is Prayer Prayer. Entreat the Lord for me: that I may see my sin and be humbled - see His

---

[95] Ivimey, *History of English Baptists,* vol IV p 421.

> love and be exalted. That I may be more resigned, more dependant and have no will but the will of my God. Blessed be His name I can call Him and pray to Him as my Covenant God in Christ. Pray that the dispensation may be sanctified to me and I sanctified by it and that my dear wife may be fitted for all His will.[96]

His wife died a year or so later in 1744. In 1748, at the age of thirty eight, he received the call to Abingdon. The first reference to his second wife appears in a list of members in 1766: 'Elizabeth Turner, wife of D.T. Pastor, 4th May 1766. An asterisk before the name indicates that she was baptised by Daniel. Her maiden name was probably Dowsett as a nephew, Robert Dowsett appears in correspondence.[97] The new minister appears to have been deeply respected in the church and neighbourhood for his saintliness and pastoral care. He became known as 'Good Mr. Turner'.[98] But it is his writings which reveal him to have been one whose influence would be felt far beyond the town of Abingdon and far into the future of his denomination. They show him to be a man of liberal scholarship, concerned with education and the embryo Sunday School movement and an advocate of open communion and wider church unity. He tackled some of the burning questions of his day and laid foundations for church organisation which have persisted for two hundred years to the present day.

**The task ahead of him.**

In 1748 he inherited a church which had been struggling for three years. It appeared to have been taken up with the weekly problem of finding a preacher for the coming services, usually working only a fortnight in advance, and dealing with divisions and problem members - a church which, for the time, had lost its way. It was perhaps a relief, before he arrived, in January of 1748, to give attention in the church meeting to something as down to earth as a walnut tree: '....desire the approbation of the Church in taking down the walnut tree adjoining the dwelling house in the property of this Church as it is looked on by some to be inconvenient and that we would appoint a time to take it down in order to sell it'. But a month later comes the

---

96 See a bound volume of MS correspondence of Daniel Turner in the Angus Library, Oxford.

97 See MS correspondence in ABC archives, Angus Library.

98 So John Evans in his memorial address on the death of Daniel Turner.

first mention in the church book of their future minister. It is thought that many in the church would approve of this young minister in Reading, but they were unwilling to 'give him a call ....unless the Reverend Mr. Turner is actually at liberty'. What today is known as head-hunting was carefully avoided in the churches of the eighteenth century. But by the middle of the year the Reading church informed the Abingdon church that they had given their minister 'full Liberty to Treat with you on the matter'. A unanimous invitation was offered and the church called for a day of prayer 'next week' to seek God's help to convince Mr. Turner of the rightness of accepting it. He was convinced and his fifty year ministry in Abingdon began.

**Immediately the new broom gets to work.**

December 20th 1748 Sunday services are to be held at 10.20 a.m. and 2.00 p.m.

'Transient members' (i.e. people temporally in Abingdon and wishing to receive communion) must bring a letter of recommendation and dismission from the churches where they belong. There will be a sermon every month at 6.00 p.m. on the Wednesday prior to the 'Sacrament day'. The Lord's Supper to be held on the first Lord's day of the month, and at no other time without the consent of the church. And finally (to delight the hearts of future church historians) the church books 'be locked up in the cupboard in the Vestry'.

The influence of the man who in ten years time will publish his great work on how a church should be organised is further seen a few weeks later:

> February 6th 1749: 'Bro. Turner acquainted the Church that as there were no persons that acted as Deacons it was most agreeable without delay to choose Deacons in order to take care of the outward affairs of the Church'. Three Deacons were soon elected by ballot.

Then the matter of poor attendance at the church meetings was addressed. They are having difficulty raising the necessary quorum of seven men - should they reduce the number? These meetings were usually held after morning worship on Sundays and it appears that few of the membership were prepared to stay on for them. The decision is made, however, not to reduce the quorum but to admonish the absentees.

Financial matters were now addressed. The church was understood to be a society and was financed by subscriptions from its members, as was any society. These entitled the subscriber to a pew. There was other income, from donations by those in the auditory who were not members, and from legacies. There were also regular collections for the poor - these being increasingly linked to the Sacrament. In June 1750 the minister raised the question whether the church 'should pay him £60 per annum or whether he should take the income of the estate and subscriptions as they come in?'. The church decided that Mr. Turner should take the donations and subscriptions as they come in (i.e. only when the money is available) but effort be made to increase the subscriptions so that arrears due to him might be paid. This appears to have been an ongoing problem and in 1759 a 'Collector' of all the church's income had his job description set out: to receive the subscriptions, rents and donations; to pay the minister quarterly from these; to keep 'faithful and clear' accounts which are to be audited every half year or as often as the church thinks proper. Two years later, when Mr. William Tomkins of Boar Street was appointed, the title 'Treasurer' was first mentioned.

**Prayer.**

In September 1751 the decision was made to hold a monthly day of prayer - 'on the Thursday after the Sacrament'.

> March 29th 1772 'The Church stayed today and a meeting for prayer proposed on account of the calamities that threaten the Nation, the aboundings of Sin and Wickedness and declension of Vital Religion'.

**Pews.**

Many of the short meetings when the church was 'stayed' after morning worship dealt with the allocation of pews. The system of having a pew allocated dependant on the size of the subscription or rent must had been fraught with difficulty. As people increased their subscription or as others died or ceased to attend, there must have been a constant shuffling of the congregation.

> July 3rd 1751 Resolved that the pew in which Mrs. Webb and Mrs. Rawlings usually sit and which Mr. Tuckwell claims as his, should be fastened up that

> nobody should sit therein till the Church's intentions are further known.
> July 11th 'Mr. Tuckwell being heard in support of his claim to the pew in question, and the question being put, it was unanimously agreed that he had no right or title to the same as his property, but that his right is forfeited to the Church and that they have the sole property and disposition of the same.

The two ladies were then allowed back into the pew on the understanding that a space be left in it for Mr. Tuckwell on the infrequent occasions he might attend.

**Property matters.**
By 1772 the old meeting house was apparently in need of some modernisation:

> Resolved that the passage at the front of the Meeting House which is now pitched with stones, be paved with brick after first having the charges. Brother Jos. Tomkins desired to apply to his workman for that purpose, and report the same to the next Church Meeting and likewise to speak to Jos. Hutt to know what he would expect by way of reward for keeping the premises without doors free from weeds and keep the house clean within doors, washing the whole twice in the summer. Likewise to enquire the expense of a cover at each door and report the same next Church Meeting.
> July 3rd 1772 Brother J. Tomkins has enquired of J. Hutt about the expense of keeping the Meeting House, Vestry, Burying Ground and Walks clean and says he wishes £3. 10s. per annum. Engaged.
> August 4th Brother J. Tomkins says that the workman's estimation for paving the walk before the Meeting House with brick is 22d. per yard laid in sand. But Mr. Butler desired to take the opinion of Mr. Wilmot on that subject and to enquire likewise the expense of paving a yard wide up the main walk to the Meeting.

It is good to know that Jos. Hutt is still the caretaker. Fifteen years before he was in trouble, as Sexton, for selling the old grave stones which were removed when he dug new graves. He was told he had no right to them and that he must return the money so earned or it would be stopped from his wages. The money so gained by the church would be given to the poor.

Another alteration which may have been made at this time was the installing of a new pulpit designed by Mr. Turner himself. There is no documentary reference to this, but it is one of those bits of information which have persisted to the present day. If one may be allowed to muddy the waters further by hypothesising on a rumour, the church has two photographs of harvest festival displays, one at least dating from the nineteenth century. Both are clearly the interior of the Victorian chapel, but the pulpits are different. When the premises were rebuilt in 1841, was Mr. Turner's pulpit preserved in the new chapel until such time as fashion or convenience demanded it be replaced?

*Figure 18 19th century chapel, Note the early pulpit.*
*This may be the one said to be designed by Daniel Turner.*

**A College at Kingston Lisle?**

Joseph Ivimey, the historian, includes in his account of Daniel Turner a letter from the Revd. Robert Robinson of Cambridge written to Daniel Turner in 1781 regarding a proposal that Turner had made for the founding of a college 'for law and physic'. Robinson writes,

> Our dissenting interest has suffered much from this deficiency by the sons of such gentlemen being sent to our universities, who of course left us to go over to the church. This was the case of Lord Barrington and several families in this neighbourhood. Mr. Atkins has a house near Wantage that would do: he might, if he would, endow it with a thousand a year: if you have opportunity, feel his pulse about the matter as fully as you can.[99]

Daniel appears to have felt the man's pulse and one of the endowments in the wealthy Mr. Atkins' will recorded elsewhere by Ivimey is for a school at Kingston Lisle which has very strong Abingdon Baptist representation in the list of trustees - Daniel Turner, Joseph and Benjamin Tomkins, William Tomkins senr. and junr., Rev. Robert Robinson, Cambridge, Rev. Thomas Dunscombe, Cote, Rev. William Wilkins, Bourton and, 'upon vacancies happening the following gentlemen have been chosen: Joseph Tomkins Esq., Abingdon, John Tomkins Esq., ditto, Edward Sheppard Esq., London'.[100] Professor Paul Fiddes discusses this in the context of the friendship of Daniel Turner with Robert Robinson of Cambridge, Thomas Dunscombe of Cote and Abraham Atkins, all of them advocates of open communion. He writes that nothing came of the scheme for the academy, nor of a similar scheme of Robinson's for an academy in Cambridge. But the four friends continued to collaborate and were instrumental in establishing the Atkins Trust in 1786, which made annual donations to poor Baptist ministers and members of their churches and grants towards their buildings, on condition that they practiced open communion.[101]

---

[99] Ivimey IV pp 421ff

[100] Ibid p 413

[101] P.Fiddes, *A Protestant Catholic Church of Christ*, ed. Rosie Chadwick 2003 p 71f and end-notes.

**The Tomkins' Company.**

It is not surprising that, following the minister, in the list of proposed trustees for the proposed Kingston Lisle project we have the three Tomkins, Benjamin, Joseph and William. Two of their sons are also listed. In the second half of the eighteenth century the Tomkins family reached the height of their wealth and influence. Benjamin (III), 1734-84 occupied The Clock House. His two cousins were Joseph (II) 1729-94 who built himself Twickenham House and William 1731-1808 of Stratton House. These three formed a Malting Company ca. 1750 to 1800. The Company opened the first bank in the town, 'Abingdon Old Bank' in 1777 which continued into the early1800's.[102]

*Figure 19 Twickenham House.*
*Built by Joseph Tomkins (1729-1794).*

**Turner's scholarship and writings.**

The Church Books move on to the last years of Daniel Turner's ministry, but at this stage we must consider his literary output. He is

102 See L.G.R. Naylor, *The Malthouse of Joseph Tomkins* pp. 13-15 . ABC archive, Angus Library

said to have published 58 works. Dr. Ernest Payne writes 'Turner's literary activities and learning had gained him the degree of MA probably from Rhode Island University'.[103] He gives no reference to support this probability, but Turner certainly had this degree, and honorary degrees were not awarded by the English universities to non-conformists in the 18th century, nor for most of the 19th century for that matter.

His writing of verse possibly began at an early stage and developed during his training for the ministry while he appears to have kept himself as a school master in Hemel Hempstead.[104] He published *Divine Songs, Hymns and other Poems* in 1746 while minister in Reading.[105] One of these hymns was composed during a violent thunderstorm and compares the power of nature with the power of judgement. Another, which recalls to us the last serious outbreak of foot-and-mouth disease in 2001 is headed 'A Hymn for Jan. 7th 1746/7. Being the Day appointed by Authority for a general Humiliation fasting and Prayer v. 3 Alluding to a contagious Distemper that had for some time raged amongst the great Horned Cattle, and destroyed many Thousands in a few months'. Verse three reads:

> The Beasts that should our Wants supply,
> Struck with thy Plagues, around us die;
> And while these hardened Hearts we feel,
> We fear more dreadful Judgements still.

This theme of judgement runs through much of his verse. This small book of hymns may not seem particularly remarkable to us, but in fact it has a significance far beyond its size. Baptists on the Calvinistic wing of the denomination (and Turner, certainly at this stage, was to be numbered among them[106]) had long debated the pros and cons of

---

103 E.A. Payne, *The Baptists of Berkshire* , 1951 Carey Kingsgate Press. p 83.

104 *Transactions of the Baptist Historical Society* vol. II pp 97ff.

105 This and other titles in this section can be sourced in the Angus Library, Regent's Park College , Oxford.

106 In 1782 Turner described his theological position to be in line with that of: 'good Mr. Porhill, Mr. How, Dr. Watts and many others .... I hold the doctrine of particular Election and general Redemption, as it may be called. that is a Redemption from a Covenant of mere works and death to a Covenant of Grace, Mercy and Life, that Christ tasted Death for *EveryMan, the Whole World* in the plain sense of the words without having recourse to figurative terms, etc. and yet steadfastly believe that the Elect only

singing hymns in worship. The hyper Calvinists argued that since, in public worship, there would always be some present who were not redeemed, it would be wrong to encourage them to sing along with the saints sentiments which they were not yet in a spiritual state to sing without hypocrisy. They argued from this that hymns had no place in public worship. But those who were seeking a more liberal and inclusive expression of Calvinism saw hymns as a means of drawing everyone nearer to Christ. It was not the only factor, but the publication and use of hymn books became an indicator in the gradual movement towards a more open, humane and evangelistic understanding of the gospel which would lead, by the end of the century, to movements such as Sunday Schools, the expansion of non-conformity into the villages and new industrial towns, and the formation of Missionary Societies. Among the Baptists, Turner's was not the greatest, but was the earliest hymn book to be published. So his little book, *Divine Songs, Hymns and Other Poems*, published in 1747 while he was still at Reading, placed him among the pioneers of an understanding of the faith which would lead to the worldwide expansion of Protestantism in the 19th century and the movement towards Christian unity in the 20th.

*The Compendium of Rhetoric* written for the use of school children perhaps supplied a need of which his early school-teaching made him aware and gives an insight to his own oratory. A publication entitled *Letters, Religious and Moral; designed particularly for the Entertainment of Young Persons* is a series of letters giving practical and moral advice to a young man who has emigrated to India. If the young person to whom the letters are addressed is a particular young man and not simply a literary device, then from manuscript correspondence discovered by Mieneke Cox of Abingdon, copies of which are now in the Angus Library, it appears that the young man could have been Mrs. Elizabeth Turner's nephew Robert Dowsett who was in business in Madras. Although this recently discovered correspondence is chiefly between members of the Rose family of Abingdon, it further reveals something of the pastoral heart of Daniel Turner. Part of this book is a contribution to one of the great debates of the eighteenth century - the relationship of faith and reason.

It was in the 1750's that Daniel benefited greatly when the Tomkins'

share in the complete and saving Grace of His Redemption'. (quoted by E.A. Payne op. cit. p 85.)

family made a gift to the church of what became known as the Tomkins' Library, a collection of some five hundred early theological books which were to be housed in the old manse for over two hundred years before being placed in the Angus Library. These were originally the library of Martin Tomkins, a grandson of John Tomkins. He was a well known Arian divine and controversialist. After his death in 1757 a member of the family presumably secured his library for Turner and his successors.[107]

Daniel Turner's main on-going contribution to the churches was the *Compendium of Social Religion.* The preface to the first edition is dated 'Abingdon (Berks.) Jan. 26 1758'. It would have been written at the manse in Ock Street. The book from which I shall quote is a second edition (1778) and inscribed on the title page 'M. Tomkins from the Author'. The 'Social Religion' of the title refers to what is done publicly in churches as opposed to private religion or devotion. Its five chapters set out how a 'true Church' should be organised and what the respective duties of its officers and members are. It would have reflected the patterns which were emerging as well as helping to establish good practice in non-conformist churches for years if not centuries to come. Its statements are backed up with numerous footnotes giving examples from the scriptures and early Church Fathers - probably drawing heavily upon his new library and so numerous that the main text is often reduced to just a line or two of each page. Most of the material still forms the basis of Baptist church life today, with the exception of his passage on the role of women in the church. However, the book really comes alive in its final section headed 'Conclusion' which occupies nearly a quarter of the book and deals with a controversy in which his decided views were at first not shared by the Abingdon church, but were later to make Abingdon a major church in the movement towards open communion - a view which was also built into the covenant of the New Road church in Oxford which Turner and others reconstituted, after a period of closure, in 1780.[108]

The early division between the view of the church and that of their young pastor is seen in an entry in the church book on 13 May 1751, seven years before the Compendium was published: 'The question

---

[107] Naylor, *The Malthouse of Joseph Tomkins (op. cit.)* p 9

[108] E.A. Payne, BQ XI pp237ff.

being put whether Mrs. Ruth Webb should be admitted to Transient Communion in this Church upon recommendation from Mr. Foot of Bristol, It was agreed by the Majority present in the Negative because that Church is not of the same Faith and Order with us'. The men present were listed. But then, in a unique entry in the margin in his own hand Turner has written: 'I witness the Resolution of the Church but not to the Justice of it, being of the opinion she ought to have been admitted. D. Turner'.

Transient Communion was part of the wider debate with those who held that only those who had received believer's baptism should be permitted to participate at the Lord's Table. This view was challenged in the previous century by John Bunyan of Bedford though 'open-communion', the view that all believers should be welcome at the Table, was strongly opposed by William Kiffin and most of his Baptist contemporaries. Turner argues in the conclusion of his Compendium that the Lord's Supper must be offered to all 'who appear to love our Lord Jesus Christ in sincerity'. At the heart of Turner's views on open communion, which he obviously held with passion, are the seeds of ecumenicalism. He sees the Lord's Supper as the one God-given activity which could demonstrate the underlying unity of all the separate denominations. No belief, however sincerely held, should be allowed to prevent true Christians sharing in communion together. He argues this for the dissenting Protestant denominations - they should be able to accept each other at the Table. But what of open communion with the Established Church? His language is guarded, possibly because he wishes to alienate as few as possible among the Baptist churches, but he does include the established church among those who love their Lord with sincerity, even though they may deny their Table to us: 'I readily acknowledge, that there are many, both of the established church, and the dissenters, who profess to make it a matter of conscience, to maintain a stricter communion than what I am pleading for; whose piety and charity in all other instances are so conspicuous, and carry with them such strong marks of Christian sincerity...'[109] And the plea for open communion being the way back for Christians to a greater unity reaches its height in the final paragraph. I allow myself the luxury of quoting this at length because it represents arguably the greatest contribution that the Abingdon church, through its minister, has made to the Church universal:

[109] D. Turner, *A Compendium of Social Religion 2nd. ed.* p 191.

> Finally, while the case is such, that through our own weakness or that of others, we cannot carry our CHARITY so high, as to partake of the Lord's Supper together at the same table; or otherwise worship together in the same forms; while I say this is our unhappy case, let us be extremely careful, to exercise and exemplify that grace in mutual forbearance, and all other offices of Christian condescension and goodness. Let us put away all wrath, strife, bitterness, anger, and evil-speaking - and put on bowels of mercy, long-suffering, gentleness, meekness; believing all things, hoping all things possible in favour of those that differ from us (Ephes. iv.31 Col. iii 6.12. 1Cor. xiii.7.) that the means used to support our (at present) unavoidable separations may not increase and aggravate them, or prove the occasions of a real alienation of heart from one another and thereby injure the internal power, as well as the external form of godliness; always remembering it is the express, the repeated command, and even dying charge of the blessed Redeemer - that WE LOVE ONE ANOTHER.

That the Abingdon church was now in agreement with their pastor on this issue is shown in the opening words of *A Modest Plea for Free Communion at the Lord's Table between Baptists and Paedobaptists,* written by Turner in 1772:

> I hear that I, and the church under my care, have been severely censured by several of our stricter brethren of the baptist denomination for admitting Paedobaptists to commune with us at the Lord's Table.

The debate would continue and be taken up heatedly a hundred years later, but the great majority of the denomination would be convinced of Turner's position. As for that greater unity, to which the prophetic parenthesis of his phrase 'our (at present) unavoidable separations' aspires, it would have rejoiced his heart that over two hundred years after his death, his house would be in use as a town-centre resource of 'The Church in Abingdon', though, alone (as yet) the Strict Baptists at Abbey Chapel remain separate.

Eight years after the publication of *A Modest Plea for Free Communion at he Lord's Table between Baptists and Paedobaptists* came a document, referred to earlier, which is both an example of the practical application of Turner's ecumenism and of the continuing power of Turner's spirit of love. This is the *New Road Covenant* of 1780 which is read in full at that church's anniversary year by year. Throughout most of the 18th century the church in Bonn Square, Oxford, which dates from 1653 and is now known as New Road Baptist Church, had been very small and for years on end had failed to use its building. Several of its members had taken to worshipping at Abingdon. Turner was one of six ministers who were present on the 16th November 1780 when thirteen people met to sign the covenant document and so re-constitute the Oxford church. He later published the sermon which he preached to them that day. It has an introduction in which he outlines the church's history - how it had begun more than one hundred years before; how its meeting house, together with that of the Presbyterians had been destroyed in 1714 'by the Rioters of those Days'; how the two homeless churches (Baptist and Paedobaptist) had come together in 1721 to build the meeting house in New Road. His sermon had the text, 'And above all these Things, put on Charity, which is the Bond of Perfectness'. It is a sustained call for love to be the hallmark of the church. We may disagree on many things, but differences are no excuse to withhold love. And to share Communion together with all who 'love the Lord Jesus in Sincerity' is where that Christian love becomes reality. This new church, where all Christians of whatever denomination were welcome to its Lord's Supper, he called, 'A true Protestant Catholic Church'. He writes,

> The next Lord's Day (Nov.19) I administered the Lord's Supper to this Church, and thereby sealed their Covenant Engagement, to our mutual Satisfaction - thus the People, so long scattered like Sheep without a Shepherd, are gathered and united again, with very pleasing Prospects of Happiness. May the Prayers put up for them be graciously heard!

Daniel Turner collaborated with John Lake, the Abingdon Congregational minister, and others in this exercise. But from the textual evidence he was the author of the Covenant document and it is there that we can detect his heartbeat. I was present at its annual reading just this past Sunday. Afterwards, one of the present members said to me, 'I can never hear those words without a tear of pride coming to my eye, that I belong to such a church'. Those New Road church people who wished to be baptised by immersion continued to come to Abingdon for this service, though their own minister officiated, until the Oxford church built their baptistery, probably when they built their new chapel in 1799.

There is so much to learn from his writings, about Daniel Turner and his influence upon the Abingdon church and the wider scene. One of his most revealing works was written in his eighty-fourth year. *Free Thoughts on the Spirit of Free Inquiry in Religion* seeks to encourage a spirit of free enquiry in matters of religion and the study of scripture, while warning against possible pitfalls his readers may encounter if they engage in such a process. But he also appeals to moderate free-thinkers both in and outside the churches and challenges the bigoted in the state church and among the dissenters. How far can the Christian thinker go with modern free-thinkers, many of whom are pushing at the boundaries which divide Christian understanding from Secularism? In this surprisingly optimistic book (Turner was no grumpy old man) he finds much to encourage him. The Protestant Reformation and the enlightenment of the 18th century are achieving great changes for the good in Anglican and even Roman Catholic circles. He is realist enough to see the impossibility of the various churches ever worshipping together, while man remains a fallen creature, but he pleads for Christian charity towards all: 'Even the *Roman Catholics* (as they are called) of the present day, very sensibly feel the power of this spirit enlightening their understandings, weakening their prejudices, enlarging their hearts, and inspiring them with a degree of candour and moderation unknown to their ancestors'.[110] Be aware of your own fallibility when judging others:

> However mistaken these people may be, yet while they continue to own JESUS CHRIST as their LORD and SAVIOUR, support his cause in general, as the cause of truth, and lead pious and virtuous lives, we should not deny them the honour of the Christian name... They have still a right to a place in our fraternal affection.[111]

---

110 D. Turner, *Free Thoughts on the Spirit of Free Inquiry in Religion,* 1793 p 10.
111 op. cit. p 121.

The weakness of his argument may lie in the limits to free enquiry that he sets. The basic tenets of the Christian creeds and scriptures, especially the doctrine of atonement, which sees Christ's death as an expiatory sacrifice, and that of grace - the work of the Holy Spirit upon each person which is necessary if they are to believe - are no-go areas for free enquiry unless examined in an attitude of deep humility and a readiness to accept that God's mysteries must remain beyond human understanding. He states that 'Hyper-critics' are doing the Church a disservice.[112]

I have mentioned Turner's optimism. So much in the past two centuries have encouraged him to believe that Europe was at the threshold of a new golden age. And the latest example of this is:

> '....the late astonishing effort in favour of civil and religious liberty, that has taken place in *France*, and which has produced one of the most extraordinary national revolutions ever recorded in the history of mankind, the deliverance of the *Israelites* out of their bondage in *Egypt* excepted'.[113]

We know that many in Britain and elsewhere were at first greatly in favour of the regime change taking place in France from 1792 onwards. But this attitude changed almost over-night as news came of the Reign of Terror. The news evidently reached Turner after he had written the above glowing approval and shocked him into adding a footnote*

> *It must be confessed that the enchanting prospect that seemed to be opening upon us at the beginning of this Revolution, (when the above was written,) has been since miserably obscured by the horrid gloom of anarchy, and such deeds of violence, injustice, and cruelty, as are, to the last degree, shocking to humanity, and cover the fair face of liberty with confusion. But it is to be hoped, after some further painful struggles amongst themselves, and rebukes from the ALMIGHTY for their national vices, they will unite in some form of

[112] op. cit. p 11.
[113] op. cit. pp 7f.

> government, consistent with the enjoyment of just and rational freedom, and that peace and goodwill towards the rest of mankind which true Christianity teaches. At present they appear to be much under the influence of a set of men of the most abandonly vicious characters that ever disgraced human nature, while the wise and the good, *deluded* by their specious pretences, or *terrified* by their savage menaces, behold the dreadful torrent of misery coming upon them unable to resist its force.
> N.B. This note was written January 22 1793 since which we have been informed, that this desperate faction have shed the blood of their late king!![114]

It must be quite rare to find such a change of mind happening as the author is writing. And his horror at the death of the French king echoes that of one of Abingdon's earliest members, the prophetess Elizabeth Poole, who in 1649 had raised William Kiffin's ire when she expressed divine condemnation of those who had executed the English king.

As public suspicion rose against British dissenters, fearing a copycat revolution on this side of the Channel, Turner called the nation to find a 'middle way' which resisted tyranny and anarchy.[115] This way is found in Divine Providence. Before this work went to press, Turner stayed his congregation after the morning service and lectured them against being led astray by the French example. This was also printed with an 'Advertisement' that its contents were supported by all the other dissenting people of Abingdon.

**Assistance for the ageing minister.**

All this time, of course, Turner was involved in the weekly care of his church. By 1778 he was sixty eight years of age and the church began to seek an assistant minister. Pumphrey records that 'the congregations attending Mr. Turner's ministry were nearly three hundred'. But as his physical powers diminished so also his congregation may have declined. On the 2nd August a letter was sent to Mr. Norman to be Assistant Minister at Abingdon. He possibly came on a year's probation, because on October 31st the following

---

114 op. cit. p 8 footnote.

115 op .cit. p 39.

year it was proposed that Mr. Norman be paid £60 as an Assistant to Mr. Turner and also to supply at Oxford. This was two years before the re-constitution of that church. It was possibly this extra work that was proving too much for Turner to manage alone. However, Norman remained only until March 1780 when he accepted a call to Plymouth.

In his article *The First Leeds Baptist Church* [116] F.W. Beckwith includes a biography of Thomas Langton. While Thomas was studying at the Bristol Baptist Academy Beckwith records: 'He spent the next vacation of 1780, however, at Abingdon, assisting the Rev. Daniel Turner, unable through age and infirmity to work unassisted, and at the close of this visit a unanimous invitation was given to Langton to become co-pastor'. Despite the generous terms - £70 a year, increased to £100 when he became sole minister, plus a house - Langton felt he should spend longer at Bristol College.

Then, in September 1781 the Revd. John Evans accepted a call as Assistant. Four years later this post was upgraded to Co-pastor. And Daniel wrote in the church book:

> Brother John Evans was ordained joint pastor with me by the assistance of the Rev. Mr. Evans, Myself, Mr. Miller, Mr. Dore, Mr. Dunscombe and many other Ministers present. Mr. Evans of Bristol gave him an excellent Charge. Mr. Miller preached to the people. A great and serious auditory, and I felt the presence of our God. Oh that the happy Fruits of this solemnity and the labour of our Brother amongst us may be abundant to the glory of God and the people's Comfort and increase of Numbers and Graces. D. Turner.

---

[116] F.W. Beckwith, BQ VI pp 76f.

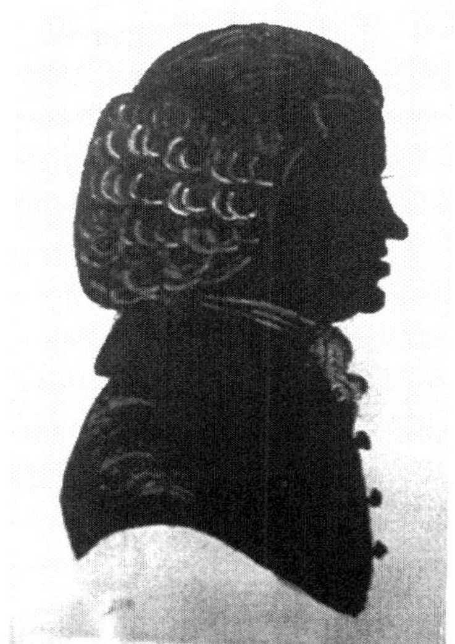

*Figure 20 Daniel Turner.*
*Ministered at Abingdon from 1748-1798.*

*Figure 21 John Evans.*
*Ministered at Abingdon from 1781 to 1813.*

**Funeral address for a centenarian.**

We shall see how Daniel's prayer was answered as we move into the nineteenth century. John Evans, a Welshman from Pembrokeshire, was to serve with Turner for sixteen years and then continue for a further fifteen in sole charge of the church. But from much later in the nineteenth century comes a memory of Daniel Turner's declining years which tells of both the low state that the church had reached and of a revival of spiritual activity which must have brought joy to the old man's heart. The Revd. Samuel Green, President of Rawdon College, came to Abingdon on 19th June 1870 to preach the funeral sermon of a remarkable Abingdon woman. Mrs. Elizabeth Leader had died aged 102. Born in 1768, she had come to Abingdon at the age of five to live with her uncle, Joseph Fletcher, a deacon at the Independent Church in the Square. The funeral address records that 'the praises of God were sung very mournfully at the Independent Chapel, as at most other places in those days, only one hymn at each service'. But young Elizabeth and others formed a choir which sang from the gallery. Alas, the livelier tunes were disapproved of by some who 'solemnly walked out of the Chapel as soon as the obnoxious sounds began'. Perhaps Elizabeth despaired of this solemn church because, at eighteen, she left to join the Baptists. But here she found the church was also 'in a very languid state'. Her baptism, in 1787, was apparently the first for years. But then, the funeral sermon continues, a new spirit of activity began. In 1792 Elizabeth married Edward Leader. Their home at Wootton Farm became a centre of activity, with evening services during the week and a Sunday School at the farm. Elizabeth provided generous Christmas treats: 'young people stood demurely around the well filled board repeating chapter after chapter of the Bible before the feast began'. Although it rightly belongs to a later stage in the story, those who listened to her funeral address in 1870 were reminded how in later life Elizabeth, despite increasing blindness, remained active and hospitable, receiving distinguished guests and the young people she loved. She had no children of her own. When the new Chapel was built, 'soon the aisle and the pew and the seat in the vestry became as familiar as her own home'.

**Daniel Turner's death.**

The decisions of the church meeting on 3rd August 1798 were signed 'D. Turner'.

But those of 1st November by J. Evans. Daniel had died, in office, on 5th September aged eighty nine. John Evans preached the memorial sermon. [117] On the title page of the published sermon is a piece of verse written for the occasion (not by John Kershaw as mistakenly claimed in the first edition of this book) :

> Of no distemper, of no blast he died;
> But fell like Autumn fruit that mellowed long;
> Ev'n wondered at, because he dropped no sooner:
> Fate seemed to wind him up for fourscore years,
> yet freshly ran he on nine winter's more,
> till, like a clock worn out with eating time,
> the wheels of weary life at last stood still.

His ministry at Abingdon spanned a period of change - both social and theological. These were years of a steady movement of the population from the countryside into the cities as the Industrial Revolution really took hold. They were also the years of the Evangelical Revival which challenged the Calvinism of the Particular Baptists. A lesser man than Turner could have resisted this change and closed his mind to the evangelistic opportunities opening up abroad and in the villages and towns of Britain. Instead he led the church into that modified Calvinism, pioneered by such men as Robert Hall and Andrew Fuller which led to the formation of the Baptist Missionary Society in 1792 and Baptist involvement in the mainstream Christian societies of the next century. Typical of Turner's contribution is a Testimonial written by the church less than six months after his death, to authorise one of their members as a preacher. It breathes the missionary spirit of the last decade of the old century, which would flourish in that about to begin.

> Our brother William Kent, having according to desire exercised his abilities before this Church by preaching on a passage of the holy Scripture, we, the members of the Church, are satisfied that he is a proper person on point of character and talents to be occasionally employed in preaching the word of God, as Providence may afford opportunities, and the Lord shall enable him. We are also sensible that religious instruction is very

[117] John Evans, *A Sermon occasioned by the Death of The Rev. D. Turner M.A.*1798.

> much wanted in country places and neighbouring villages and indeed everywhere. Impressed with these circumstances, we think it right that the occasional labours of our Brother William Kent, in preaching the gospel of Christ, should be encouraged by the sanction of this Church. And we do hereby give them our deliberate and willing sanction; desiring that our Brother will be engaged in preaching the word of God as often as he shall find it practicable and expedient, in hopes that the Lord will bless his efforts for the furtherance of the Redeemers Kingdom and the Salvation of Mankind.

It would appear that among today's theologians there is an increasing appreciation of the importance of Daniel Turner of Abingdon, together with his circle, in the movement towards openness to all Christians in his day and the quest for Church unity in ours.[118]
Professor Paul Fiddes, former principal of Regent's Park College, Oxford, concludes a recent study of Turner with the challenge:

> ...we should honour Turner's intention of holding all true gospel churches together in the invisible catholic church, on the basis of *both* word and sacrament, and it sets all Christians a challenge to work out in new ways for our own day.[119]

---

[118] For an example of one theologian's assessment of Daniel Turner's contribution to modern ecumenical theology see Prof. Paul Fiddes, *Studies in Baptist History and Thought,* vol. 28, *Pulpit and People, Studies in 18th cent. Baptist Life and Thought,* Ed. John Briggs, chap 7 p 112.
[119] ibid.

# Chapter 3
# The Nineteenth Century

**The Rev. John Evans:**
For 17 years John Evans had served alongside Daniel Turner. Then, from 1798 to 1813 he continued in sole charge of the church. Our chief source of information for this major ministry is a volume of his sermons, published posthumously by subscription, with a preface by his successor and, more informatively, a memoir by his contemporary the Rev. James Hinton, minister of New Road Church, Oxford.[120]

John was born on September 17, 1755 at Fynnon-Adda, Miline, Pembrokeshire. His parents were members of the Baptist church at Kilowyr where he was baptised c. 1776. At the age of 23 he entered Bristol Baptist Academy where he excelled as a student. From there, after three years study, he accepted the call to Abingdon to be assistant to the aging Daniel Turner. As we have seen, he was promoted to Co-Pastor in 1782 and, the Memoir continues: 'soon after, he married Miss Anna Robarts, daughter of a respectable family in his own congregation'. He often preached at New Road. In the new century his ministry flourished and the Abingdon church grew to the greatest numbers it had ever enjoyed.

In his historical lecture of 1895, Pumphrey spoke of two major developments during John Evans' ministry. It saw the beginning of 'good work' in nearby villages, and he was involved with the start of Sunday Schools. We know little about the village work in Evans time and will return to it when we come to the ministry of his successor. But we can note Pumphrey's reference to it and recognise that the chapel-building and growth of the village churches of the 1820's and 30's had its beginnings nearer the start of the century. Regarding the Sunday (or Sabbath) School, Pumphrey places the start of this in 1805 - 'held in an upper room, and the first teachers were Thomas Grain and Miss Tomkins'. He goes on to say that despite every effort he has been unable to track down any more information of the Sunday School's earliest days.

---

120 *Sermons on Various Subjects, adapted chiefly for Domestic Reading.* London. 1814.

Yet this might be the place to introduce a fascinating document which has recently come into my hands, dated December 27th 1785. This is printed as Appendix C. in this book. Mieneke Cox was aware of this document and interprets it as the establishment of the St. Helen's Sunday School.[121] This may well be, but it appears to have a wider application than St. Helen's alone. It reads as if the Town Council, which has Dissenters as well as Anglicans on its membership, is electing a board of governors to encourage and oversee the establishment of Sunday Schools - 'as many schools, having 30 scholars in each (separating boys from girls) be established as the funds raised will support'. That these are not exclusively Anglican is made clear in the paragraph concerned with the role of the clergy in these schools: '...the children of Protestant Dissenters shall be instructed by a Minister of such persuasion'. I have not been able to trace the denominational affiliation of most of those listed as forming the committee, but at least the three Tomkins were Baptists and possibly one or more of the un-named office holders that head the list. The Revd. Jn. Cleobury was rector of St. Helen's and the Revd. Wm. Kennedy headmaster of Abingdon School. This document is dated just two months after John Evans was appointed Co-pastor. Two years earlier Daniel Turner had preached, and published, a sermon based on Abraham's instruction of his children and pleading for the wealthy to support Sunday Schools so that they can offer *free* education to the children of the poorer classes. So if in fact the document (appendix C) does indicate that a Baptist Sunday School is envisaged, or even already in existence, it places it within five years of the start of the Sunday School movement.

The month by month concerns of the church under John Evans' leadership are recorded in the new church book which begins in the year 1800. They are chiefly concerned with applications for membership or transfer of membership and with matters of discipline. Immoral behaviour of the more serious kind was still punished by exclusion from the church. Lesser wrong-doing would be dealt with by exclusion from communion for a period. The church looked for remorse and repentance before full communion was restored, and it is a mark of the acceptance of the church's right to exercise such discipline that there are many instances of members being restored. And despite the class system that prevailed, poor and wealthy were treated alike. As the century progressed there is evidence that the

[121] M. Cox, *Abingdon, an 18th Century Country Town,* pp 149-50.

church became increasingly uneasy with a system which put them in the position of having to judge the morals of their fellow members. But while it continued, and was accepted as part of the mutual care which the church exercised for each other's spiritual welfare, it must have been a strong influence for moral rectitude among the membership.

In these early years of the century the church had four Deacons and a new Treasurer. In 1807 William Tomkins, who had taken on the new post of Treasurer back in 1761, offered his resignation after 46 years in office. Benjamin Kent, who with William Kent, the village preacher, ran the Wantage Bank, was appointed in his place.

Then another ministry ends: 'July 1 1813 Mem. Rev. John Evans the beloved Pastor of this Church died - deeply lamented by an affectionate Church and Congregation'. In the year following his death, subscriptions were raised for the printing of a book of his sermons.[122] This book appears to have been used in the village churches of Drayton and Fyfield.

**Revd. John Kershaw, M.A.**:
The Welshman was followed by a Scotsman as, in 1814, John Kershaw was called to supply the pulpit on three months' probation. At the end of the three months he was invited to stay a further six months with a view to becoming Pastor if that is still the feeling of the church. A large majority of members and subscribers issued a call to him in November and on January 1st 1815 he began as 'Pastor and Minister'. 1816 records the sending of 'our young friend Frederick Evans' for ministerial training at 'the Education Society at Bristol'. This is Bristol Baptist College which had been training ministers since 1679. Frederick Evans may have been the youngest son of the previous minister, who had left a widow and four sons. He was the first of four young men sent by the Abingdon church to the Bristol college during Mr. Kershaw's ministry. 1816 was also the year when the church had to handle the repercussions following the failure of the Wantage Bank, of which William Kent and his son Benjamin were partners. The story is told in detail in the biography of Benjamin Kent

---

[122] *Sermons on Various Subjects; Adapted chiefly for Domestic Reading, by the Late John Evans*, 1814. John Kershaw provides a Preface and James Hinton a Memoir.

junr., *Benjamin's Son.*[123] The collapse of the bank, causing financial loss to Baptist church members and perhaps the church itself among others, was considered, after careful examination by the church, to have been the result not of 'intentional fraud' but of 'culpable negligence'. The judgement was that these two members, one the Treasurer of the church and the other a preacher to the villages, are to 'be separated from its communion during the period of one year' after which, 'with an acknowledgement of their fault' a request to be 'restored to the privileges of Christian Communion' will be gladly considered. Meanwhile the church assures them of their affectionate interest, sympathy and prayers. A year later Benjamin was restored to communion and William after a further six months.

**Baptist schools.**

A major part of the story of the Baptist church in Abingdon during the nineteenth century is the story of three institutions which had their premises and achieved their work on the Ock Street site. The first of these was the church itself, whose year by year life, recorded in three church minute books, we shall return to later. But alongside the church, staffed by its members but in other ways quite distinct, were the schools - the Sabbath School and the British School. Even this was not all. Beyond the Ock Street premises, the minister and his friend Benjamin Kent founded a private school which began in 1817 in premises somewhere in Ock Street and moved two years later to Radley Hall.

---

[123] P.H. Schurr, *Benjamin's Son* pp 4ff. Pub. Royal Soc. of Medicine.

*Figure 22 The Kent memorial, in the position to which it was moved in 1995.*

**The Sabbath School.**

Although there are earlier examples of schools for poor children on Sundays, the Sunday School movement owes its origins to Robert Raikes whose first school started in Gloucester in 1780 for the teaching of scripture, reading and other elementary subjects. Drawing on volunteer teachers from the churches, it was possible to offer free education to the poorest of families. But as schools for the general education of the poor were established in the nineteenth century, the Sunday Schools began to limit their teaching to scripture and encouraged large numbers from all classes of society to attend. As mentioned already, there are no early records of the Abingdon Baptist Sunday School, but a letter to the Berks. Association dated 1852 mentions three elderly members who have died, 'one indeed having for full fifty years been connected with our Sabbath Schools'. So a date very early in the century is indicated. The use of the plural - 'Sabbath Schools' - refers to the boys department and the girls department, kept quite separate. Then we have Mr. Pumphrey's comments placing its beginning c. 1806. Where did they meet? Pumphrey says, 'in an upper room'. One wonders where this was located. The most likely room was the upper floor of an extension against the north wall of the 1700 chapel. Later, they certainly met on the church premises, probably from 2.00 p.m. to 3.00 p.m. Since the church's communion service was held on the first Sunday afternoon of the month, the church minutes record the problem of the noise of the children leaving after their lessons and disturbing communion. In 1849 the problem is resolved by a decision to start communion half an hour later, at 3.15 p.m. That the noise would have been quite considerable is indicated in a report to the Association in 1850: 'In our Sunday Schools we have 25 teachers and about 200 children'. Two years later, speaking of the children's work, the Association is informed: 'The dying testimony of one child and the admission into the Church of two young persons in the senior class afforded some encouragement'.

Apart from these snippets of information, the Baptist Sunday School organised its life and taught its generations of children with hardly a mention in the church minutes.

However, the Minute Books of the Sunday School do survive from 1859. When the 1859 Minute Book begins, the Revd. Edger, as President, chairs the quarterly teachers' meetings and the A.G.M. The officers are a Superintendent, Secretary, Treasurer, Librarian, and Visitor who calls on absentees to encourage them back. The Visitor, Mrs. Gubb, has the added responsibility of sitting with the boys in the gallery on Sunday mornings to keep them in order during the service. There is an infants class during this service, held in the hall, which the female teachers of the other classes take it in turn to lead. In 1860 a young men's class was started to receive 'Miss Sopwith's elder scholars'. The quarterly meetings constantly dealt with the movement of children among the classes, to ease the problems of older children getting restless or classes getting too large. The Sunday School met at 10.00 a.m. and 2.30 p.m. The size of the Schools, though probably reported at each A.G.M., was only rarely written into the minutes. However, the annual report for 1862 is stitched into the Minute Book and gives the following figures:

| | |
|---|---|
| No. of scholars | 208 |
| Average attendance | 95 - 150 |
| No. of teachers | 31 |
| Average attendance | 20 - 27 |
| No. of library books | 450 |
| Amount of children's pence | £18. 1. 2d. |
| Distributed to children in clothes | £4. 15. 0d. |

In October 1867 there was a Tea for the parents of scholars. Eighty parents sat down to tea at 5.30 p.m. The male teachers acted as waiters, the female teachers were interspersed among the parents at the tables. At 7.00 p.m. the company moved to the church for a service at which the minister preached. This appears to have been an annual event. In 1881 the School affiliated to the Oxford Sunday School Union. In 1883 a serious decline in the number of boys was noted. These were mainly in the 14+ age group. Plans were made to visit them, but the lack of male teachers was seen as a contributory cause. The decline appears to continue and it is likely that the early 1860's saw the height of Sunday School attendance. Robust efforts were made in the new century to stem the decline sometimes with good success. The 1915 A.G.M. heard that 129 names were on the role - a gain of 13 on the previous year - and that an average of 100 attended in the afternoon. Treats and outings were arranged. In the 1930's a Farthing Sunday, held just before Christmas, was the occasion when children brought the farthings (a quarter of the old penny) which they had been collecting for the Baptist Missionary Society throughout the year. In 1931 a record 4,368 were gathered - a challenge for any Church Treasurer to count!

The two Minute Books of the Sunday School tell the story of the year by year plans and problems, achievements and disappointments of an organisation dedicated to sharing the Christian gospel with children and young people. It continued for over 250 years in much the same form until 1970 when it was reorganised as 'Family Church'. But the same gospel is still taught and the same dedication of the teaching staff is still called for.

**Benjamin Kent's School.**

Although quite independent of the church, the school started in premises somewhere in Ock Street by John Cashew and Benjamin Kent in 1817 is further evidence of Baptist interest in education and of

Kershaw's readiness to be involved in it. After taking the lease of Radley Hall in 1819 the school flourished until it closed in 1844, in Benjamin's sixtieth year. In 1847 new tenants of the Hall opened St. Peter's College, today's Radley College. Kershaw appears to have had an active role in Benjamin's school throughout his Abingdon ministry. The prospectus of c. 1832 begins:

> In the Academy at Radley Hall, Berkshire,
> conducted by Mr. Benjamin Kent, with the
> regular assistance of the Rev. Jn. Kershaw, M.A.

Benjamin's son, also named Benjamin, went from his education at his father's school to the Medical School of Edinburgh University (the English universities would still not take non-conformist students) from where he received his doctorate and went on to a medical career in the pioneering days of Adelaide and the founding of its General Hospital. His story is the subject of Peter Schurr's biography cited above.

**The British School.**

The Quaker, Joseph Lancaster, was a pioneer of education for the children of the poor. In 1808 his efforts resulted in the formation of the Royal Lancastrian Institution for Promoting the Education of the Poor. 'Royal' on account of George III's patronage and approval of the non-sectarian principles of his work. This later became the British and Foreign School Society. The Established Church reacted by founding the National Society of 1811 which was overtly Anglican. At its launch the Baptist Magazine marvelled that leading churchmen 'should wage an implacable and relentless war against us teaching poor children to read the Bible'.[124]

In contrast to the lack of information on the early Sunday School, there are two books which cover the British School from the inaugural meeting in the Baptist Church Vestry on the 24th November 1824, 'for those interested in education', to its take-over by the state and move to new buildings in Bostock Road in 1902. The first book contains the minutes of the Managers; the second is the Log Book which all principal teachers were instructed to keep from 1863 and records the many day to day events of school life.

---

124 J. Briggs, *The English Baptists of the 19th Century*. p 341 quoting *Baptist Magazine* 1811 p 117.

Strangely, no mention is made in the minute book of the erection of the schoolrooms. These were purpose built as the stone strip set in the brick facade between the first and second floors indicated. This was deeply inscribed:

BRITISH SCHOOL. ESTABLISHED MDCCCXXV.

After demolition, parts of this inscription were saved and later built into the wall in front of the Kent family memorial in the church forecourt in 1996.

However, in the intervening years since I wrote the book of which this is a revision, I have been able to discover two indentures[125] and a number of photographs which together show how and when the property was acquired and developed by the school. The first indenture is dated 1828 and deals with the lease of a house and land from the trustees of the church to the trustees of the school. This is the house and garden to the E of the Minister's house, divided from it only by the pathway to the chapel and, for nearly a century rented by the Watt's family. Both the minister's house and the Watt's house were bequeathed to the church by Benjamin Tomkins. The garden of the Watt's house was about as wide as the plot now occupied by Richard Coxeter's curtain and carpet shop and ran back as far as the northern boundary of the church plot. But this indenture also speaks of a 'lately erected school-house' in the garden. This would be the school-teacher's house, still standing in the 1960's. The second indenture (1837) refers to the demolition of the Watt's house and, in its place, 'all that newly erected building now standing on the said... parcel of ground used as a school and called 'The British and Foreign School'.

[125] Originals held at the Baptist Corporation's office in Baptist House, Didcot.

*Figure 23 Rear view of British School and Teacher's house. Note the two chimneys, beyond rear of chapel*

*Figure 24 South frontage of British School and Teacher's house.*

So we can trace the development of the school building. Land is leased from the church after the meeting which established the school in 1825 and immediately the school teacher's house was built on it. From aerial photos taken before the demolition of the British School in 1960 and the School-teacher's house shortly afterwards, the house was a large twin-gabled construction. The western gable has large neo-gothic windows which give the impression that this was in fact a classroom with the school-teacher's accommodation in the eastern gable. Another such photo, showing the rear of the building, reveals equally large windows on the rear gable on the western half, which appears to confirm its use as a classroom. Classes perhaps began to be held in this room and probably in rooms in Watt's house when the Watt's lease expired. By 1837, either because the growth of the school required it or the sub-lease of the Watt's house having expired, the new, purpose-built classroom block was erected on the street frontage. From these and other photos and maps we can see the square block of this new schoolroom set back about three metres from the pavement to the right of the chapel gate, behind a low wall with railings (later a brick wall). The building consisted of two storeys in brick with round-arched windows. A double doorway adjacent to the church gateway probably led to an entrance hall or directly into the ground floor classroom which was lit by two windows onto the street and one facing east and warmed by a fireplace or stove in the centre of the W. wall. To the right of the frontage an arched door opened into a covered passage which probably led to stairs to the first floor. There appears to have been a stair-case window and the upper room enjoyed light from four south facing windows. It had a fireplace above the one below. The older children were taught upstairs; the younger downstairs.[126] There was space behind for a playground. But the cramped site was to prove a problem for the next seventy five years.

The inaugural meeting agreed to start a school along the lines of the British and Foreign School Society - for the children of labourers and mechanics. Revd. John Kershaw chaired the meeting and the seventeen people present formed themselves into a committee to manage the school. Although the school appears to have been a Baptist initiative, the committee was drawn from a cross-section of dissenting denominations, who also contributed financially, as indicated below.

---

[126] See Interview with Mrs. E.E.M. Cockshead below.

The School was started with daytime and evening classes for girls and evening classes for boys. Daytime classes for boys were started a little later. The first teacher for the boys, Mr. Luff, seems to have been recruited locally, but the managers wrote to 'Boro' Road' for a Mistress for the girls. Borough Road Teacher Training College, Isleworth, was founded by the British and Foreign School Society and was the usual source of supply to the Abingdon British School, for both staff and advice, throughout the century. It is now part of Brunel University. Although the School management was an all-male committee, a Ladies Committee was formed from the start to oversee the girls side of the school. These were only consulted when, in attempts to accommodate the growing numbers they were asked to move to other rooms or even to the Independents' church hall - the women usually refused such requests. In the early 1850's the boys outgrew their classroom and the church permitted the use of its vestry. The children were charged a penny a week. Annual sermons with collections for the British Schools were preached in the Baptist and Independent chapels, and subscriptions sought from the townspeople. The Wesleyans, whose church was also in Ock Street, on the site of the P.O. Sorting Office, and the Abbey Baptists were also contributors. After the Wesleyans had moved to their new church in Conduit Road and the Primitive Methodists moved to the old Wesleyan premises, they also were approached for financial support. The Rev. Lepine, a long serving minister of the Independent Chapel, was a member of the management committee for much of its life. A.G.M.'s were open to the public and held in the Council Chamber.

The 1870 Education Act sought to improve conditions in schools and also established School Boards to provide democratic control and Board Schools which would fill gaps in schooling where no school existed, or would take over failing schools. At this stage, conscious of the cramped conditions, the managers considered building a new school and approached Christ's Hospital, a major town charity, for the gift of a site. The Charity replied that it was not empowered to give land. The estimated cost of new buildings was beyond the managers' means or faith to provide. In 1874 an Infants' department was added, no doubt to meet popular demand but putting a further strain on facilities. The 1874 O.S. map shows a classroom attached to the rear of the original square building. This may have been built to house this Infants' department. In September 1875 the managers decided to close the school and gave notice to the teaching staff. But the decision was reversed in the December. Adjacent land was purchased and new red brick classrooms built, probably in 1876, while the recent extension was demolished to make more room for them. In 2011 these still stand on property no longer owned by the church. The relief was short lived. The possibility of using the old Wesleyan chapel for the Infants was unsuccessfully explored. Attendance averaged 87. But the school continued. In August 1891 the Elementary Education Act is noted and it is agreed to receive the grant of ten shillings per child for all children aged three to fifteen and that from then on education will be offered free.

*Figure 25 ca. 1876 additional classrooms, still standing 2011.*

In 1896 the Baptist Church hall was authorised by the Education Department for 46 girls or 56 infants, but a damning report by the E.D. inspectors that same year complained that the hall was too far from the school, that the girls' main classroom was too narrow with only one window and there was insufficient cloakroom accommodation for what was now a school of 191 pupils - there were only three W.C.'s for all the girls and infants and no urinals for the infant boys who, consequently, used the wall of the boys' schoolroom in a narrow passage leading to the girls' playground. Plans for new cloakrooms were submitted to the Education Department.

On 3rd May 1897 there is a final entry in the manager's book with no indication that an end has come. But the head teacher's Log Book provides the answer, 'Sept. 13 1899 This school was taken over by the School Board for Abingdon with the approval of the Education Department, as from the 12th Sept. 1899 and was opened this morning as a School under the management and control of the Board'. The final entry in the Log Book reads:

July 17 1902 Children assembled at 9 o'clock. They were then dismissed, acting upon an Order (made by Dr. Woodforde M.O.H.) signed by two members of the Sanitary Authority. An epidemic of Scarletina seems to be spreading in the town, though there are only three boys ill belonging to this Department. The School Board decided that the holidays should be prolonged for a little over a fortnight so that we can begin work in the New Schools on Sept. 8. The Order for the closure of the Schools was for a period of 3 weeks.

The 'New Schools' had been built in Bostock Road, just a few hundred yards from the old premises. Jackie Smith, the town archivist, records the existence of a school on the Carswell/Bostock Road site in the late 19th century, before it was enlarged by the building of the Board School in 1902. The school continues as Carswell Community Primary School. The senior children's education being moved to Larkmead School in 1954.

From the management minutes the impression may be got of three quarters of a century of problems. But through their efforts, the school not only continued to run, but inspector's reports were usually of good work and a happy atmosphere, especially in the Infants' classes. On a loose sheet in the managers' book someone has typed, in 1960, an obituary to the school premises as they are being demolished. There is a useful account of how the building was used during the fifty years between the move of the school to Bostock Road and its demolition. Then the writer adds two sentences:

> One of the last holidays enjoyed by the school was for the coronation of Edward VII - June 26 1902. Looking up at the British School the other day, with evident

affection, an elderly lady was overheard to remark - 'Ah, they were happy days, happy days.'

A less approving memory has been preserved in an undated and anonymous fragment:

> Here is the Manse and, set back, the Baptist Chapel. In front, facing directly onto the street, is a square and forbidding building known as the 'British School'. This, in so far as I can find out, was an attempt to give some sort of an education before the Council Schools reigned.

Finally, the following interview came to hand in material being gathered for display in the Exhibition, *Ock Street Remembered; An Abingdon Community.*[127] The author was responsible for that part of the exhibition devoted to the churches and schools of Ock Street and found the following a fascinating insight to one school-girl's experience ca. 1902:

**4th August 1977**

**Mrs. E.E.M. COCKSHEAD**
**(Ella Bonner b. 1899)**

Mrs. Cockshead, who is my grandmother, very kindly agreed to being interviewed on her life in Abingdon.

> *Were you born in Abingdon Nanny?*
> Yes, at number twelve Ock Street.
> *What did your parents do for a living when you were a child?*
> My mother kept a shop. She sold sweets, fruit and she also did refreshments. And my father was a carrier from Abingdon to Oxford. He had a carriers van and two horses and he just travelled backwards and forwards

[127] This was mounted by The Ock Street Heritage Group which was a sub-group of the Abingdon Area Archaeological and Historical Society. See *Ock Street Remembered* - an illustrated guide to the exhibition, pub Ock Street Heritage Group 2008. pp 26, 30, 43.

every day.

*What age did you start school?*

Well I started when I was three and a half years old, the school was not very far away from where our house was and I used to go down with my elder sister to take me to school and I wouldn't let her go home so the head mistress said just leave her she'll be alright and I was three and a half so that was when I started.

*What school did you go to?*

It was called the old British School in those days, and then there was some new schools built further down the road, in Conduit Road, and when they were opened we were moved from the Old British School into what they then called the council schools, and I think I went there when I was five and a half.

*How big was the Old British School?*

Well it was a building with one big room downstairs and there was an upstairs room as well so the bigger children had their lessons upstairs and the younger ones had them downstairs.

*What size were the classes?*

There was about thirty or forty in the bigger classes and about the same in the smaller classes. It was not a very big school really.

*How big were the new schools when you went there?*

[The interview continues with a description of the Council Schools.]

*Figure 26 - A class of girls at the Bostock Road school ca. 1902/3. The girl in black, front row right, is Elizabeth Emily Bonner, 1897-1973, big sister of Evelyn Ella Mary Bonner 1899-1986.*

Evelyn Ella Mary Cockshead (nee Bonner) was the second daughter of T. Bonner, Carrier, of 12 Ock Street, Abingdon. The new schools began classes on Sept. 8 1902. Ella would have been three and a half about then.

These accounts of the Sunday Schools, the school at Radley Hall, and the British School have carried us to the end of the century. But we must go back to John Kershaw to record other aspects of the church during his ministry, and then hear of the other ministries which spanned that busy century.

## Mission in the Villages.

*Figure 27 Cothill Baptist Chapel.*

The Revd. John Kershaw's twenty five year ministry also saw the building of the village chapels at Fyfield, Cothill and Drayton. These appear to have remained within the care and oversight of the Abingdon mother church. Reference has already been made to the work of John Evans in the early years of the century, in the villages from which many of his members and congregation came. But Pumphrey states that the chapels were built in Kershaw's time, in the 20's and 30's.

*Figure 28 Fyfield Baptist Chapel.*

I have recently had the privilege to examine a dusty oak box, in the storage area of the Angus Library. The box overflows with a library of some fifty nine published volumes. These works fall into three categories: sermons (36), commentaries (21) and one or two books of prayers. My attention was alerted to these when reading a brief history of Marcham chapel written by Gordon Lewry in 1994, who was probably the last person to study them. He describes them as I found them with the exception that when he saw them in the Angus Library in 1993 they were in two boxes labelled 'Fyfield' whereas now only one such box remains, not large enough to hold all the books. It is oak, 2ft. 6ins. x1ft.x1ft. with brass lock and escutcheon, with 'Fyfield' painted in black Victorian lettering on the lid. All the books have been given brown-paper dust jackets and are numbered in ink from 1 to 82 on the spine. Mr. Lewry lists the missing numbers. These dust jackets are fixed with red sealing wax inside the covers and look original to the 1820's to 1840's, within which years they were all published. Many of the volumes have 'For Drayton' or 'For Fyfield' written inside the front cover. A good number are also inscribed 'John Tomkins'. One book of prayers is inscribed 'For Fyfield and Drayton'. This, and most of the Drayton books have pencilled dates above the start of each sermon as well as shorthand notes in the margins. Most of the Fyfield books, by contrast, have no marginalia. The earliest date I have found for Drayton is 1828; for Fyfield 1831. But I have not given myself the time to work through each book, and I am not in the position to translate the shorthand notes. Until such further study my preliminary conclusions are that this was originally part of the library of John Tomkins (1764-1846) who frequently led the worship in the larger Drayton chapel, though also in Fyfield. He was not averse to including in this worship 'read' prayers. When his active ministry to the villages ended, or after his death, the books were deposited in two boxes and placed either in Abingdon, for the use of the village preaching team, or else in Fyfield or Drayton or both.

*Figure 29 Drayton Baptist Chapel*

Apart from the fascination of indicating what each village congregation was listening to on given Sundays in the 1820's to 40's, there is little information of the chapels themselves. But above Sermon 1 in book no. 37 John Tomkins has written 'Drayton New Chapel July 20 1834' which suggests that the first meeting place has been replaced with, presumably, the chapel that stands today. Perhaps a more complete study of all these volumes will produce more glimpses into those early years. Cothill is mentioned in an indenture, held by the B.U. Corporation, dated 1842 where it is described as 'lately' erected. This village work will continue to the present and beyond and this book will pick up its story from time to time. But from the beginning we should remember that the story is less about building chapels and preaching or listening to sermons, as the creation of warm and life-building fellowships. In the 20$^{th}$ century the Cothill congregation was serviced by a team of twenty lay preachers, drawn largely from the Abingdon church (see appendix F). In 2002 I talked with one of these. I had retired and was feeling my age. Charles Orland was 90 paying his old minister a pastoral visit. He had cycled down from north Abingdon, as for years he had cycled or walked out to the village chapels to lead their worship. He talked about those days.

> There were ten elderly people in the congregation at Cothill. Mr. Fairbrother was caretaker and leader of the church there. He and his wife lived at Rose Cottage, opposite the chapel. Mr. Fairbrother had lost both his legs in the First World War and was now the grounds-man at Cothill School. We lay-preachers loved to go to Cothill because of the great Sunday teas in Rose Cottage before the 6.00 p.m. service. There was a fine grandfather clock in the cottage and one Sunday I said how much I admired it. But I got the response from the old caretaker, 'Young man, thou shalt not covet thy neighbour's goods'.

Young men, cutting their teeth in village work - caring and being cared for; teaching and being taught; encouraging faith and having their own faith challenged and strengthened; from the 1830's to the 1930's and beyond; the Ock Street church has nurtured and been nurtured by its work in the neighbouring villages.

**The death of John Kershaw.**

As his ministry continued, John Kershaw, supported particularly by Dr. Charles Tomkins and John Tomkins, took a vigorous part in politics calling for political freedom for non-conformists. This trio were also active supporters of the Bible Society. An Auxiliary of the Bible Society was formed in Abingdon in 1813. Copies of the Bible were delivered freely to poor families. By 1824 4300 had been distributed in Abingdon. The death of John Kershaw in 1842, two years after concluding his ministry at Abingdon, was just within living memory of the church of Pumphrey's day. He records that the late Mr.

Williams, who was a Deacon during Kershaw's ministry, remembered him as 'a polished scholar, a perfect gentleman, genial in his deportment, and for many years highly esteemed by all who knew him'.

**The ministry of the Revd. Edward Smith Pryce B.A.**
There is suddenly a modern feeling in the church book with the coming of Mr. Pryce.

He is obviously an administrator. The church book, which begins in 1800 and is scarcely a quarter filled, was abandoned. On the opening pages of the new book, dated 1840, accepted practice regarding Church Membership and regulations for the conduct of Church Meetings is set out. From now on the minutes of the monthly church meetings will be read and confirmed at the following meeting. Notice of motions must be given at the previous meeting. Those applying for membership will now be visited by two members - even those with a letter of transfer. Members moving to other places will be encouraged to find a new church to join and not keep their membership at Abingdon.

**The New Chapel.**
Within a year of his coming a new chapel was required. The purpose was not stated. But the size of the membership and the congregations was increasing. The building of chapels at Fyfield, Cothill and Drayton may have partially been an attempt to make space at Abingdon. A Building Committee was set up. From the Trustees' minute book:

> '13 March 1841 An application from the Building Committee was read requesting the consent of the Trustees to pull down the present Chapel and erect a new one on its site....'
>
> '24 March 1841 Proposed: That the Trustees unanimously consent to the pulling down of the present chapel and the re-building of another....'
>
> '5 November 1841 That in consequence of the removal of the old chapel' the Tomkins' 'Private Burying Ground' shall be extended to form a quadrangle'. 'That the Trustees having inspected the newly erected Chapel are satisfied...'

*Figure 30 The 1841 chapel in the 21st century, after the renovation of its façade.*

From the Baptist Magazine of Dec. 1841 we have an account of the opening celebrations and a description of the Chapel. On the Wednesday evening prior to the opening on the 21st October a meeting was held in the Vestry (i.e. church hall) at which prayer was offered by three of the eldest members. On Thursday morning Rev. W. Jay of Bath preached on Matthew 5:15 - 'Neither do men light a candle and put it under a bushel, but on a candlestick; and it giveth light unto all that are in the house'. This was followed by a meal when all the members dined in the Council Chamber. In the evening the Revd. J.H. Hinton of London preached especially to the young from Ecclesiastes 11:9 - 'Rejoice, O young men in thy youth; and let thy heart cheer thee in the days of thy youth and walk in the ways of thine heart, and in the sight of thine eyes: but know thou, that for all these things God will bring thee into judgement'. The Baptist Magazine continued:

> The Chapel, which is erected partly on the site of the old building, is situated in the principal thoroughfare of the town, having a wide approach of the length of a hundred

> feet from the street. On one side of the entrance is the British schoolroom, on the other side the minister's house. The front, which is remarkable for the substantiality and chastity of its appearance, is a classic specimen of the Roman Doric. The chapel is sixty feet by forty one, capable of conveniently accommodating 800 persons. At the back is the vestry, to hold 200, with minister's room adjoining. The cost of the building, with fence, walls and other outlay on the premises is about £2000, of this the sum of about £300 has yet to be provided.'

The architect was John Davies of Devonshire Square, London, and the builder John Chesterman of Abingdon. John Davies, a versatile and well known architect, was also responsible for the Tilehouse Street Baptist Church, Hitchen, which was built within a year or so of the Abingdon chapel and has an identical façade.

*Figure 31 Tilehouse Street Baptist Church, Hitchen.*

John Chesterman was born in Marcham in 1796. He was a carpenter and married Elizabeth Coleing in the Marcham Parish Church in 1815. By 1841 they had lived for some years in Abingdon and John was the head of a firm of builders. He and his growing family were already members and active in the Baptist Church when he was given the task of building the new chapel.[128] The new chapel was in danger of destruction almost immediately. Twelve days after its opening there was a gas explosion. The Trustees Minute Book records: 'That a staircase and two windows having been damaged by the explosion of Gas in the New Chapel on the 2nd of November instant, Dr. Tomkins be authorised to make a claim for the sum of £13. 10. 0. being the estimated damage on the County Fire Office'.

**House Groups.**
In April 1844 Mr. Pryce placed before the church meeting a 'Plan for promoting social intercourse and religious improvement amongst our members'. The membership of the church was divided, by alphabetical order, into six sections each with a convenor. Each section was to meet twice a year in the home of the convenor ( i.e. one section would meet each month). The meetings would be held from 6.30 - 8.30 p.m. in the winter and from 7.00 to 9.00 p.m. in the summer. No refreshment to be served. The minister to be present at all meetings. After six months the church decided to hold these meetings fortnightly. Each group would therefore meet four times a year. There was then no further mention of the scheme. These meetings may have lasted only during Mr. Pryce's ministry or continued on through the century.

**The Revd. Edward Pryce's departure.**
In January 1845 the minister informed his church that he had been invited to a new church being constituted in Zion Chapel, Gravesend and asked for the church's opinion. The church met four days later and decided that due to 'the success attending his ministry' they would want Mr. Pryce to continue with them. However, a week later Mr. Pryce tendered his resignation.

**The Revd. Robert Humphrey Marten.**
April 1st 1845 'Resolved: That the Revd. Robt. H. Marten be requested to supply the Pulpit of this Chapel on probation for three months'. Mr. Marten accepted and his ministry will last ten years.

---

128 I am grateful to Malcolm and Gwyneth Moore for this and other information which they gathered as they researched their family history in 1997. A copy of their research and family tree will be placed with my archive in the Angus Library.

**Close links with the Independent Chapel in the Square.**
That same meeting on 1st April proposed that the afternoon services in future be alternated with 'the people attending the Upper Chapel' and this was agreed at Mr. Marten's first church meeting. Seven years later a yet closer link was proposed by the Baptists: 'Resolved that the Independent Church be requested to unite in the re-establishment of the 'Preparatory Lecture' to be held at the Baptist Chapel on the Thursday evening and at the Independent Chapel on the Wednesday evening before each first Sabbath, alternate months.' This preparatory lecture was designed to prepare the congregation for holy communion on the coming Sunday.

**The Two Institutes.**[129]
In the middle decades of the century concern for adult education resulted in the formation of societies which sought to involve the working classes in self improvement activities. The churches were among those who saw the value of such Institutes, as they were called. Abingdon had two. The earliest, founded 1843, called The Literary and Scientific Institute, had the Baptist Dr. Charles Tomkins on its board. The second, which opened in 1854, was named The Mechanics' Institute and met in the British School. This proved to be the most popular and appealed more to the working community. The two non-conformist ministers, Robert Marten of the Baptists and Samuel Lepine of the Independents were involved in the early preparation for the Mechanics' Institute. Both Institutes had a library and reading room, with copies of the London newspapers available. Lectures, readings (of special help to the illiterate) and entertainment all offered an alternative to Abingdon's fifty or so public houses. The Mechanics' Institute closed in 1879 in Abingdon, but such societies were the fore-runners of modern libraries, Workers' Educational Associations, Open University and even radio and television.

**The death of John Tomkins.**
In December 1845, when it was agreed that in future the Deacons would serve for terms of five years, John Tomkins was made 'A Deacon for life' - the first of several who would be given this honour over the next hundred and fifty years. But John was to live only a further five months. He had been a Deacon for thirty four years. His

[129] See J. Dunleavy, *The Mechanics' Institutes of the Home Counties: The Two Abingdon Societies Compared.* Article in *The Vocational Aspect of Education* (April 1985) vol . XXXVII, no. 96 pp.17-22.

commemorative plaque is one of only three which remain within the walls of the church; the others being those to Daniel Turner and John Kershaw. A copy of the funeral address and a sermon preached the following Sunday 'to improve his departure' has recently been found and added to the church archives. It gives an insight into both John Tomkins' character and his minister's eloquence.

The Church now met on Tuesday evenings for prayer. It had Communion Tickets - a system in which twelve dated tickets would be issued to members each year which they would place in the offering plate at the monthly communion service, so indicating their presence or absence. Continued absence without good reason could lead to their dismissal from membership. The membership in 1846 was 172. On the 9th March 1847 special services for the revival of religion were proposed for the last week in March.

**Joining the Berks. Association.**

Fellowship with the other Baptist churches in the county, if it existed at all, received no mention in the church books until the year 1850. Then, on the 14th May:

> Resolution: That in order to promote as much as possible, the spirit of union and friendly co-operation in the cause of Christ especially between ourselves and the Churches of the Redeemer in our County and neighbourhood, it is deemed in the judgement of this Church desirable that application be made for the admission of the Church into the Berks. and West Middx. Association, with the understanding that mutual assistance and fraternal intercourse are considered as the objects to which its operations are confined.

The pastor and two representatives were appointed for the Association meetings in a week's time. The initiative came from the Association and the wording of the resolution, and the letter which follows, suggests that Abingdon felt that the Association had not confined its programme solely to religion, and that for this reason they had held back from joining the Association until now. With this warning shot across the bows, the letter then recounts Abingdon's history, details of the Sunday School, mentioned above, and then tells of the church's village work:

> There are three village stations, statedly supplied by our brethren Rev. S.V. Lewis and the Rev. Geo. Best at which the average number of hearers would be about 250. In these villages there are about 70 scholars and 11 teachers.

**Another change of minister - the Revd. Samuel Edger.**

By 1855 the Abingdon membership stood at 190. There were probably as many again who attended Sunday worship but were not yet in membership in Abingdon. The 170 who worshiped in the three village chapels and their pastors were partly Abingdon members, partly 'hearers'. At this point in his successful ministry Robert Marten accepted a call to 'a chapel recently erected in the neighbourhood of Blackheath, London, where both a congregation and a church have to be gathered in the midst of a large and rapidly increasing population'. The decade of his ministry in Abingdon, he writes, has been years of 'goodness and mercy'.

The process of finding their next minister was difficult. There was disagreement as to whether a Mr. Edger or a Mr. Stalker be invited. Mr. Burry, a Deacon, resigned. His resignation was not accepted. It was proposed to recall Revd. Pryce and Revd. Marten to preach on consecutive Sundays to try to overcome their division. The proposal was defeated. Finally 95 members and 85 subscribers invited Mr. Edger. And three members submitted a written protest against Mr. Edger. Fortunately, the Revd. Samuel Edger is a peacemaker.

*Figure 32 Revd. S. Edgar 1855 - 60.*

**A fresh approach to church discipline.**

The practice of bringing the names of members whose behaviour is considered reprehensible before the church meeting, usually resulting in expulsion from communion for a number of months or, in severe cases, exclusion from membership, has been a regular feature of the church meetings. But during Mr. Edger's ministry a new attitude, which was eventually to become the norm, first emerges. A member has been caught stealing a small sum from his employer. It is a first offence and the employer has forgiven him. But the matter, as usual, is considered by the church. They decide that their minister should write to the man, but the matter will be left at that. In his letter Edger says that he will leave the matter of his attendance at communion to the man's own conscience and continues, 'That is with God and yourself. It is Christ's Church not ours. All religion must spring from Conscience and divine love. What they prompt you to, we have no right to forbid'.

We learn from the church book that those who had protested against Mr. Edger being the minister had left the church. A year later Mr. Edger wrote to them to encourage their return. He brought their replies to the church meeting with the report: 'One is expressive of much good feeling' but the other two letters are 'undesirable to be made public'. But when these two hear that their letters had not been read to the meeting they strongly object. So they are read next time.

In 1857 it was agreed that there will be a Members' Tea Meeting and Church Meeting twice yearly to hear and approve the accounts. In September of that year it was agreed unanimously 'That the Hymn Book just issued - published by Mr. B.L. Green be used, in place of all that are at present in use by the Church and Congregation - and that it be adopted on and after next Sunday'.

**United Communion services.**

March 30 1858 Mr. Edger suggests and Mr. Coxeter recommends (and accepted almost unanimously):

> The followers of Christ here assembled, feeling the many advantages that must result from Christian Union, and conscious that our annual united Communion Service has a tendency to promote this union, would suggest to their fellow Christians meeting at the Upper and Wesleyan Chapels the desirability of holding a quarterly united (communion) service, or in the place of the one for each third month.

No answer was reported from the Wesleyans, but that from the Independents of the Upper Meeting put a damper on the plan:

> April 22nd Dear Sir, In compliance with your wish I have conferred with my deacons in reference to the resolution we have received from you. And while fully estimating the advantages of Christian Union we are of opinion that it would be inconvenient to make any alteration to our Sacramental Service. Signed on behalf of the Deacons, S. Lepine.

Two years later the Baptist church decided to move its monthly communion service from the afternoon of the first Sunday of each month to 'after the morning service and the ordinary service shortened so as to close at 12.30 at the latest'.

**Lukewarmness and spiritual awakening.**

February 1859 The minister 'entered at length into the condition of the

Church both as to its state of lukewarmness etc. - its need of more life - and appropriate means of awakening it'. He gave notice of this as a subject for the next church meeting. His plan involved the Deacons getting to know their people much better and ways of applying for membership which would ensure a better understanding of what might be expected of members. In the letter to the Association the following year, however, Mr. Edger was able to rejoice in;

> that general awakening of religious thought and feeling which we regard with such pleasure and hope'. He realised that this was not confined to Abingdon but that many of the Association churches must be experiencing it. And since this has come about without any 'extraordinary or special efforts' it was hoped to be truly a movement of God's Spirit. The following year Abingdon reported congregations 'much increased both in numbers and apparent thoughtfulness.

**Desire for more open membership.**

The old debate about open or closed communion had long been settled in Abingdon. But the fear of those who maintained that allowing paedobaptists to receive communion (open communion) would lead to open membership was still allayed by trust deeds and church practice. Under Mr. Edger's ministry he and the church began to ask the question, If a believer is regularly sharing communion with us, why should they not be welcomed into membership with us? Today we see no problem; then it was dynamite.

October 1st 1861 Several friends who regularly commune with us and attend worship 'be invited to the Church Meeting for three months to see if they will then enter membership'.

November 7th 1861 Notice of motion: That those of other denominations who take communion with us for six months 'be regarded by that act of fellowship as full members, unless any objection to the contrary should appear'.

At the 29th November meeting Mr. Lewis and Mr. Williams put a counter proposition - that no alteration be made for admitting members, because the proposition amounts to 'communion constitutes membership'. They feared 'the Church would lose its liberty'. However, the original proposition was carried by a large majority and, accordingly, eleven were named as members. But Mr. Lewis and Mr.

Williams had a trump card yet to play - they appealed to the law.

A Special Church Meeting was called for February 6th 1862 when the minister informed the church that 'in consequence of the liberal character it had assumed' they had been threatened with legal proceedings because their resolution had broken the Trust Deed. Therefore the eleven were to hold their membership in abeyance until the matter was resolved. But then the minute adds, with the frustration of a church held to ransom by just two of its members, 'At the same time this meeting would wish it understood that our friends, not being Baptists, who, in accordance to these resolutions surrender their claim to a participation in any legal rights, do not thereby lose any of that communion, fellowship, sympathy or co-operation with us; that essentially belongs to Christ's true spiritual Church'. It is obvious that the church wants open membership. Mr. Williams has won his case, but must have realised how out of step he was with the majority of the church. He responded by resigning his offices of Deacon and Treasurer of the church. But he remained a member and will accept office again in the future.

**Temperance Movement.**

1861 saw the founding of the town's Total Abstinence Society. Samuel Edger was among those who encouraged this, using the Mechanics' Institute as a place where this Society could be advocated. In its first year it was claimed that four hundred and fifty had signed the pledge, that two hundred had joined The Band of Hope and a brass band had been formed.[130]

**Ecumenical sympathies.**

From a church meeting minute in 1861 we hear of a committee known as the Town Mission which was organising services in the Town Hall. It is not clear who made up this committee, but the Baptists wrote to them to point out the problem of the Town Hall meetings clashing with the Baptist week-night service. And they added that, while fully appreciating the motive of these meetings, they regret 'the lack of catholicity' on the committee. They suggested the Town Mission committee would be better 'if all the ministers of all denominations were invited to co-operate in the arrangement and conducting of these services'.

[130] J. Dunleavey, op. cit. p .18.

**Samuel Edger leaves for New Zealand.**
Abingdon had a prophet in its midst, but prophets move on. In the autumn of '61 the members wish to express to Mr. Edger 'their high appreciation of his labours among them for the last six years and to assure him of their warmest sympathy amid all the difficulties with which he has had to contend and also their deep regret that there is a possibility of his leaving'. They send a delegation to encourage him to remain. He agreed to do so. But in April of the next year he informed the church of his expectation to emigrate to New Zealand. The church responded with a 'requisition urging him to remain in the town and signed by more than 500 on Sunday evening' - an indication of his popularity and the size of his evening congregation. He agreed to consider it, but left in the summer. He was to be followed by a very different man.

**The ministry of the Revd. W.T. Rosevear.**

*Figure 33 Revd. W.T. Rosevear 1862 - 69.*

On October 31 1862 the church was informed of the acceptance of their call to Mr. Rosevear of Coventry. A year later the church withdrew its membership of the Berks. Association. On March 27th 1867 the *Berks and Oxon. Advertiser* reported a meeting in Abingdon

Council Chamber 'on behalf of the funds of the Sunday Schools at the Baptist Chapel'. The Revd. J.J. Brown, of Birmingham, had been invited to deliver a lecture on John Bunyan. Mr. Rosevear was in the chair. At a similar occasion the following year the lecture was on Isaac Newton. In 1867 the church book recorded the first exclusion from church membership since 1855, and matters of discipline again became a regular feature of church meeting agendas. Mr. Rosevear then informed the church that he intended to withdraw from his customary fellowship with the Revd. Lepine, minister of the Independent Chapel, on account of his 'unchristian behaviour in connection with the Abingdon Town Mission'. The church felt they must support their minister and agreed they would not join in the monthly 'United Missionary Meeting' with the Independents and the Wesleyans until 'the cause of the present disunion ceases to exist'. Mr. Rosevear's problem with Mr. Lepine now influenced relations between the two Sunday Schools, causing the Baptist teachers to write to the Independent Sunday School to withdraw from united prayer with its teachers. A copy of the reply to that letter is preserved in the Baptist Sunday School minute book:

> Independent Sunday School Abingdon. At a teachers meeting held on July 12th 1867 it was unanimously resolved that the underwritten communication be signed by the Superintendent and Secretary and forwarded to the Secretary of the Baptist Sunday School.
> 'To the teachers of the Baptist Sunday School Abingdon. Dear Friends, We have been pained to receive your Resolution of the 2nd July and to hear that you have set aside our meetings for united prayer which had been uninterruptedly held for above 30 years. We shall thankfully remember that this was not our act and we shall continue to pray for you as before. Our beloved minister has our full confidence and regard. It is a small thing to be judged of man's judgement, he that judgeth is the Lord.'
> W.P. Cousins, Superintendent
> Chas. Glanville, Secretary.

We do not know what it was about Mr. Levine's behaviour regarding the Abingdon Town Mission to which the Baptist pastor took exception. In July 1869 Mr. Rosevear stated that he had received an invitation from Blackfriars, Glasgow and would be leaving. The church meeting appointed a committee to 'draw up a reply to M. Rosevear'. The usual practice of the church to copy their letter of gratitude to departing ministers into the church book is broken on this occasion. It is easy to misjudge a situation from what is recorded, or not recorded, in church minutes, but the impression is left that the church were not sorry to see him depart. Membership remained at about 200 and no doubt there were many good aspects to his ministry. In the weeks following his leaving the resolution regarding the Independent Church was rescinded, to leave any new minister free to join with them.

**The ministry of the Revd. G.H. Davies.**

On July 18 1870 Mr. Davies was invited to be pastor and accepted. For the nine years of his ministry the church book is filled almost exclusively with details of the coming and going of church members. In 1874 notice of a conference is given 'for the deepening of the spiritual life' and neighbouring churches and their ministers are to be invited.

*Figure 34 Revd. G.H. Davies 1870 - 80.*

In December 1879 the minister expressed the wish to see the interior of the Chapel renovated. Presumably, after thirty nine years, the new chapel was looking dowdy. A committee was formed. On 28 June 1879 Mr. Davies resigned and in their letter of acceptance the church thanked him for the teaching they have received during his past ministry.

**The founding of Marcham Baptist Church.**

In his pamphlet on the history of the Marcham church,[131] Gordon Lewry reminds us of the lectures delivered by John Pendarves at Marcham in the summers of the early 1650's. Then, 'by, and perhaps well before, the 1860's a group of persons of Baptist persuasion were meeting in a cottage in a lane leading to what was known as Plum Tree Acre.' The group's first purpose-built chapel came in 1871, by train and wagon - "a second-hand corrugated iron chapel building of the well known 'tin tabernacle ' style". Apparently this had been organised by a Mr. Holloway, who taught at the British School and had been holding children's meetings in the village, together with Mr. L.S. Worth of Willesden, a trustee of Abingdon Baptist Church. It was set up more or less on the site of the present chapel. A lease had been acquired on the plot and this was sold first to the Revd. G.H. Davies and then to a trust made up of the Abingdon deacons and others. It was opened in 1872, the first minister being the Revd. W. Pontifex who also had care of Fyfield and Cothill. The tin chapel would not be replaced until 1928. The church would have strong ties with the Abingdon Church, and its three other village churches, to the present time.

[131] Gordon Lewry. *Marcham Baptist Church, A brief history.* June 1994 (3 sheets of A4) A copy in the Abingdon archive, Angus Library, Oxford.

*Figure 35 Marcham Baptist Chapel 1895.*

**Association evangelism.**

During the period between ministers the church agreed 'That we unite with the Association in the evangelistic services to be held in October' and at the September church meeting they agreed to obtain Bills with details of the meetings and Tracts to be delivered house to house. This is the first indication that the church had returned to the Berks. Association.

**The ministry of the Revd. Robert Rogers.**

On the 19 October 1880, by unanimous decision, the Revd. Robert Rogers of Chesham was invited to the pastorate for a term of seven years. Involvement with both the Association meetings and the annual assemblies of the Baptist Union now received regular mention in the church minutes. Mr. Williams and J. Coxeter were appointed delegates to the Association, and to the Assembly meetings in Liverpool.

*Figure 36 Revd. R. Rogers 1880 - 93.*

In 1882 a Finance Committee was appointed 'to conduct the financial affairs of the church and to devise and carry out some improved system of collecting the subscriptions'. In November of that year another name that will appear frequently in the church minutes in the years to come is seen for the first time as the book records the transfer from Bingley of Mr. J.C. Smallbone.

**Parental responsibility.**

Discipline is still being administered. On February 1st 1887 Ann Paynton is excluded from communion for six months for immorality - 'The Church further desires to express its sorrow that our friends James and Sarah Paynton have not exercised more watchful care over their daughter and hopes that in future they will more zealously exercise proper parental supervision.'

**The minister's library.**

In June 1892 the church wrote to thank the widow of its former minister, Revd. E.S. Pryce, for the gift of his books to the minister's library. These would have been added to the Tomkins' bequest and are now in the Angus Library.

**Restoration of the Chapel.**

Following the request of his predecessor in 1879, the chapel was thoroughly restored in 1881 at a cost of nearly £900. In 1893 a further £500 was spent on a new roof.[132] This has stood the test of time and serves well nearly a hundred and twenty years later. But the purist can only regret that the fashion of the late nineteenth century dictated that a wooden, gothic ceiling should replace the classical, plaster ceiling of fifty years earlier. The line of the cornice of the original ceiling can still be clearly seen.

The church had renewed their invitation to Mr. Rogers to serve them for a second seven year term, but in 1893, after a thirteen year ministry, he announced his resignation following a call to the English Presbyterian Church, Abergele. In a warm letter of response the church spoke of a 'testimonial' they intended to present to him. In the 'interval' (the church studiously avoiding the Anglican term interregnum) the Wednesday night meetings would take the form of special Prayer Meetings for the guidance of the church. It was to be a very problematic Interval.

**Breach of promise.**

The church invited the Revd. James Crosby Rogers as their next minister. This was accepted, and no doubt he gave notice of resignation to his church. But then, on what grounds is not mentioned, further enquiries were made about him and the invitation withdrawn. The committee which was responsible for finding the new minister received a vote of confidence from the church and the matter was finally settled, after Queen's Council had become involved, by the church taking out a loan for £150 to pay the distressed minister to drop all charges of breach of promise. The same meeting that heard this resolution of the affair passed the proposal that in future ministers be elected for four years by at least two thirds majority; the church to have the right to terminate the contract at any time with six months' notice; the minister must give similar notice of resignation.

---

[132] T.H. Pumphrey, op cit p 20. In a brief memoir, written in the 1960's, the minister W.H. Cox writes, 'before the work [ i.e. the £900 restoration] was finished the white plaster ceiling of the Church crashed down during a Service and this meant a new roof with open rafters at a further cost of £500'. I believe Pumphrey's dates are more reliable than Cox's later memories, but the dramatic collapse of the ceiling may well be a story still being told in his childhood in the church. The memoir is in the Abingdon archive, Angus Library, Oxford.

On Tuesday 22nd May 1894 the Revd. Harold Doggett was invited for four years - he will serve three such terms.

**Ministry of the Revd. Harold Doggett.**

This ministry was to span the Jubilee celebrations of the old queen, the turn of the century, the funeral of Victoria and the coronation of Edward VII. Although church attendance across the denominations and throughout the land was already falling from its peak in the 1870's, it was still in many ways the golden age of Victorian spirituality and of the authority of the 'non-conformist conscience'. At his Induction Service on 13th September 1894 reference was made to Harold Doggett's successful work in Cambridge as a winner of young men to Christ, and in South Africa as the founder and first pastor of the Baptist Church in Bloemfontein, Orange Free State. In Abingdon, membership had fallen to 113 but Mr. Pumphrey, in his lecture the following April, had high hopes for the future - 'In addition to the Young People's Guild, a Society of Christian Endeavour was commenced in the Autumn of 1894, and already justifies its claim to be a link between the Church and the Sunday School'. This 'Young People's Society of Christian Endeavour' would play a major role in the church's life for years to come. W.H. Cox, in the 1960's, records that in 1895 a junior section was added. This was 'greeted by the [Sunday] School with enthusiasm and flourished successfully for many years and when the Congo Mission steamer was launched we were honoured by collecting for the flag inscribed 'Endeavour' which for many years graced the steamer in Africa'.[133]

**Thomas H. Pumphrey's historical lecture.**

*History of the Baptist Church, Abingdon* by T.H. Pumphrey with preface by the pastor Rev. W. Harold Doggett. Price one shilling, is the published text of a paper on the early history of Abingdon Baptist Church read on 4th April 1895. Only one original copy of this is known to survive. It is a slim A5 hardback, bound in dark green linen with its title in gold leaf on the front cover. This, now delicate, one hundred and sixteen year old volume has, on the inside of its cover, the stern statement, 'Church property not to be taken away'. It obviously had been taken away from the church safe over the years, to be transcribed by typewriter; to be photocopied and, later still, to be digitised; and the original has recently been placed in my hands, from

[133] Source - see footnote 11 above.

which it has now been placed in the church archive in the Angus Library - there, hopefully, not to be taken away. Apart from the brief references to the Abingdon church in Crosby and Ivimey, and a few sentences of history in the letter to the Association on 14th May 1850, Pumphrey's lecture is the first serious attempt to research the material available to him and publish a History. He uses Ivimey, often quoting verbatim. But his chief source was what he could find in the vestry cupboard, or more likely in the cellar of the church secretary's grocery shop in Stert Street, a year after the great flood of 1894. It could have been the flood that brought the archive to his attention or impressed upon him the vulnerability of the old records and the need to write a history from them while they still survived. He also, in the final two pages, was able to draw on living memories of old members, reaching back to John Kershaw's ministry in the 1820's and 30's and could also benefit from his own memories of more recent times. Bound into the end of his little book is a list of ministers from Pendarves to his present day. This has been added to, in ink, up to 'Adrian Thatcher 1969 -'. Finally we are given a photograph of the pulpit end of the chapel interior by W.J. Vasey of Broad Street, Abingdon. Most, if not all, of Thomas Pumphrey's sources of information survive. But the value and influence of his booklet lie in the fact that he was for many years part of the story he was telling. Like myself, he was very much an amateur historian, but by living in the town and within the on-going story he would have imbibed the folklore and developed a feel for the place, which the professional researcher is often denied. The twentieth and early twenty-first centuries would see a steady flow of learned papers, especially on the first fifty years of the church. But the church's view of its own history showed little awareness of these. For most of the twentieth century, the generations marked their anniversaries by relating to themselves or to the local media, Pumphrey's 1895 paper.

**The life of the late Victorian church.**

The church meeting minutes are becoming ever more detailed. Earlier in the century a page of the church book recorded the transactions of several meetings, now a meeting can fill three pages. And these pages speak of the weekly life of a late Victorian church. Decisions about payments to the organist - £10 per annum plus £2 for instructing the choir - representatives on the local Committee of the Nonconformist Council - Brethren Pumphrey and Cullen with the pastor - appointment of an Organ Committee - that the New Year Sacramental

Collection be for the widows and orphans of the Baptist Missionary Society as usual - that 'The Village Mission Committee, now consisting of the pastor and officers, be increased by the addition of the Evangelist, one member from each village, and one member from the Home Church'. Marcham is now included in the list of village causes. 'That a committee consisting of six ladies be formed to assist the pastor and Deacons in a systematic visitation of all members of the Church and Congregation, and other works of usefulness.' The Sunday School numbered about 150 with about 20 teachers. The pastor announced his intention to hold a Sunday evening Prayer Meeting for the next three months. 'During the winter months the Communion service to be held alternately morning and evening.' The new system of 'pew-to-pew' collections would be further explained. Shelves to be placed in the entrance lobby of the Chapel 'for the depositing of the visitors hymnbooks within reach of brethren who - one at each door - should attend to their distribution'. And so on. The church is busy with its committees, money-raising social events, appointing representatives for numerous town, association and national gatherings, the minutiae of its organisation and its on-going village work.

**The Organ Committee.**

The brief mention of this committee, above, prompts an outline of the three organs which have been installed in the chapel. There is no mention of an organ in the days of the 1700-1841 chapel. The first known organ appears to have been installed either when the new chapel was built, in 1841, or shortly afterwards. A strong tradition claims that when this was replaced in 1899 it was rebuilt in Fyfield chapel, where it is still in weekly use. Its replacement served the church for nearly a century until the present instrument was purchased in 1991. The first two organs probably occupied the platform in the rear gallery before the second was moved to the NW corner of the ground floor, where the manual of the present organ is. Details of the three instruments are as follows:

1. The organ now at Fyfield has this inscription attached:

   > British Institute of Organ Studies. This organ has been awarded a Certificate Grade II in recognition of its being an important organ by R.W. Rowse c. 1850. Largely in original condition.

2. The organ which resulted from the 1899 committee was a Martin & Coate organ, built in Oxford in 1899 at the cost of£110. It was dismantled in 1991.

3. The present organ cost £12,000. It is a Makin, of Oldham, Toccata - two manual, digital, computer, electronic church organ. 14 stops, 16 swell, 8 pedals, with usual couplets. At the same time a Rogers electronic piano was purchased.

**The work in the villages continues.**
July 1897; Mr. Shipley was invited to accept the oversight of Cothill, Fyfield and Marcham. November 1897; The Village Mission Committee invited Mr. Harberd to take the oversight of Drayton. April 1905; 'It was suggested that a few friends might give sixpence weekly to help the Miss Suttons of Drayton who are greatly in need'. January 1909; Mr. Edward Hall, Evangelist at Drayton, received for membership.

**A further step towards open membership.**
November 30 1898; 'The pastor having intimated that two sisters, members of UMFC at Liskeard, desired their transfer to our fellowship, and that he was advised by the Deacons that such transfer from a paedobaptist Church was not inimical to the letter or spirit of our trust deeds, provided that every member so received was informed that he or she has no power to vote in our church meetings...' It was resolved to apply for their transfer.

**The death of Mr. Coxeter and the end of the century.**
The Coxeter family appear to have occupied, from the second half of this century, the position held by the Tomkins of the previous two hundred years. In January 1900 Mr. C. Coxeter of Chesham House, The Park, died in his 94th year.

*Figure 37 Mr. Charles Coxeter.*

He had been a member of the church for 72 years; a Sunday School Teacher 70 years; a Deacon 50 years and a local preacher. The *Temperance Worker* printed his obituary in its March edition, reporting, 'His religion was a reflection of his sunny nature' and recording his two favourite maxims: 'The morning is the time for work' and 'A Sabbath well spent is a week well begun'.[134] His life had spanned the nineteenth century and the obituary speaks of how he fulfilled what might be expected of a good Christian in that century. He was a successful businessman - fair, honest and kind to his employees. In his church he was humble, committed and always ready to support its work. He was concerned to encourage his fellow citizens to improve themselves, by hard work and avoiding alcoholic drink He preached the Christian gospel in the town and villages, and practised what he preached. The obituary offers us a man who was a microcosm of that century. The elderly man in the accompanying photograph looks into the camera with the comfortable confidence of a man of his time. The new century would be very different.

[134] *The Temperance Worker,* March and April 1900. Copy in Abingdon archive 14/3 titled *Memoirs of a Deacon.* Angus Library.

# Chapter 4
# The Twentieth Century

**New Year's Soiree and A.G.M.**
An insight of the life of the church at this time and of the success of Mr. Doggett's ministry can be had from the detailed programme of the meeting held on Thursday 3rd January 1901 at 6.30 p.m.:

Hymn: 'Come Thou Fount of every blessing'
Reading from the Psalms and Prayer
Business and statistics -
membership stood at 145, with additions from the Mother's Meeting and the Christian Endeavour
Reports on the YPSCE, Village Mission etc.
Hymn: 'Come let us join our friends above'
followed by memorials of friends who had died in the past year
Refreshments
Reports of the Sunday School and Mother's Meeting
Financial Statement and details of the Twentieth Century Fund
All above interspersed with solos:
Mrs. Kendall - 'Will the Lord absent Himself forever'?
Miss Argyle - 'Walking with Jesus'.
Miss Farmell - 'The Gift'.
'A most inspiring meeting closed just before 9 o'clock with 'Hail! sweetest, dearest tie that binds' and the Benediction.'

**250th Anniversary.**
On 12 December 1901 a special church meeting began to plan for the 250th anniversary of the church next year. It should be noted that until research was done later in the century into the life of John Pendarves, the earliest record of the Abingdon Church was in the 1652 minutes of the 'Abingdon Association'. Special anniversary services were held on the 14th and 21st of June 1902 recorded in detail in the Abingdon Herald. While celebrating the old struggles with the establishment of the seventeenth century, Mr. Doggett still had a bone to pick with them in the new twentieth: he spoke of the United Service for Nonconformists to be held in the Congregational Chapel on Coronation Day (June 26th) 'and he had explained to the vicar that their action was not antagonistic to the general rejoicings, but they

believed that the coronation service went to the root of their Nonconformist principles, for much as they honoured the King, they could not recognise him as head of the church. (applause)'.

*Figure 38 An Abingdon Baptist Church outing ca. 1900.*

**An attempt to reach the working classes.**

December 1903 'Mention was made of the success of an experiment undertaken in connection with the evening services of our Church; and testimony was thankfully borne to the way in which many of the class sought to be reached were now attending God's House. The service is well advertised as lasting one hour, with Sankey's hymns, string band assisting choir, free seats and no collection.' These special services appear to have been held monthly for, after two months of these 'new' Sankey hymns, the church meeting agreed to revert to old hymnbooks for the evening service and use Sankey's only for the special monthly service. There is nothing more designed to upset a church than the introduction of new hymns!

**Individual Communion Cups.**

February 2 1905 'The system of the Individual Communion Cup was brought forward and discussed and it was resolved to leave it for a time'. But if the church is reluctant to face inevitable change in the details of its worship, it still had a strong heart for evangelism and in the June of 1905 they agreed to support the 'Special Mission of this county during 1905-06'.

*Figure 39 Cast of The Mikado.*
*A church performance in the early 20th century.*

**The end of Mr. Doggett's ministry.**
On 7th March 1906 a letter of resignation from Mr. Doggett at the end of his third term of four years was read to the church. A warm letter of appreciation was written and a copy entered in the church book. However, in June, since he had not yet received a call to another church, he was invited to remain at Abingdon for a while. The call eventually came and in March 1907 the Revd. Tedeschi was invited to the pastorate for a four year term.

*Figure 40 Early 20th century church leaders.*
*Unknown deacons and possibly minister (fourth from left).*
*Could this be the Revd. J. Tedeschi?*

**The ministry of Revd. J. Tedeschi.**

The new minister appears to continue the momentum of Mr. Doggett's ministry. It is an energetic time of building improvements and work with young and old. Immediately the weekly envelope scheme of giving to the church is introduced. A Coffee Supper for young men will be held after the third Sunday evening service of every month. A new building scheme for extra classrooms and for lavatories is discussed and agreed to be started as soon as £100, half the total cost, is raised, though the classrooms appear to be dropped from the plan. New ceiling lights are ordered for the Chapel. A 'Pleasant Sunday Afternoon', to become known across the country as PSA's, is started for women, presided over by Mrs. Tedeschi, with an average attendance of sixty women. The 'Village Station at Drayton' (i.e. the Baptist Chapel) is renovated. A series of special meetings for 'the Deepening of the Spiritual Life' are led in the church by Revd. H. Oakley of Tooting. And the pastor and C.E. Society have 'very often' conducted open air meetings on the village greens. By 1910 membership has increased to 157 and it is small wonder that the following year the church invites the Revd. Tedeschi Wilson (for he has now changed his name by deed poll) to continue for a second term. But in June 1911 the church accepts with sorrow the news that their minister has accepted a call to Belfast. They decide that 'money in a purse' should be the form of the testimonial to their departing minister and 'if money exceeded £15, an illuminated address as well'.

The memoir of W.H. Cox has been mentioned earlier. This is not a finished work but five pages of unpunctuated notes in an exercise book. One of its most valuable contributions concerns Mr. Tedeschi's ministry, which fell just within Mr. Cox's childhood memory but probably reflects church gossip, or group memory which still circulated when he was a young man. He writes in the mid 1960's:

> In 1906 the Church was again bereft of its pastor but in the same year the Church heard of a young minister from Brightwell not far away Rev. J Wilson Tedeschi and he came with his wife and three young daughters staying until 1911. He maintained a very active ministry but was handicapped by his nationality so helped by his friendship with Rev. J.B. Meyer he easily changed [his name] to Joseph Tedeschi Wilson but some were still prejudiced (as he was of Italian parentage, his wife was English) even among his deacons and in 1911he left for St. Albans and eventually he went to Australia when a few months ago at the age of 90 the Church received his greeting through the visit of one of his daughters.

**The ministry of the Revd. Charles Deal.**

The letter of acceptance from Mr. Deal was received by the church on 31st March 1912. He would be called to minister in Abingdon through some of the darkest years of the century and as we read through the church book, in which the small details of normal church life continue to be recorded, we begin to sense the terrible toll that these years were taking not only upon the young men whom the church was proudly sending to their death, but upon the spirit of those who, in the young men's class had taught them the way of faith, hope and love and now saw them returning cold eyed and disillusioned from the killing fields.

**New ideas in children's work.**

On July 1st, a month before the declaration of war, an excursion to the seaside for the Church and Sunday School was planned. Baptists were aware and concerned that the Sunday Schools could exist almost independently of the church and this joint outing was possibly seen as a way of bringing them together. But a far bolder approach was suggested to the church meeting on 30th September: 'The Pastor in his remarks said the Sunday School should be in closer touch with the Church and suggested that the morning scholars should assemble at 10.45 for marking registers and then proceed to the service and that part of the service should be essentially for the children. Proposed the scheme be brought to the Teachers for consideration'. There was, of course, no suggestion that the larger afternoon Sunday School should close and join them, and we don't hear what was the reaction of the teachers or whether the scheme was acted upon. But we have here the seeds of the Family Church movement of fifty years later.

**The effect of the war.**

The war receives no mention until the annual letter to the Berks. Association is composed in May 1915. From it we learn 'eighteen men from the Mother Church and the Villages have joined the colours'. The September church meeting agrees that a roll of honour of all members of the Church and Villages should be placed in the schoolroom for prayer. The following meeting insists it is more prominently displayed in the Church vestibule. In December 1915 the Revd. 'Chas.' Deal is invited to continue for a second four years.

The Association letter of 1916 tells of 45 men from the Church who have now joined H.M.'s Forces. And the arrival of 800 troops in the town was 'opportunity for service not missed'. 'Provision was made for the men during the week and after Sunday evening services. Meanwhile the women of the Church have been busy and a case containing a large assortment of clothing was despatched for the relief of the Serbians'.

The letter reports that the village work continues and 'In Mr.W.J. Webber, the newly appointed Village Missioner, the pastor has found a true and devoted colleague'.

The Sunday School roll stands at 102, a loss of 27 being mainly due to the Young Men's Bible Class being decimated by the war.

In June 1916 the pastor is ill and the church writes to assure him 'That supplies for the Church having been arranged for July and August, he must now think only of himself, his health and those near to him.'

July12 1916 Carried - 'That the Free Churches combine and hold special Mission Services simultaneously with the Anglican Church from the 5th to the 12th of November inclusive'. It is not clear whether this is an attempt to work as closely as is possible with the Anglicans, or in direct opposition. On the 4th August the Baptists accept an invitation from the Wesleyans to meet for prayer on the second anniversary of the war.

The church minutes record the life of the church continuing much as ever during the war years, but there is evidence that income is low as well as morale. When Mr. Hainsworth retired as Secretary in 1917 no replacement could be found. For over a year there was no entry in the church books. This was the first break in nearly two hundred years. The explanation was written by Mr. Deal in February 1919. In a 'Note by the Pastor' he writes that as no successor was found for Mr. Hainsworth, Mr. E. Coxeter and the Pastor tried to fill the post. They decided to discontinue the monthly Church Meeting and only call a meeting when business demanded it. Meanwhile the deacons would deal with church business. And he concludes. 'We feel that it has been an honour that from a Church such as ours no fewer than - men responded to the call of King and country in the great war and with sorrow record the fact that of that number - lost their lives in the Great European War. It is suggested that a Welcome meeting for the returned men associated with us should be held when demobilization is completed'. The blank spaces were not filled in, as the pastor no doubt intended, but the memorial plaque listed four names of those who had died.

**A change of minister.**

The church meeting on 19 September 1919 began to set things in order. With the end of Mr. Deal's ministry possibly in sight they unanimously agreed 'that we become affiliated to the Baptist Union Federation for Ministerial Settlement'. Mr. Smallbone was elected secretary and six Deacons were elected. A Ladies Sewing Meeting was launched which would seek to raise money for a new chapel at Marcham. To complete Marcham's story, in 1928 an asbestos building replaced the tin chapel. This new chapel was clad in brick in 1950.

*Figure 41 Marcham Baptist Chapel.*

On 4th March 1920 the A.G.M. and Social would 'be also our farewell to Rev. and Mrs. Deal'. The new Ministerial Settlement process began to operate with letters suggesting names of likely ministers being sent by the Area Superintendent Revd. C.T. Byford. The September 1st meeting sent an invitation to the Revd. Penfold Morris of Lewes. W.H. Cox recalls, 'In 1912 Rev Chas Deal came and exercised a faithful but not brilliant ministry... The Church experienced a time of stagnation but came alive again in the ministry of John Penfold Morris from Lewes.'

**Preparing for the new minister**.

Mr. Morris was sixty three when he accepted the call to a four year term of office at Abingdon. He would find the church in a run down state. The war had removed so many of the young men who might now be coming into leadership positions. Only four names were recorded on the Memorial which would be erected to their memory - Donald Cullen, Stanley Harper, Frank Lupton and Fred Pusey. But how many more members of the Young Men's Class in 1914 were too disillusioned or their lives too disrupted to return we do not know.

The flu epidemic of 1919, which is said to have killed more people than the war itself, though many of these would have been the elderly and weak, had no doubt taken its toll. And now a deepening recession with its consequent unemployment was taking hold. Firm evidence of the decline may be seen in the Attendance Register which from 1889 to 1919 was kept as a record of when members attended communion. This indicates that in 1889 the membership stood at 106 and of these 61 attended the January communion service. In 1913 numbers had dropped, but not drastically - 97 members of which 52 were at communion. In 1919 we have 93 members yet only 23 at communion. But the church had called the right man for the moment. Before he came, however, a church, with no financial reserves, struggled to get its house in order.

November 17 1920: The manse was in a bad state and the estimate for repairs greater than the church reserves - a social afternoon and evening with stalls and side shows would be held to raise funds. There was a shortage of hymn-books - one assumes this is from dilapidation rather than increased demand. Again a sign of the low state of the church is seen in the suggestion 'that no doubt there are several churches in our Association who have changed their hymn book for the Baptist Hymnal and who would consequently have some Psalms and Hymns to dispose of'. 'The chairman brought forward the matter of Individual Communion Cups, there was general opinion that it was time we adopted this more hygienic method and it was decided a price list and samples be obtained.' December 29 1920: Good news - ninety copies of the old hymn book had been obtained from an advert in the Baptist Times. But the cost of Communion cups is too high for the church at present.

*Figure 42 Harvest display, 20th century.*
*Minister is unidentified though he bears similarities to the Revd. J.P. Morris*

**The ministry of Revd. Penfold Morris.**
On April 7 1921 the Recognition Services for the Revd. Penfold Morris were held. Miss Margaret Hardy, President of the Baptist Women's League preached the sermon.

> The Vicar of Abingdon, as minister of the oldest standing in the town, welcomed Mr. Morris. If there was one thing clear about things as they are at present, it was that the churches could not do without one another. They had each to contribute their bit to the common purpose - the extension of the Kingdom of God. There were many things on which they differed, but there was that fundamental ground of fellowship that they were alike believers. A great many were coming to realise that they must - as the Prime Minister had said - 'probe every avenue to greater union'. That could not be secured by mechanical means, but by the Spirit of God.[135]

20th April, Individual Communion Cups to be purchased 'as a memorial to the members of the Church and Congregation who had lost their lives in the European War 1914 - 1918'.

There was a new spirit about the Association letter for 1921. Between thirty and forty young people are attending Christian Endeavour, the Sunday School is outgrowing its rooms. 'We say with humble thanks to God that our Pastor came in January to a Church that was alive and just ready for development.'

**Money for ministry and mission.**
Shortage of money and ways to raise it continued to be a regular feature of the church minutes, but there was a growing sense of achievement throughout the 1920's.
The church decided to accept a grant from the Baptist Union Sustentation Fund to bring the minister's salary to £250, of which £25 was considered the value of the manse. But the church itself raised the money for the renovation and furnishing of the old British School buildings, having first checked the trust deeds to ensure it was indeed

135 *Abingdon Herald*

Baptist Church property. From now on it was to be known as the Baptist Hall. The facade of the chapel was renovated. The deficit of £200 which the church had at the start of the new ministry was cleared by 1923. They were steadily raising money for a new chapel at Marcham. Contributions to the Baptist Missionary Society were boosted by a 'One Thousand Shillings Fund'. And then in 1925, after Mr. Webber's retirement as village missioner, a Co-Pastor, Mr. Charles J. Lipscombe, was appointed, with Sustentation Fund help, to oversee the four village churches and a second manse at 40 Tesdale Terrace, Bostock Avenue, was purchased for £310. Donations of £10 towards the cost of this were being sought. In 1927 the decision was taken to build the new chapel at Marcham - it will cost £400 but there is already £300 in the bank and promises totalling £75. Finally, in 1929, the Abingdon church felt able to purchase new hymn books, four years before a revision makes this book out of date again.

*Figure 43 Revd. J. Penfold Morris 1921-31.*

*Figure 44 Mr. C.J. Lipscombe,*
*Co-Pastor to Mr. Morris and his two successors.*

**Ministry.**

In 1923 and 1927 Mr. Morris' four year term of office was renewed. The Co-Pastor, also called Assistant Pastor, Mr. Charles. J. Lipscombe, was a tall man who had lost an arm in the war, he is remembered for his energetic cycling from Abingdon to the villages, even in the snow. In some notes of conversations with Mr. R. Caudwell which Ken Read made in 1973 he records Mr. Caudwell saying that when Mr. Lipscombe visited he would call on every house in the village. When not wanted he would always call again to see if they had changed their mind! Charles Orland remembered him as 'a saintly man, aided by a good wife'. He would work with three successive ministers and retire after twenty two years.

In 1923 Mr. Morris recommended to the church, for baptism and church membership, a young man Mr. W.H. Cox. He was said to be a member and local preacher of the Wesleyan Church but his study of scripture had led him to a Baptist position regarding baptism and churchmanship. Four months later, after baptism and reception into membership, he was appointed lay pastor of the Leafield Baptist Church. A year later the Abingdon church recommended W.H. Cox of Leafield church, aged twenty one, to Spurgeon's College to train for the ministry.

*Figure 45 Young men's Bible Class in 1920's or 30's.*
*Possibly on the same day as the Spring Cleaning Party below.*

The old 'Village Committee' was now reformed into 'The Abingdon Fellowship' to forge yet closer links between the mother and daughter churches. A deacon was elected by each of the four village churches and these, with the Abingdon deacons and the two pastors will form one diaconate.

**The cenotaph service.**
The decision, in October 1923, to support the United Memorial Service at the cenotaph in the Square was a milestone in the march towards church unity. This is the first record in the Baptist archives of a united service which brought together both the non-conformists and the Anglicans of Abingdon.

**A splendid spirit.**
As the decade progressed, in spite of the difficulties of the Great Depression, the Abingdon letters to the Association were buoyant. 'There is a splendid spirit in the church', the 1923 letter records. The youth service and social hour every third Sunday evening is flourishing; a Junior Christian Endeavour is started in addition to the Senior which had been in operation for nearly thirty years now; the Primary Department of the Sunday School has grown to the point that more chairs have to be purchased; forty women meet on Monday evenings at the Women's Meeting; the Ladies Working Party are beavering away to raise funds for church and village work.

*Figure 46 Spring Cleaning Party 1920's or 30's.*

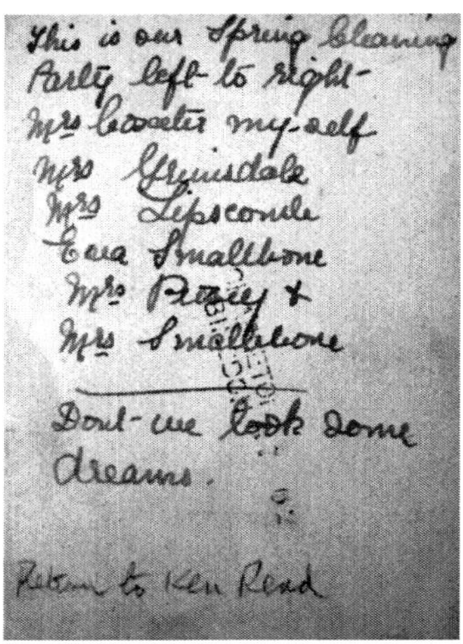

This is our Spring Cleaning
Party left to right-
Mrs Coxeter my-self
Mrs Grimsdale
Mrs Lipscombe
Cara Smallbone
Mrs Pizzey &
Mrs Smallbone

Don't we look some
dreams.

Return to Ken Read

*Figure 47 Reverse of Spring Cleaning Party.*
*Names to be read L to R rear row first [my-self is Minnie Spokes].*
*Schoolteacher's house in background.*

**Death of the Revd. Penfold Morris.**

On 1st July 1930, pen in hand as he worked on his sermon, the minister suddenly died. He was seventy three years old. A fortnight later the shocked and saddened church agreed to continue his stipend to Mrs. Morris until September, since the Sustentation Fund grant would continue until then. The *Baptist Times'* In Memoriam speaks of his organising ability. While working in the Post Office, he had served in an honorary capacity at the Lewes Church for ten years to enable that church to continue to pay its minister, W.K. Armstrong, whose health had broken down. At Abingdon, the article continues, he prevented the sale of the old British School and furnished it for the Sunday School so that the Church Hall could house the Primary Department. He renovated the church premises which were badly run down on account of the war years, and his energy was largely responsible in finding funds for a co-pastor and the purchase of a second manse.

**Electric light.**

The church consulted with Mrs. Morris regarding a suitable memorial to her husband, suggesting the installation of electric light in the church. She said this was the next objective that her husband was planning. After the work was completed, the last of seventeen memorial plaques was mounted inside the chapel:

In Grateful Memory of John Penfold Morris
for ten years the pastor and friend of this church,
suddenly called to higher service July 1st 1930.
Under his inspiring ministry much progressive work
was accomplished here and in the villages.
The electric lighting was installed in 1931 as a
permanent memorial of the high esteem in
which he was held by all.

BAPTIST CHURCH, ABINGDON.

**Memorial to the late Rev. J. P. Morris.**

The Church Officers cordially invite

Mr & Mrs J D Godfrey

to be present at the RE-OPENING SERVICES on

THURSDAY, SEPT. 17th, 1931,

after the installation of electric light, and the renovation of the Church.

DIVINE WORSHIP, 3.30 p.m.,
Preacher: REV. J. A. SMALLBONE.
(of Kings Heath, Birmingham).

TEA in Hall, 5.0 p.m. PUBLIC MEETING 6.30 p.m.

MRS. MORRIS will unveil a memorial tablet at the evening meeting.

**The ministry of the Revd. John Robins.**

Mr. Robins, called for a five year term, began his ministry at Abingdon in 1931 and immediately introduced Special Services, on the second Sunday of each month, using Sankey hymns. A thousand cards advertising these services were printed for house to house visitation with personal invitations. The following year the church agreed to join in the Baptist Union's 'Discipleship Campaign' which involved grouping the Abingdon and village churches with the churches in Wantage, Wallingford and Faringdon. Each church was to appoint a representative for the committee.

*Figure 48 Revd. John Robins 1931-38.*

In addition to its Sunday worship and village work, the church records in these inter war years were concerned with the details of an annual round of events - choir concerts, sales of work, rummage sales, garden parties, the pastor's anniversary, Sunday School Anniversary, Church Anniversary, Harvest Festival. In 1933 special services in Holy Week leading up to Good Friday were held. The following year the pastor reported that he had attempted to get the Free Church Council to organise these in Holy Week but he had 'not met with much success'. Miss Trotman, who had taken over as organist from Miss Baum in 1925 and was to continue to lead the music for years to come, put in a plea in 1934 for an electric blower, since she was finding it difficult to get a human blower to pump air through the organ on her practice nights. In 1935 the decision was taken not to apply for the Sustentation Grant for the following year onwards. And Mr. Coxeter was asked to represent Revd. Henry Forty in the town's procession to celebrate the king's jubilee.

**Open membership.**

On January 13 1936 the church meeting needed to decide whether to invite Mr. Robins to continue for a further five years. This led to the church raising the question: Could only baptised members vote on this issue? The right to vote on the call of a minister was probably one of the last privileges denied to church members who had not been baptised as believers.

The Secretary agreed to write to the Baptist Union seeking advice regarding what the Trust Deeds might say on this matter. The church met next on February 3rd and the Secretary reported that he had received no reply from the Union. The chairman then put it to the baptised members, whether they were willing for the paedobaptist members to vote on this matter. There was a unanimous vote in favour. The long journey to open membership, which had begun nearly three hundred years before in the ministry of Daniel Turner, had reached its destination.

*Figure 49 Church gateway in the 1930's.*

In the event, Mr. Robins remained at Abingdon a further two years before accepting a call to Watchet Baptist Church. Mr. Lipscombe, it was agreed, should continue to have oversight of the village churches without time limit.

**Manse repairs**.

Before a new minister could take up residence in 35 Ock Street the Deacons informed the church that alterations were 'absolutely necessary to make it more tenable'. As work began the decision was made that the time had come to install electricity, and the estimated cost rose accordingly. The existing kitchen and scullery were demolished and the cellar filled in. The larder was altered to form the kitchen. The elaborate window of the present kitchen would go into the new kitchen and 'look up the chapel yard'. At the same time electric radiators were installed in the church.

**The ministry of Revd. Cecil J. Nelson.**

The Revd. Cecil Nelson of Northampton was invited for a five year term on the same stipend as Mr. Morris fourteen years before. It was the eve of the Second World War and his ministry would see the church through the war years and into the years of austerity which followed.

*Figure 50 Revd. C.J. Nelson 1939-49.*

**The war years.**

On October 4th 1939 the church made the necessary decisions to conform with the black-out regulations - i.e. that no lighted window should be visible after dark. The evening service would be moved to three in the afternoon and the shutters in the schoolroom would be overhauled. It was also reported that the Hall (i.e. the old British School rooms) had been taken over by the Free Church Council as a canteen for the troops stationed in and around Abingdon. There is no indication in the minutes that this would be inconvenient for the Sunday School, but ten days later the Teachers held an emergency meeting, prior to going on to the Methodist Church for the regular Sunday School Union meeting, 'to discuss the best means of sustaining interest in the school during the days of the War as in the National upheaval the usual place of meeting, The Baptist Hall, had become a Free Church Canteen'. Mr. Nelson, who like his predecessors always attended the Sunday School meetings, suggested that since the evening service had been moved to three o'clock, the children could come to that service for a short address before going into the schoolroom for classes. Further concern was expressed over the 'loss of interest' since the outbreak of war. The teachers' meetings were now held in people's homes, including the manse, because of black-outing problems. Reference to evacuees was made in the minutes when Mr. Charles Orland advised that in the classes: 'so far as possible the London visitors be equally mixed with our regular scholars'. Perhaps the arrival of evacuees boosted the flagging numbers, because space was found in the Canteen for the Primary Department and a teacher and pianist to staff it. A picnic and ramble was organised to help to overcome the reluctance of the regular scholars to welcome the evacuees. A book of remembrance was started, with the names of all those of the church and Sunday School serving in the forces - to be on the communion table and read each month alternately at morning and evening services. As the second winter of the war approached it was decided that the afternoon services had not been successful and so panels of black-outing would be fitted to the church windows. An Associate Membership roll was started for church members evacuated from their home areas.

**Celebrating a centenary.**

A bright spot in these dark years was the celebration of the centenary of the 1841 chapel. A Centenary Fund was set up for renovation work on the chapel. Copies of the 'new' (1933) hymnbook were ordered and a week of meetings and services drawing on preachers such as the Revd. Ruffel Laslett and Dr. Townley Lord were held from 28th October to 2nd November. Miss Trotman gave an organ recital.

In the summer of 1942 members of the Abingdon church shared in a mission at Drayton. Later that year Miss Joyce Hainsworth became church treasurer. She was the first woman to hold this office and thus to serve on the Diaconate of the church.

In 1943 the church heard that another of their members, David Mingard had been accepted for training at Spurgeon's College. The church railings were removed to be melted down for weapons, but the iron gates were spared. Regents Park College provided preachers while the minister was in hospital. And a 'Forces Service' was held after the evening service on the last Sunday of the month, with a pamphlet advertising this to be circulated among the forces. In his memory of Charles Lipscombe, Charles Orland writes (and try to imagine his gentle Northants accent as you read) 'He used to work in the Canteen during the war, collecting plates, cups and saucers etc.

dispersing words of love and cheer to the forces at the same time. The Canteen was open after Church on Sundays as well as week days, closing at midnight. As we cleared up we used to sing, Another Sabbath ended/ Its peaceful hours all flown. It was anything but that.'

By 1944 Charles Orland had been called up for war service in the Royal Devon Yeomanry which was involved in the Italian Campaign of that year. From Sicily they had crossed to the mainland and dug in for the long and costly Battle of Cassino. Like so many who witnessed the horrors of warfare, Charles rarely spoke of his experiences. But in his regimental account of that battle,[136] which he must have purchased after the war, he has been moved to write a brief note in the margin. The book reads:

> On the night of the 18th/19th [of May] there was a short but concentrated air attack on the bridges. The Regiment was still only a few hundred yards from Oxford Bridge, but despite several bombs in the vicinity, the only casualty was Lieut. Kiddy of 384th Battery who was hit on the head by A.A. shrapnel while extinguishing a flare which had fallen near some ammunition.

Charles has written, 'A very uncomfortable night. C.O.'.

There would have been many others whose lives were deeply influenced by this war - those who fought and those who suffered at home. Some of these went from Abingdon to have their faith tested in the chaos of war, while others were drawn to the town and its Baptist church where they would enrich its fellowship for years to come. One such was Selwyn Bryan. Born in Spanish Town, Jamaica, he served his 'mother-land' in the R.A.F from 1941 to 1978. This brought him to the R.A.F. station at Abingdon and to the Baptist church. A modest man, his family were surprised to find among his possessions a medal achieved by being the Combined Services Featherweight boxing champion. His cheerful Caribbean nature overcame any prejudice the church may have had regarding their first black member and he served the church in many ways until his death in 2010.

---

136 *Royal Devon Yeomanry, The Story of 124 Field Regiment R.A. 1939-1945.* Baskerville Press 1947 p 90 para. 3

Another soldier whose character and faith were honed in the war years, but who came to Abingdon fairly late in life, was Peter Clarke, OBE, MSc. As an eighteen year old Territorial Army volunteer, he was called up to join his Field Ambulance at the outbreak of war and while on loan to the RAF at Manston Kent in 1941, was selected for training as pilot. While the army halted transfers that year, Peter accepted the invitation to learn to fly with the Glider Pilot Regiment which he joined in 1942. The sudden illness of his second pilot following briefing for D Day, frustrated his taking part in that operation but as a Staff Sergeant first pilot, he flew a glider to Arnhem in September 1944, setting up and manning a Regimental Air Post in Oosterbeek. His decision to remain caring for four wounded soldiers as the German army overran his position, capture, escape and recapture are recorded in various publications.[137] He was imprisoned from October 1944 and in February 1945, joined the 'Long March' of allied prisoners of war westwards as the allies tightened their grip. His diary records the day to day privations of that march covering some 330 miles between February 9th and April 13th. At one of his lowest moments, Peter lists his dwindling stock of food but remembers one of the slogans chalked on his glider the day they flew from Britain:

> We've got little less than a half loaf left - a bit of swede and a few onions and some salt. This is now <u>11.30 a.m. Sunday 19th March 1945</u> - Roll on the day of liberation! I've spent the last two days delousing myself to the best of my ability - having had no delousing since 1st week of January... I won't forget those two words chalked on glider 184 on <u>Sunday 17th September 1944</u> 'Jehovah Jireh' - truly, God can be our only hope of deliverance and to his only son our only hope of both temporal and eternal salvation to whom be the glory.

These three men must represent the many more who lived on to blend their experiences with the on-going life of the church over the next sixty or more years.

---

[137] For example *The Eagle*, regimental magazine of the Glider Pilot Regiment, Summer 1957 p. 16. This and other papers relating to Peter Clarke are in my archive, which will eventually, I trust, be placed in the Angus Library.

**Thanksgiving.**
A line is drawn under the war years with an entry in the church book of 1945:

> On May 8th this year a thanksgiving service was held in this Church, giving thanks to Almighty God for the end of the war with Germany. Also on August 15th a similar service of thanksgiving was held for the termination of the war with Japan. Thus was brought to an end the long years of bitter warfare, with victory to the Allied Cause. In placing on record these historic events, we do so with humility of spirit, as well as with gratitude of heart, praying that these great occasions may not only have marked the end of the most devastating and costly war the world has ever known, but also the beginning of an era of real peace between the nations of the earth.

**More united action.**
The Baptist deacons now took the initiative to call together all the non-conformist ministers in the town, including those of the Salvation Army, 'to create greater unity between the churches'. They agreed that in the Week of Prayer next January all non-conformist meetings would be closed and services held at the Baptist Church. There was also a large Harvest Social evening to which all the village members were invited and many came - 'quite a unique occasion'.

In 1946 there was yet more emphasis on work with young people. David Mingard asked for his membership to be transferred to Stevenage Baptist Church where he was starting his ministry. A Youth Club was formed 'to try to capture the interest of young people who had been in the Sunday School' and was held on Sunday afternoons in the WAAFS Canteen. A Youth Committee was formed and a Boys Brigade proposed. Charles Orland became Sunday School Superintendent. A Cub Pack was launched which, within a year, would lead to a Scout Troop and a Scout Management Committee.

**The Scouts.**
The minutes of the deacons' and church meetings from August 1946 onwards include several references to the growing Scout Group. There is a possibility that this had a previous existence. In *A Brief*

*History of the Group*[138] Miss Smallbone, writing in 1966 begins, 'The present 30th North Berks Scout Group was *reformed* in the ministry of Rev. C.J. Nelson...' and at a church meeting in January 1948 Eric Baxter, the scoutmaster, stated that it was hoped to *recommence* Church parade. But whether 1946 saw the beginning or a new beginning the minutes of the church record the steady growth of the Group, which had its headquarters in the old British School Hall until its demolition in 1960, after which the scouts and cubs met for a while in the church hall until the first hut was built by voluntary labour on the site to the west of the chapel. The 'Misses Whitehead and Mr. E. Barnet' were the first cub leaders. These, together with the Revd. Nelson (chair), Mr. Orland and Mr. Eustace formed the first management committee. The scout troop, a year later, was led by Eric Baxter, a scientist working at Esso House. When he eventually left to become a missionary teacher in India, the assistant minister, the Revd. Jenkins, briefly took his place. From time to time the question appears to have been raised as to the place of the Group within the life of the church. The Group was 'open' (i.e. not confined to children of church people). At a deacons' meeting in 1951, 'In reply to a question, Rev. H. Jenkins stated that although the gain to our church through the Scouts had not been great, the gain to the Church Universal was incalculable'. Dennis Rhodes, described by Miss Smallbone as 'a very keen Scouter' joined the church soon after and became scoutmaster, his wife helping with cubs. These were greatly supported by the arrival of Ken Clifton and Bill Stevens, both ex servicemen. Ken took responsibility of the cubs, Bill was scoutmaster and Eric group scoutmaster. Over the years leadership changed and patterns of activity were established - Massive Jumble Sales, the sale of Christmas cards and Bob-a-Job Week all raised funds for the local Group and the national body; there was participation in national and inter-national events; monthly parade services with a Grand Parade at the evening service twice yearly. A congregation of 300 attended the first of these. Then there were the camping weekends at Youlbury, the Oxford camp site. They travelled further afield for the annual camp. In 1972 the Group's name was changed to 30th Abingdon (Baptist) following the county boundary changes. Later in the century the younger boys would be catered for in a Beaver Scout Colony and older Scouts, boys and girls, would form a Venture Scout Unit.

---

[138] A copy of the typed original, occupying one side of foolscap, will be placed in the Abingdon Baptist archive in the Angus Library of Regent's Park College, Oxford.

The immense contribution of Scouting to the boys' physical, mental and spiritual growth, and therefore to the church, is incalculable. Let one boy's story speak for many. David Lloyd Carter, 1973-1998, suffered from muscular dystrophy. That having been said he threw himself into scouting with enthusiasm. Aged thirteen he was awarded, by the Chief Scout, the Cornwell Badge 'in recognition of his high standard of character and devotion to duty under great suffering'. Later, when working for his Queen's Scout Award, for his expedition he chose to journey in his wheel-chair to Glasgow; London having been dismissed as too easy an option. Accompanied by fellow Venture Scouts Sharon McIntyre and Paul Coleman they made the journey, sleeping on scout hut floors. On his return, he wrote up his experiences highlighting the suitability or otherwise of facilities for disabled travellers at every stage of the journey. He received his Queen's Scout Award at Windsor Castle and it was celebrated in the Abingdon Baptist church on the 23rd February 1993. As chair to the Venture Scout Unit (the unit ran its own affairs) he put forward the idea of a winter camp in Snowdonia. When the response was very negative he replied, 'Well I'm doing it'. They all went. It was a great success. He did not speak much about his faith. He was not a church member. But early in 1998, he is remembered as saying to his mother, 'I know I'm going to die - I'm looking forward to it; don't worry'. He died on Easter Day.

In the first decade of the new century all the units were opened to girls as well as boys. The Venture Scouts were renamed the Explorer Scout Unit and were organised at district level. Stephen Bodey became Group Scout Leader in 1986 and twenty five years later continues as such. A second long-serving leader, Hazel Telling, joined as an assistant Cub leader in 1975 and then was leader from 1978-2001. Stephen led the Scout troop for a while before Alan Wood took over with Royston Telling as assistant. The original scout hut was destroyed by fire in the late 70's. Its replacement began life as a workmen's hut for the builders of the Didcot Power Station. John Atree, assistant Cub leader until 2001, worked at the power station and secured the hut after the builders had finished with it. As with most youth organisations, the strength of the 30th Abingdon Scout Group has fluctuated, but at the time of writing they are reported to be thriving in all units. Geoff Soord leads the scouts, David Mann the Cubs and Julie Kelly the Beavers.

**The Office of Elder.**

Mr. Thompson resigned as church secretary in 1946, replaced by Mr. Eustace. As the Deacons were also elected and Mr. E.B. Coxeter retired after many years service, the church decided to create the new office of Elder and Mr. Coxeter was appointed the first Elder. This office is not to be understood in the early eighteenth century sense - a post which Benjamin Tomkins held - nor in its modern sense. Mr. Coxeter was to be what today is called a Life Deacon.

**Football.**

'Jan. 16 1947; The invitation to Spurgeon's and Bristol Baptist Colleges to hold a meeting following an inter-college football match was endorsed, the church to provide the party with tea.' This was the first of an annual occasion warmly remembered by both players and church people. The match was played on the town field, just over Abingdon Bridge, Abingdon being fairly centrally placed between Spurgeon's College in London and Bristol. Referee and linesmen were supplied by Regents Park College, Oxford. The tea at the church was followed by a service in which the students and college staff were involved and to which the local congregation was invited.

**Help for German Baptists.**

'The action of Mrs. Nelson and Miss F. Smallbone in providing a centre for the making up and dispatching of food parcels for German Baptists was endorsed.'

**Resignation of Mr. Lipscombe.**

In April 1947 Mr. C.J. Lipscombe resigned as Assistant Minister. The church placed on record 'its gratitude to God for our brother's long and faithful service'. Charles Orland recalls, 'When Mr. Lipscombe died, after he had left Abingdon, I was privileged to conduct a service of thanksgiving for his life, at Marcham. I remember how I referred to him as another Barnabas who was described as a Good man full of the Holy Ghost and of faith (Acts 12:24 A.V.). We who knew and loved him will always treasure his memory'. In his *Brief History*[139] Gordon Lewry records that Mr. Lipscombe's ashes and those of his wife are scattered at Marcham on the little memorial plot created for the purpose in the SE corner of the church garden. The minutes of the Abingdon church now indicate a weakening both in the life of some of

---

139 Gordon Lewry, *Marcham Baptist Church, A Brief History, op. cit.*.

the village churches and of their links with Abingdon. There is discussion regarding increased contributions towards the salary of the next Assistant Minister. Marcham agreed to an increase of £15. But it was thought that Cothill 'with only three or four members left' could not be expected to make an increase, and Fyfield would have similar difficulty with only seven members. A committee was set up to investigate the possibilities. In the Association Letter the church reports that the war years have weakened the links between 'the five communities that compose the Abingdon Church'. However, in October of 1947, the Revd. Hubert Jenkins was invited to be Co-Pastor with C.J. Nelson, a Sustentation Grant having been obtained towards his stipend.

In 1949 a Women's Club was formed. Two more young men were sent from the church for training - Mr. E. Baxter to St. Andrews' College, Selly Oak prior to service with the Baptist Missionary Society; Mr. J. Nelson (the minister's son) to Spurgeon's College for the home ministry. On 31st March 1949 the church hears of the resignation of Mr. Nelson. He was a popular minister and is remembered especially for his ministry of encouragement during the war and his commitment to the Forces Canteen.

**Attempt to start a Fair Service.**

In September Mr. Thompson urged the church to consider holding 'a Special Service for the show people in Abingdon for the October Fair'. The Secretary is instructed to make contact with them and to endeavour to arrange such a service 'and to advise the Free Church Federal Council that we desired the matter discussed for 1950'. But in January 1950 the Revd. Jenkins reported that the Free Church Federal Council had decided 'it was inadvisable to hold any service in connection with Abingdon Fair'.

**Friction between the ministers.**

In 1950 The Revd. S.J. Cowley was called as Co-pastor with Mr. Jenkins. Mr. Caudwell and Mr. Thompson wanted Jenkins to be understood as the senior minister but the Area Superintendent over-ruled. The scene was set for a disgraceful rivalry between the two men, and their wives. The next two years were remembered as a time of bitterly divided church meetings. The Deacons Meetings of January, February and March 1952 drew up a plan of respective duties. One minister was to serve Drayton and Abingdon for six months while the other served Fyfield, Cothill and Marcham - then they were to change over for the next six months. One wonders how this could have worked. But on hearing of it Mr. Jenkins resigned, announcing this from the pulpit. Mr. Cowley accepted. But the Deacons felt that both must stay or both go. Mr. Miller, the Area Superintendent was called in. He pointed out that the Home Work Grant is for village work only and therefore cannot go to two ministers - the grant would not be renewed. So the Deacons recommended to the Church Meeting that Mr. Jenkins' resignation be accepted and Mr. Cowley be asked to offer his. In future, they recommend, one minister with local preachers and students helping to cover the villages. The Fyfield chapel representatives were very unhappy with this solution and wanted Mr. Cowley to stay, but the Church Meeting accepted the recommendation.

**The ministry of Revd. Relfe.**

The Church had been greatly weakened by this unholy interlude and needed a good leader. The Revd. Relfe was called in 1953 and appears to have been unable to be what the church needed. He was in a poor state of health when he came, according to Rowland Caudwell's recollections. On one occasion he collapsed in the pulpit. At the Deacons Meeting on 8th November 1954 it was noted that Mr. Relfe, 'acting on advice of his doctor', had gone away for a few days' rest. The December meeting heard a report of a small committee appointed to visit Mr. and Mrs. Relfe. They had a 'frank talk... the most outstanding statement of Mr. and Mrs. Relfe was the lack of support in the work they had suggested or undertaken'. There seems to have been some difficulty in Mr. Relfe fulfilling the expectations of the villages. His preaching schedule appears to have been quite demanding. A preaching plan of the time, which covers Abingdon and its four daughter churches, shows that over the first three months of the year there were 104 services. Mr. Relfe is responsible for twenty four of these, mainly at Abingdon, and Mrs. Relfe for eight. Between them, the Relfes were down for thirteen services in the villages. A Church Meeting was called to ask if the villages wanted to be independent or remain within the Fellowship - and also to discuss Mr. Relfe's future in the Fellowship. Mr. Relfe pre-empted the decision by resigning in a letter to the meeting on 14th February 1955. The representatives of the village churches reported 'a general feeling among the members of these churches that they did not desire in any way to sever any connections with the Mother Church at Abingdon'.

At this low point, perhaps for financial reasons, the meeting decided to look to the Colleges for a final year student to accept the pastorate. Perhaps the church needed a more experienced minister.

*Figure 51 The chapel in the 1950's, reflecting its low state.*

**Ministry of Revd. David T. Daniell, M.A.**

A year passed before David Daniell, a final year student at Regents Park College, accepted the churches' invitation. Plans were made for his ordination and induction later in the year and there was a decision to stock the manse larder as a wedding present.

Meanwhile use of the slowly collapsing Baptist Hall was restricted to the ground floor rooms and an offer for the purchase of its site is considered. But at the first church meeting attended by the new minister, the decision was made that 'it would not be wise at the present time to sell any part of the site of the Baptist Church grounds'. If Daniell was in any way instrumental in that decision, the church must be grateful to him. In the Abingdon Herald report of the ordination and induction services in October 1956, tribute is paid to those who had led the church through the previous eighteen months - Mr. J. Cooper, chairman of the Diaconate; Miss. Smallbone, secretary; Miss. Hainsworth, treasurer, and the Deacons. The mayor of Abingdon, councillor Polly, spoke of the 'close harmony of the churches in Abingdon'.

Over the next year Mr. Daniell was busy with Sunday worship, the Tuesday evening Bible study and prayer time and with work in the villages. A Daniel Turner Society was formed, mainly for young people and meeting in the manse. A Church Library was established. As the Cubs and Scouts move out of the Hall, now altogether too dangerous for use, into the Schoolroom, the Church Meeting is moved to the manse - an indication of its small size. But though small in number, the meeting began to think in big ways.

**The birth and death of a vision for growth.**

> December 3rd 1957. A long discussion followed concerning the condition and future of the Baptist Church property. Mr. Daniell said a great opportunity in a new development could be ours if we launched out fearlessly, and eventually amid great enthusiasm Mr. A. Eustace proposed, seconded by Mr. Porter it was agreed that Rev. D.J. Daniell formally approaches Mr. Nicholson the Town Clerk requesting that if and when the site previously mentioned and situate between Harcourt Way and Darrell Way becomes available it first be offered through the Free Church Council to the Baptist Church in Ock Street.

This site, on the southern side of Northcourt Road, was an area of housing development which was to gradually fill the fields to the north of the town. It was a vision which would have revolutionised the life of the church. A decade or so later the Anglicans would restore the old tithe barn not far from this site and grow perhaps the strongest church in the town from those northern housing estates. But the possibility of the Baptist church taking that initiative was to be dealt a death blow just a month after the vision was so enthusiastically received.

> January 21st 1958 Mr. Daniell then made a statement which staggered the Church members. He said that for several months the conviction was borne upon him that he had misinterpreted God's call in being a minister of the Baptist Church and after much prayerful thought he was convinced that God's plan for him lay in a different

> direction and therefore he asked the Church to release him at the end of March. The meeting remained silent for some time and then one after another, Deacons and members, expressed their appreciation of Mr. Daniell's ministry and concern for the Church in such sudden darkness. Although much business remained on the agenda it was agreed that all should be postponed and after our Elder Mr. Caudwell had offered prayer the meeting closed and all went to their homes sad, bewildered and perplexed.

David Daniell is remembered as a popular minister who obviously had the ability to inspire his church to great things. He moved into a different Christian ministry in the Social Services - one of so many theological students or ordained ministers who would move into community service or the teaching professions in the coming decade, when the role of the minister was undergoing such change and morale in the Baptist ministry was as low as the stipend.

When the church met a fortnight later, although two suitable sites in the Northcourt area were available for discussion, the meeting considered that the minister's resignation had altered everything. They began to see, or imagine, possible problems in selling the church site, with its burial ground. Enquiries would be made but the decision was to postpone any action meanwhile. A week later, on the recommendation of Douglas Hicks, the new Area Superintendent, Mr. B.R. White, M.A. of Regents Park College, who was looking for a student pastorate while he studied for his Ph.D., was invited to live in the manse and 'undertake as much pastoral work and leading of worship as his studies permitted'. Dr. W. Morris S. West, a tutor at Regents Park College, agreed to act as Moderator during the student pastorate. Barrington R. White later recalled how low the church had become - 'Miss Smallbone [secretary] and Miss Ainsworth [treasurer] and Ken Clifton, who lodged with Miss Ainsworth, kept the church going'.

**Miss Florence Sophia Smallbone.**

These three, and others like them, really deserve their life-stories to be recorded in detail. Their contribution to the church in these difficult years was very great, both in the offices they held and in their countless acts of love and care. I have to hand, the details of just one of them - Miss Florence Smallbone. After her death, on the 30th November 1971, Frank Massey, who had succeeded her as Church Secretary, gave a tribute to her at an evening service of the church. From this we learn that she was born in Abingdon in 1887 and baptised in 1903. She joined the Women's Army Auxiliary Corps in 1914. During the war years and onward she worked in the church with the Christian Endeavour Society and as a Sunday School Teacher. After demobilisation at the end of the war she began work at Webbers of Oxford where she remained for forty years. During the year 1924-5, Frank records, 'she caused a sensation in the church and the denomination - she and Miss Argyle (i.e. Mrs. Olive Caudwell, present this evening) were elected together as the first lady deacons of the Church and almost the first in the denomination. They worked hard together to clear the debt on the building of the new Baptist church at Marcham'. Through the next decade, with the encouragement of the Berks Baptist Association, Miss Smallbone (never, Dr. White later recalled, to be addressed as Florence!) together with Mr. Caudwell, worked as the Abingdon representatives on The Didcot Baptist Fellowship Committee, a committee of twelve, formed to establish a Baptist Church in the rapidly expanding town of Didcot.[140] Always a hands-on person, she helped to start and became a teacher in a Sunday School, held in a Red Cross hut in Didcot from 1935. The church opened in 1938. Miss Smallbone's efforts, in this and other ways, were rewarded by being declared a personal member of the Berks. Baptist Association and she was elected to serve on the Central Area Committee of the Baptist Union. Back at Abingdon she led a Boys' Bible Class and established a Youth Club. Another great interest was Scouting, serving for many years on the Group Scout Committee and as a Cub Scout leader. She became secretary of the Baptist Missionary Society work of the church and then Church Secretary for eight years until 1961. She was made a Life Deacon in 1965 and was still active in Deacons' meetings. Remembered also for her keen interest in Baptist history and theology and in the ecumenical movement 'before it became popular', she was a member of the group formed to discuss and finally launch the 'trial of union' between the Congregationalists and Methodists which resulted in Trinity Church. As she grew weaker, in the final year of her life, she would make her way to the chapel on sunny days and sit in a chair on the church lawn, watching the progress on the church extension.

[140] Source - Didcot Baptist Church archive courtesy of Mr. David Williams.

Legal problems had arisen over the demolition of the old British School due to a small part being now owned by an Oxford firm. Both the search for a new site for the church and the demolition of the British School were put on hold. Mr. White was not asked to work in the villages, but Mr. Caudwell produced a preaching plan for Abingdon and all the villages.

**Mr. Roland Caudwell, 1880-1982.**

Mention has already been made of Roland Caudwell, another great character and supporter of the church through much of the twentieth century. He was grandfather of Margaret Bradshaw, nee Caudwell. There is apparently no record of his ever becoming a member of the Abingdon or any other Baptist church. He always claimed to be a Quaker. Despite this, he was elected a deacon of the Abingdon church when in his seventies and later made a life deacon. He died aged 102. He was the youngest of a large farming family and served in the Boer War, caring for the cavalry horses. He began farming and was not called up for the First World War probably because farming was a reserved occupation, though by then he had adopted pacifist views. Forced to sell his farm in the early 1920's farming recession, he was a tenant farmer on several farms in the Besselslea area before moving the family to a new council-house in Bowyer Road, Abingdon. Then in his forties, he re-trained as a carpenter, cycling to Chelmsford each week for this training. He was taken onto the workforce of Kingerlee's, the Oxford builder, and built his own house, 52 Thesiger Road, part of the estate built on the old Workhouse site. He lived there for the rest of his life. He was respected and loved in the Baptist church where he and the family worshipped. Roland had long been a lay-preacher in the Primitive Methodist, Wesleyan and Baptist churches and organised the preaching rota for the Baptist chapels of Drayton, Cothill, Fyfield and Marcham. Following the death of his first wife he employed Olive Argyle as his housekeeper. They eventually married. At sometime in the 1970's, Roland Caudwell, in response to a request from the Revd. Cox, by then retired, wrote of the early Methodist farmers and preachers in a fascinating letter which has survived. The text of this letter is printed as appendix E. to this book. He took to knitting blankets for Christian Aid. As he grew older and his fingers became less nimble, he invested in a knitting machine, increasing his out-put and attracting much praise in the local press.

As the completion of Mr. White's studies drew near, a Special Church meeting was held in March 1959 to consider the future of the church. The members were informed that Mr. White did not see himself continuing as minister at Abingdon after his ordination. In the light of this, and since an early settlement seemed unlikely due to the shortage of ministers nationally, it was agreed that no progress could be made in the relocation of the church at present. Dr. Robert L. Child, recently retired as principal of the College, was appointed Moderator. Perhaps surprisingly, the search for the next minister met with early success. In August the church gave a unanimous invitation to the Revd. W.H. Cox, B.D. and by the A.G.M. in February 1960 Mr. Cox was in the chair.

**Ministry of the Revd. W.H. Cox, H.C.F., B.D.**

Although it receives no mention in the church book, Mr. Cox was no stranger to the Baptist Church in Abingdon. This was the young man who, 37 years before, had left the Wesleyan Church in Conduit Road and sought baptism and membership in the Ock Street church. He was now 57 years old and would continue at Abingdon to his retirement.

In 2010 I met the daughter of Mr. Cox, Margaret Wyatt, at Thatcham Baptist Church, when attending the farewell service of their minister, the Revd. Andrew Hall, who was about to emigrate to ministry in Australia. Subsequent correspondence with Margaret resulted in her sending me a copy of a letter from Roland Caudwell to her father giving a fascinating insight of Primitive Methodist preaching and sheep farming in the nineteenth century, and also her publication of a tribute to her father with the following account of his life:

> Rev. William Harold Cox, H.C.F., M.A., B.D. was pledged to the Lord even before he was born.
>
> A letter from his Father sent to him on entering Spurgeon's Collage in November 1925 states '…and fitted for that service to which your Mother and I dedicated you before you were born.'
>
> His first pastorate was to Arnold (Notts) then to Oundle Road, Peterborough prior to serving as an Army Chaplain throughout the Second World War (1939/1945). In particular, in France, Belgium, Northern Ireland, India and the Far East. The events

surrounding the evacuation at Dunkirk (1940) which he recorded in a detailed diary, have since become his Regiment's written history. (Oxfordshire & Buckinghamshire Light Infantry).

Whilst serving in India he gained his B.D. Degree from Serempore College (an establishment steeped in history surrounding William Carey). Upon his safe return after the war years he held pastorates in Walsall, and then in Alcester, where in 1956 he was elected the High Bailiff of the town, being the first non-conformist minister to hold this office. Then followed the pastorate at Abingdon, the church where he himself had been baptised.

Upon retirement in 1969 his love of learning, and desire to continue giving his best, led him to Regent's Park College Oxford where he obtained his B.A. degree in the Honour's School of Theology. In 1973 he moved to Bromley to be near his family and he continued to use his pastoral gifts as a member of Park Road Baptist Church. He was a modest man with a great interest in football and cricket. William Cox died in 1988.

*Figure 52 The Revd. W.H. Cox, BD.*

Mr. Cox brought to the church what it seemed to need so badly, a period of stability. At that February meeting in 1960 the decision was made not to proceed with the re-siting of the church - 'considerable relief was expressed as it was generally felt that in no respect is the Church ready for such an undertaking'. Mr. Eustace had been running a Sunday School in the Fitzharry's Community Centre in the Northcourt area, but lacking any help from a church which had now abandoned that vision, he reported that he was handing it over to the Salvation Army, though he would continue a small Bible class in his home on Sunday mornings. The demolition of the old British School was at last under way, Mr. Cox reporting that he had procured the inscribed stone which would be mounted elsewhere, and the 30th North Berks. Baptist Scouts were 'reluctantly' allowed to build their new head-quarters on part of the minister's garden. Mr. Cox, however, was not living in the manse. He lived in his own house, in South Avenue, the manse being considered too damp for Mrs. Cox's rheumatism. The manse, which for years had been considered hardly fit for habitation - the attics shut off and the occupants advised not to lean against the front walls - was offered on a two year lease (the time probably reflecting the short ministries of the 50's) to Messrs. L. Jayne & Co. solicitors.

**The churches struggle to keep going.**

The Church Meetings of the coming years show the Fellowship of Churches struggling to maintain their premises with very little income, and their activities with very little staff. Mr. Cox came to be respected and loved. He was a hard worker who saw little success except, perhaps, briefly and right at the end of his ministry. 'Sheer persistence' was how one member remembered his ministry. There were 32 members when he came. Sales of work and other money raising events enabled the church to see to the most pressing repairs, and gifts were also sent to the Baptist Union's Ter-Jubilee Fund and regularly to the B.M.S. and Home Work Fund. Returning to his daughter's correspondence:

> I do remember how burdened my father was when he accepted the call to Abingdon: he realised the situation. Both of my parents laboured hard and did much 'spade work'. Father was thankful that the church later grew and had stability.

It came as both a joy and a challenge when, in 1961 Mrs. Whittington of Bromsgrove gave £600 towards a kitchen in memory of her husband who had had close association with the church through the British School. In 1962 the church accepted an estimate of £1,800 for the new kitchen and a Finance Committee was formed. The kitchen was opened by Mrs. Whittington on 20th October 1962 and called The Heber Whittington Room' - a name which was not to catch on; 'The Kitchen' being the more obvious description!

1963 saw the first of a series of 'Practical Bazaars'. The Women's World day of Prayer received a first mention as did the Gift and Self Denial Week for the B.M.S.

The church was regularly represented at the Abingdon Council of Churches (founded in 1961).[141] A concern for evangelism led to the decision to canvas 360 houses in Ock Street, Conduit Road and Bostock Road, with a leaflet followed by a personal visit by pairs of men and women to invite people to church. Following Miss Smallbone's retirement as secretary two years earlier, Mr. Frank Massey had taken on the task. He now retired and Geoffrey and Pamela Pratt were elected 'Joint Secretaries' - two secretaries was an anomaly which would continue to serve the church well for over thirty years. There was an attempt to re-start the old Christian Endeavour, but this ended after six months through lack of interest. The minister's stipend had dropped below the recommended minimum and the church supported an appeal to the B.U. for a long service grant to their minister. With this £10 secured, they rejected the suggestion that the church become a Home Work Fund supported church and managed to raise the £20 per annum needed to reach the minimum. But as in the coming years the B.U. sought to increase the minimum stipend faster than the cost of living, every year's increase was a problem to the Abingdon church. By 1964 membership had risen to 56, but the quorum for the Church Meeting was reduced from fifteen to twelve - a sad reflection on the church. Early in 1965 the Church Meeting agonised for an hour over 'the spiritual life and work of the church'. But apart from defending the leaders who were working hard and a general call for more hospitality and readiness to invite people to the services, no way forward was achieved. Membership had fallen again to 49, with 3 at Cothill and 11 at Fyfield. A student ministered at Drayton. Putting on a brave face the minister reported 'Our expansion

---

141 The Revd. Michael Goode, *The Origins and Development of The Church in Abingdon 1988-1998. P 6.*

is gradual but our witness is evident in the town'. 1966 saw the membership lift to 55 and there is a Youth Club of 30 - 40 members. 31 scholars make up the Sunday School and the Women's Meeting attracts 18-20 each Wednesday. Now Mr. Massey and Mr. Walters are joint secretaries. These figures, especially those relating to the youth club, reflect a very 1960's activity. Douglas and Margaret Bradshaw, now grandparents but then in their upper teens, gave me some of the details.

**The Youth Club.**

Mr. and Mrs. Jay and their three teenage boys had joined the church around 1964/5. They lived in a large bungalow at the west end of Caldecott Road with an extensive garden running down to the canal. Young people from the church were made welcome here and this led to the formation of the youth club. The Baptists were the first, and for some time the only, Abingdon church to allow such a potentially subversive activity. They frequently held discos! It drew youngsters from other churches including Catholics and members of the new Christ Church in Northcourt. John Bampton, a young staff member of the Barnardo Home in Caldecott Road, assisted the Jays. Douglas and Jill Ratcliff joined the leadership. At first it attracted the older teens, but as younger children showed interest, Rodney Carr began an 'Inters' section. In time Gilbert Payne added his support while, as Sunday School Superintendent, he was in touch with all the younger church. When, early in Adrian Thatcher's ministry, the church closed its Sunday School in favour of Family Church, the youth club became part of this under the overall leadership of Gilbert Payne and Pamela Pratt - meeting on Sundays for worship and teaching, then on Thursday evenings for a social and games programme. The overall children's and youth work of the church was given the name 'Searchlight'. Many members were involved in the teaching and social activities in this organisation which continued through the remainder of the century. The name 'Searchlight' has not been used for some years today, but Helen Pratt and John Marshall continued to care for the youth of the church into the 21st century, meeting on Saturday evenings for games and social events.

**Communion plate display case.**

In 1967 Miss Hainsworth donated an oak and plate glass display case which was mounted in the right front corner of the chapel. This was given in memory of her mother, Kate, who had been a member for 72 years. Until his departure to Nottingham in 1990 Mr. Ken Clifton placed the communion silverware in this case each Sunday, returning it to the safe after the evening service. It was in Mr. Cox's time that communion came to be celebrated in the morning as well as the evening.

**Mr. Cox announces his retirement.**

At the 1968 A.G.M. Mr. Cox said that he had come to an unsettled church in 1960 and had tried to give it stability. He intended to retire in the coming autumn. In June Charles Orland chaired the Church Meeting when two decisions were made - that they would apply to the B.U. for a loan of £4,500 towards the purchase of a manse, and invite Rev. Dr. Child once more to be Moderator. The following month the decision was taken to purchase 16 Thesiger Road at the cost of £6,000. In October the Covenant Scheme of giving was explained and introduced, and a decision to hold a Mission sometime in 1969 was taken. By the A.G.M. of 1969, before a new minister was called, there were forty members attending, the Youth Club reported an increase from 18 to 42, an average of twenty attended the Young People's Fellowship on Sunday evenings, and there were 42 Cubs (in two packs) and 24 Scouts. The church may still have been poor and its membership low, but Mr. Cox had left it in a far more confident mood than he found it.

**Ministry of Revd. Adrian Thatcher, M.A. begins.**

With the decision, made in March, to call Adrian Thatcher, a young, intelligent, handsome minister, the confidence grows. A Youth Council to co-ordinate all the youth organisations is formed. The gallery is to be cleared of 'rubbish and old pews' in readiness for a United Service in the Week of Prayer for Christian Unity in January 1970. (Thirty years later the gallery appeared to generate rubbish and old pews as fast as they are cleared.) There is a World Poverty Sign-in; the Sunday School finances are integrated with those of the church as Family Church replaces Sunday School; there will be six Church Meetings a year in place of twelve. Six young people attending baptismal classes are to be visited regarding membership because 'baptism and membership are an integral act'. Membership is growing.

**A change of Association.**

For some years, it appears, the church had retained its membership of the Berks. Association while being an associate member of the Oxon. and E. Glos. Baptist Association. In April 1970, after boundary changes put Abingdon into Oxfordshire, the church applied for full membership of O.E.G.B.A. and left the Berks. Association.

**Building extensions.**
A scheme was drawn up for extending the rear of the premises in a westerly direction to provide a lounge, minister's vestry and extra toilets. The cost for materials would be £1,150 and the work done by the men of the church. The church agreed to this.

**Church music.**
A music group was formed which Mrs. Margaret Ricketts agreed to lead. This must consist of not less than twelve but is not to think of itself as a choir. Its task will be to learn new music and introduce hymns and even chants to generally enrich the worship and singing of the church.

By the 1970 AGM. the Family Church numbered sixty children and young people with an enthusiastic teaching staff using new materials and visual aids. The Youth Club had eighty members aged 14-21 years and a waiting list. The Scout Group had 110 cubs and scouts and needed more help! The Ladies Contact Club met monthly with 35 members.

**The church looks outwards.**
To raise money for a dispensary in Brazil a sponsored football match was held - a 24 hour 5-a-side marathon - the minister playing in the Deacons' team scored a goal and £252 was raised. The Abingdon and District Churches gathered at the Baptist Church to present the Abingdon M.P. Mr. Airey Neave, with a petition on World Poverty. The church unanimously agreed to respond to the Anglican invitation, sent to Roman Catholics, Methodists and Baptists to join in a Stewardship and Mission Campaign to draw people in from the fringe to the heart of church life. Although links were now weak, Abingdon offered help to the ailing churches at Fyfield and Cothill. A Missionary Committee and a Pastoral Care Group were formed. And with the approach of the 1970 Abingdon Fair, plans were made for an Open Air Evangelistic Service on Monday evening, with invitations to all the town's churches.

**The challenge to change.**

Early in the new ministry the church minutes recorded the desire to 'change to meet the challenges of the seventies'. In April 1970 Mr. Thatcher had produced a nine page document headed: 'Suggestions for a Possible 'Re-Structuring' of Church Organisation'. This could mean the end of new as well as ancient ways of doing things. Within two years of its formation the Youth Council was abandoned because it was 'serving no useful purpose'. When the Sunday School Superintendent resigned it was decided not to replace him - the minister and Family Church secretary could do his work. Pews were removed in the front corner of the church to create a 'Prayer Room'. It was considered whether communion might be celebrated weekly and a single loaf of bread, instead of small cubes, was introduced. A Duplicator was purchased in preparation for a monthly magazine which Mr. Blair would edit, beginning in January 1971. And in that year a crèche was started; the extension built, and an unused room in the old manse, with the tenant's permission, brought into use for the senior Family Church group. There were plans for a Playgroup and House Groups.

**Joint Mission.**

In early 1972 the church agreed to join a Joint Mission, with Trinity Church and St. Michael's Anglican Church, to the houses in the western quarter of the town. The outcome of this was not recorded in the church minutes, but this joint action was but part of the wider vision for church unity. For in June the church supported the resolution, coming from the Council of Churches, 'That the Executive Committee be asked once more to explore the implications of Abingdon's becoming officially recognised as an area of ecumenical experiment'. About this time Adrian served as President of the Abingdon Council of Churches and recalls: 'One powerful memory of this was that I was invited to preach at the Roman Catholic Church, at Mass on Sunday evening (probably during the Week of Prayer). The Baptist Church cancelled its evening worship and the whole congregation came willingly to the Catholic Church, well aware that history was being made'.

**Christian Life Campaign.**

This was the name given by the Abingdon church to a method of increasing personal commitment and financial support much in vogue in the 1970's and usually called a Stewardship Campaign. The

Abingdon church followed the usual pattern of an introductory free meal which sought to gather the entire church. At this meal the scheme was explained and pledge cards distributed. On these the people could commit themselves to increased giving of money, time or skills. In May 1972 the minister was able to report that the returns indicated an immediate increase in weekly offerings of 32% rising to 45% in the following year. In the event it amounted to 53% by November 1972. By the end of 1972 most offers of service had been placed - the offers helping to complete the various committees of the new structure of the church.

*Figure 53 The freshly decorated exterior of the chapel ca. 1974.*

**Plans for a new interior for the chapel.**

This same productive year saw the decision to redecorate the exterior of the chapel and re-design its interior. This was achieved over the next four years, the final redecoration of the interior being completed in Adrian's successor's ministry. The pulpit and platform were removed together with two rows of pews. Seventeen memorial plaques were taken from the walls of the sanctuary and vestibule. An open Baptistery was surrounded by removable copper rails. A copper railed pulpit on a small portable plinth was placed to the right of the Baptistery. A lectern, made by Mr. Thatcher's father, stood to the left, somewhat out of sympathy with the modernity of the pulpit. A prayer stool, also the work of the minister's father, was placed behind the Baptistery. An ICI colour scheme, in blue and grey with a large illuminated cross filling the arch and an octagonal symbolic depiction of the sacraments, designed by members of the congregation, placed under the rear gallery completed the refurbishment. If a later generation, in an era of conservation and nostalgia, sees much of this as architectural vandalism, they must try to appreciate the spirit of the sixties and seventies. They were brave, modern years when the churches, along with society as a whole, were concerned to throw off the traditional image and old fashioned ways. The language of prayer dropped its 'Thees' and 'Thous'. Colour replaced the browns and creams. Modern script replaced the gothic of church posters. Christian names were used - even the minister's. Guitars were heard in church.

*Figure 54 Chapel interior before the 1970's alterations. This image is taken from the Pumphrey History.*

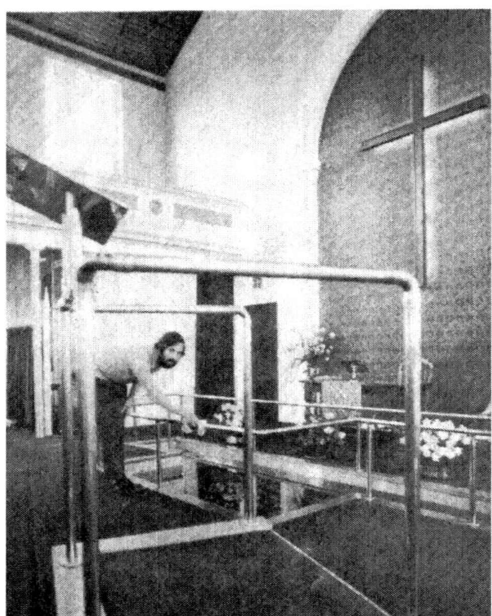

*Figure 55 The re-designed interior, showing the copper piping pulpit and baptistery rail, and the illuminated cross.*

The year 1973 saw the completion and consolidation of many of the innovations of the first three years of Adrian's ministry. Five House Groups were started in five sectors of the town. This group study was supported by individual Bible reading - seventy people using the IBRA daily study notes. The church magazine was now integrated into an ecumenical magazine in which each church had eight pages. Weekly communion was introduced and two communion trays, matching the existing pair, were given in memory of Miss Hainsworth. An 'Apprentice Minister', in training at Regents Park College, was placed with the church for the first time. This was Ken Stewart who was also ministering at Drayton, and who was to do his summer placement that year at Kings Langley. And another young member, David Saunders, was commended for training at Spurgeon's College.

# BAPTIST MINISTER LEAVING

Abingdon's Baptist minister, the Rev. Adrian Thatcher, is to leave Abingdon at the end of January to teach in Cheltenham.

He will lecture in the philosophy of religion at a teacher training college. The college takes students for degree courses, and Dr Thatcher will also teach students for a B.Ed. degree.

Dr Thatcher has been at the Abingdon Baptist Church for four years. "The main reason

*Dr Thatcher*

I am moving is that this year I became a Doctor of Philosophy, which now enables me to teach. But I will be sorry to leave because I have had a very happy time here."

He was chairman of the Council of Churches in 1972, and during his time here the membership of the council has more than doubled.

Extensions were built to the church in 1972 and opened by the president of the Baptist Union of Great Britain.

**Adrian Thatcher's resignation.**

In November1973 the church was informed that their minister would be leaving in January to take up a lectureship in Religious Studies at St. Paul's College, Cheltenham. In less than five years he had modernised the church and established structures of life and worship which would provide the pattern for decades to come. Despite its brevity, his was surely one of the most significant ministries in the long story of Abingdon Baptist Church.

**The church prepares for a new ministry.**

After being raised several times over the years, the decision was reached to start the morning service half an hour earlier at 10.30 a.m. At the 1974 A.G.M. Frank Massey and Gilbert Payne were re-elected joint secretaries and Ken Read treasurer. On the 5th May the church called the Revd. David Wilcox to the pastorate and appointed the Revd. Irwin Barnes Moderator. The church voted £100 per annum to support David Saunders at Spurgeon's.

**The ministry of Revd. David Wilcox, M.A.**
The Induction Service was held on 15 September 1974. Early in his ministry the first of several meetings was held with the village churches. Links with these had declined and Cothill was in a very weak state. David would work to try to maintain Abingdon's role as mother church.

At the 1975 AGM Mr. Massey retired after twelve years and Alan Clark took his place as joint secretary. The Christian Life pledges were renewed. And plans were made for a Sound Amplification System and the creation of more car parking by removing the garden wall of the old manse.

**The minister's illness.**
In June the minister was suffering from Sarcoidosis and was relieved of all duties until September, although he was given permission to begin a post-graduate study course providing his church work and health were not adversely affected. The Revd. Herbert Stapely, a church member, was appointed Moderator to the end of the year. By the September church meeting Mr. Wilcox was well enough to be working full time. While the Playgroup was still flourishing, Ann Wilcox reported that there had been a Toddler's Club since November 1974 which now had forty five mothers of which ten were church members.

**325th Church Anniversary.**
Two major events had been planned to mark the 325th Anniversary. An Exhibition of Arts and Crafts, with flower arrangements in the church and craft displays in the Hall was held on 26/27th April. Then a Harvest of Industry and Industrial Exhibition on the 27/28th September. This last had an MG car on the raised lawn in the forecourt of the church, a display of farm implements on the car park, displays of all the church organisations in the windows of the church and other industrial stands in the hall. Both these events laid the emphasis on the present life of church and town, reflecting the feelings expressed by the Secretaries in the Anniversary literature: 'A fine past and history to be proud of. What kind of history are we the present community of Christians in 1975 establishing? ....Our lives are creating history each day, may each step we take individually and as a Church be firmly set upon the road of love and service for our Saviour'. Thirty six years on, their words challenge the historian to

make the present day count for God.

**Another call to greater unity.**
In 1976 David Wilcox quoted to the church meeting an extract from a recent sermon of the bishop of Reading preached at a united service in St. Helen's: 'There is a degree of ecumenism in Abingdon beyond all credit. I want the Synod, in consultation with other churches in the area, to consider how this fellowship can best be strengthened'. Meanwhile there was much evidence that the hearts of minister and church were at one with the bishop's call. There is a joint visitation of the Barton estate by the Baptists and St. Nicolas' Church and shared services with Trinity and St. Nicolas.

**Girlguiding.**
At Mrs. Wilcox's suggestion a Brownie Unit was started under her leadership in the late 1970's. In the course of her sixteen years in Abingdon this would mature into a full Guide Company. Ann Wilcox and Peggy Lee, a friend from St. Helen's Church, now led the guides, which included Susan Field, Verity Brown and Harriet Carr among others.

In 1983 Veronica Webster, Frances Lee and Pat Hudson had become assistant guide guiders. Jenny Webster and Helen Lee achieved the Queen's Guide Award. Early leaders of Brownies were Margaret Bradshaw and Rosemary Brown. Many leaders have followed[142]. Rainbows was started in 1990 under the leadership of Rosemary Jardine. Following Ann Wilcox's sudden and premature death in 1993 while at a Gloucestershire guide camp, a Mountain Ash was planted in the church forecourt in her memory.

**Looking out and looking in.**
The church meeting agendas throughout this period were arranged under the two headings 'Looking Out' and 'Looking In'. The church took a lively interest in concerns beyond its immediate fellowship - Home Mission and the Baptist Missionary Society were well supported financially and with prayer interest. The ecumenical situation was now reported at every meeting and in 1978 David Wilcox is made Chairman of the Abingdon and District Council of

---

142 A detailed list of leadership within the Abingdon Baptist Church guide company has been placed in the church archive, Angus Library, Oxford.

Churches. The Villages were still on the church's heart, though Cothill finally closed and was sold in 1977. There were students now at Drayton and Bayworth. The Bayworth chapel, founded in 1900 as a mission station of New Road Baptist Church, Oxford, but geographically close to Abingdon, began to look to Abingdon for support. And concern for Fyfield was expressed when it began referring to itself as an 'Independent Evangelical Fellowship'. Village chapels were easy prey to unattached, zealous Christians looking for a church they could mould to their own outlook and in 1977 Fyfield felt strong enough to go its independent way. In 1984 it was given its independence as its Abingdon Trustees handed it over to trustees at Fyfield. But in January 1989 it was small again and would welcome Abingdon help - for a while.

'Looking In', the church sought to lease the old manse to a property developer - a saga which will appear on every agenda for year after year. In 1979 the second visit of the London Emmanuel Choir was a highlight of the year. There was an exchange of ministers arranged with a church in America in 1981. And in that year the student placement system changed into a two year cycle involving a first year student coming to the church in an observation role, then in his or her second year being given a project planned by the church. A Project Group would help the church decide the project and support the second year student through it.

**Church and Manse Appeal.**

It was estimated that £10,000 needed to be spent on the church, for insulation, the treatment of woodworm, repairs and the restoration of the facade. The manse figure was estimated at £23,000, for new windows, insulation, kitchen fittings and the extension of kitchen and living room. The Church and Manse Appeal was launched in March 1985 with a working group headed by Harry Bridges. The family which would be the first to benefit from the manse improvements decided to undertake a week long bicycle tour of all the churches of every denomination (mostly Anglican) in The Vale of White Horse District. Sponsored by people from the Baptist and other Abingdon churches, and with many donations from the churches visited, David, Stephen and Derek Wilcox raised a considerable sum for the manse appeal.

**The Care Group Scheme.**
This was set up sometime between 1975 and 1980. The town was divided geographically into twelve areas, with approximately fifty members of the church and congregation in each group. Two care coordinators (later re-named pastoral friends) were appointed for each group. These were expected to visit the people in their group and be a point of contact for pastoral need. They met with the minister three or four times a year to share news and pray for the fellowship. Looking back to his time as minister, David Wilcox says, 'It was an invaluable way of sustaining the care of church members for one another, of drawing new-comers in and ensuring no one was forgotten or fell off the edge. The Care Group scheme was for me, one of the important developments during my ministry'. This scheme continued through the next two ministries to the present day.

For much of the 90's Stella Hambleton took overall responsibility for this scheme. In 1999, each month one whole group was invited, through their pastoral friends, to Sunday afternoon tea together in 35 Ock Street. Stella and Rosalind Hall provided the tea.

Among the many members who held no high office in the church and yet whose contribution to pastoral care was great, Queenie Thompson is a name that stands out. She, with Mary Carr, ensured that there was always a vase of flowers in the chapel on Sundays. These were taken to the housebound or to sick or distressed people, after the evening worship. But Queenie's ministry of care and eye for detail continually helped to hold the church together. In the days before e-mail, her little notes, phone calls or visits and her memory for anniversaries, happy or sad, were invaluable to minister and people alike.

**Church Records.**
David Wilcox was one of those who looked into the long history of the church. His research was fed into his Schism Sermons. These have been preserved by him to date, though I have not had the opportunity to read them. It may be hoped that they will eventually find a place in the archives. He also wrote a brief history of the church, covering two sides of A4, which was available for visitors to read and take away. During this ministry Tony Valente was appointed church archivist and he drew up an index of all the books, manuscripts and papers which at the time were stored in two metal filing cabinets in the rear gallery of the chapel. Later, Jon Spiller, when church

secretary, organised the binding into several volumes of all the minutes of the church from the 70's onwards, which were in loose-leaf folders or ring-binders. Before the end of the century, the church's historical archive was placed, on long term loan, in the safe keeping of the Angus Library.

**_Contact_, the magazine of Abingdon Baptist Church.**[143]

There had been earlier magazines and news sheets, for example Adrian Thatcher with the help of Mr. W. (Bill) Blair, launched an edition in October 1970 for a 'trial run'. It ran for several years.

The first edition of *Contact* was prepared by David Hudson, Glenda Slaymaker and Christopher Brown in 1986. David had one of the early computers and enjoyed setting out the format, Glenda typed the material and Chris gathered it together. Issue one, February 1986, consisted of one sheet; strange, considering our terms of reference were to replace the ever increasing pages of notices on the Sunday service sheets. Glenda and David then put it all together, printed a master and photocopied around 80 copies. That was in the days of early machines when you had to copy one side; then put all your sheets back in (the right way round) to copy the other side. Soon Chris began to get more involved in designing the covers and other parts, as it grew into a magazine. It was in 1988 that the Church in Abingdon was formed and a few years later their 'News' was incorporated in *Contact*.

Sadly Glenda passed away in 1999. Chris took over as editor and produced the magazine on a typewriter. Later he was grateful to be given his first computer. Issue 100 was circulated in November 1995 and from then on he was allowed to print the covers on coloured paper! All copies were folded and stapled at home and named by hand. Chris handed over the editing to Rachel Pollock in 2006, and she and her husband Rodney are currently preparing issue number 254.[144] They are produced on a modern machine at Baptist House by Helen Pratt. Recently church members have designed a cover for each year, and distinctive Christmas covers have been designed by David Fleming and printed in colour by Mike Coleman.

---

[143] This paragraph is copied verbatim from a report submitted by Christopher Brown.

[144] For April 2011.

**35 Ock Street - disappointment and opportunity.**

In September 1985 the property developer's application for planning permission to demolish 35 Ock Street and build new offices on the site was finally rejected by the D of E. The minutes of the church meeting record, 'Great disappointment, after five years of working on this project, was expressed but members were requested to hold before themselves the possibility that God may be giving them an opportunity as well as a disappointment'. It is not recorded who spoke these words, but, whoever it was, subsequent events were to prove her or him a prophet indeed. But for the time being the church could only try to assess its options, and common-sense led them to the 'reluctant' decision to sell the property on the freehold market, asking the Vale of the White Horse Council to place some appropriate limitation on its future use. However, the property developer had second thoughts and asked the church to delay any sale until he had had time to seek planning permission to renovate the building. This would take time. And then a great recession would delay matters further. Then, when the time was right, the day of 'opportunity' arrived.

**The Church in Abingdon.**

At this same Church Meeting the members were introduced to a paper written by the Revd. David Manship, rector of St. Helen's Church, entitled 'Growing Together Locally', in which he set out the basis for a 'Local Covenant'. The paper concludes, 'In this way we would be giving the fullest possible expression to Christian unity while our churches are still separated, and we would be pledging ourselves to work towards full unity in the service of God and his people'. The meeting was asked to take the paper away and make their responses on the questionnaire attached. In fact the whole of the following year was given to the churches to consider their response to the paper. Meanwhile we hear of the first courses being offered by the Abingdon Christian Training Scheme (ACTS) which was organised by an ecumenical committee and offered courses of eight to twelve lectures on biblical studies, doctrine, church history, indeed any subject which might be considered as Christian training. By January 1987 the draft constitution for the Abingdon Local Ecumenical Project was being worked upon, with the encouraging news that the initial response of all nine churches considering this was positive. On 4th May 1988, at a gathering of the nine churches in St. Helen's, the local covenant was signed. The number of worshipping communities making up this one church would grow. The founding churches were All Saints Methodist Church, The Baptist Church, Christ Church, Peachcroft Christian Centre, The Church of Our Lady and St. Edmund, St. Helen's Church, St. Michael's and All Angels, St. Nicolas' Church and Trinity Church. They had entered into a legal covenant agreeing:

- to work together to proclaim the gospel and encourage neighbourly care;
- to pray for unity and yet to value the spiritual traditions of all the churches;
- to share the ordained ministry and Holy Communion according to the discipline of each denomination.

The Church in Abingdon was structured with a representative Assembly which was to be both visionary and have the final authority. There was an Executive Committee. The clergy and ministers agreed to meet monthly for prayer and fellowship and to them fell the general oversight and care of the Church. Lapel badges were designed and sold, as were window stickers which now appeared on front doors or prominent front windows all over town, on car rear windows and increasingly on the public notice boards of the participating churches.

**Action in Mission.**
Meanwhile, 'looking in', the Baptists were submitting themselves to Action in Mission (AIM) a project which invited a team of Baptists from outside to visit and assess the church's life. They would visit and talk to all the church groups, the deacons, minister and many individual members. At the end their critical but constructive report was offered to the church with advice as to how their recommendations might be implemented. The second year student, Nick Wood, was given the Project of preparing the church for this and working with the team of visitors. This was undertaken in a busy year when David Wilcox was President of the Association. The report was submitted at the end of the year and its repercussions are heard in church and deacons' meetings through the whole of 1989.

**The end of a long ministry.**
The ministry of David Wilcox at Abingdon was the longest since that of John Kershaw in the early nineteenth century. While continuing the regular work of a preacher and a pastor, the last eighteen months of his ministry were dominated by exciting preparations for the first

great mission of the Church in Abingdon on the one hand, and the pressure for change, one suspects largely unwelcome, which the AIM report appeared to release on the other hand. The Project Group rightly considered that it was its duty to follow up the AIM recommendations and not to allow them to be set aside unexamined. But some of these, especially as they related to worship, were considered to reflect the unbalanced make up of the visiting group, which had not appreciated the form of worship which had developed over many years at Abingdon. The AIM recommendations, it was argued by some, represented a 'shallower and', the emotive word hangs in the air, 'charismatic form of worship'. The minister reassured the meeting that he was committed to structured worship, though he was looking forward to some new songs which would be included in the proposed new hymn book. The Project Group invited Revd. David Coffey, Secretary for Evangelism of the Baptist Union, to meet them. He told them of his concern about the lack of evangelism in the church. He felt that the church was being led by the head rather than the heart and asked how they might feel about a resident missioner working with the church. He recognised that the church was fully committing itself to the Abingdon Mission next year, but the church would need to respond to the ongoing missionary task after that was over. David Coffey suggested he might talk with the minister about the resident missioner idea.

The minister meanwhile called the church to put AIM behind them and concentrate on preparations for the mission, now called 'Abingdon Alive!'. Each of the communities was given items in the programme to work on. The Baptists took on a Holiday Club and activities in connection with the October Fair. At the same time the Baptists started a series of monthly Sunday evening meetings called 'Christian Viewpoint' which sought to interest the general public in current issues of general concern - an expert in the field being invited to speak at each meeting. These proved popular among members of other churches as well as some of the general public. The Baptist Headquarters was moving from London to Didcot and the first members of staff began to transfer their membership to Abingdon - especially those to whom its more structured form of worship and the emphasis on informed biblical preaching appealed. So in the last months of his ministry in Abingdon David saw the membership, which having risen to 129 in 1977 had now dropped to 97, begin to rise again, reaching 114 by his departure. The task of ongoing mission after 'Abingdon Alive!' was, of course, part of the Church in Abingdon planning and Doug Bradshaw was the Baptist representative on the group which was planning this. David Wilcox's resignation was given in May 1990. This came at a time which was felt to be right for both the church and family situations and was not influenced by the painful effects of the AIM report, as suggested in my book.[145] The Revd. David Rowland of Botley was appointed Moderator. Then came the four weeks of mission which in many ways crowned the vision of this ecumenically committed minister. At the November 1st Deacons Meeting, Mr. Wilcox heard the Deacons' very positive review of the mission of which 'The torch light procession was a tremendous climax'.

The church said farewell to David and Ann and their sons Stephen and Derek at a social evening on 10th November. A few weeks later a coach was hired to take the Abingdon church to his induction at Broadmead, Bristol.

The transition to the next minister appears to have been swift and easy. A name was being seriously considered before the farewell social for the departing minister. This resulted in the recommendation from the Deacons to a Special Church Meeting on 20th November that Michael Hambleton, recently returned from work with the Baptist Sangamaya of Sri Lanka and presently doing deputation work with the BMS, be invited. The recommendation was agreed, the invitation sent, and accepted, with a starting date 1st March 1991. Meanwhile the church appointed a co-ordinator to regenerate the House Groups, heard the recommendations of an Organ Working Group to replace the old pipe organ with an electronic one, and organised the redecoration of the manse. And the old manse, with plans for its conversion into offices now accepted, but the recession making it ever less likely to happen, was boarded up and draped with plastic sheeting while pigeons roosted in its rain-sodden attics.

**The Ministry of Revd. Michael G. Hambleton, M.A.**

Michael was 55 when he and Stella moved into 16 Thesiger Road in February 1991. Behind him was a childhood in Shropshire and Devon and a youth in Dorset. He was converted during National Service in N. Wales and baptised a year later in Pontypridd. After five years study in Bristol University and Regent's Park College, he had

---

145 Hambleton op cit p 94.

ministries in Thrapston, Kings Langley and Colombo before accepting the call to Abingdon. Stella had combined a teaching career with the work of motherhood and the multi-facetted tasks of minister's wife. This latter was chiefly youth and children's work, women's work, Christian Aid and drama. Then, from 1988, in partnership with Michael, there had been study at St. Andrew's Hall, Birmingham before language study and heading up the Sri Lankan Sangamaya's Leadership Training Institute in Colombo. Family tragedy had brought them home, much earlier than intended, in 1990. They were privileged to receive the call to minister in Abingdon.

**The 150th anniversary of the Victorian chapel.**

Early in the new ministry Charles Orland produced a hymn sheet used at the opening of the Chapel in October 1841, pointing out that this was 150 years ago. A planning group got to work and a week of activities concluding with a Sunday morning service took shape. 'A Seventeenth Century Experience', with mannequins dressed as Puritan and Cavalier, and oak chest, jail etc. was set up in the rear Gallery for school parties to visit, while the old books and communion plate were displayed on the communion table before the filled Baptistery. User groups and the church organisations also mounted displays of their work and the chapel was open from Monday to Saturday to visitors from the town and schools. Meals were served, a lecture, 'The Abingdon Baptists of the Seventeenth Century' was delivered by the Baptist historian the Revd. Roger Hayden, and the Mayor of Ock Street and his Traditional Morris Men danced under the ash tree in the chapel forecourt. On the Sunday, 20th October, most of the congregation wore Victorian costume and, following a Service of Thanksgiving which used two of the hymns sung 150 years before, ended with the congregation moving outside, encircling the chapel, joining hands and singing the doxology.[146]

**New music:**

The new organ was installed before the end of the year and with the publication of *Baptist Praise and Worship* in 1992 the worship began to take advantage of the musical talents within the church fellowship and the wealth of new music coming from the charismatic movement,

---

[146] The minister was presented with an album of photographs of this event. It is a a valuable pictorial record of many of the congregation on that day, though their form of dress was exceptional. This will hopefully be placed in the church archive.

Taise, African, Latin American and so many other sources. This was greatly helped by a Band, of strings, wind and percussion, which had been formed towards the end of the previous ministry. It would be fair to say that by early 1991 there was a head of steam for change in the worship of the church. While structure and an emphasis on preaching was still required, a wider selection of music and the involvement of more people was wanted. The new minister didn't change things so much as allow change to happen. And despite one or two disasters, the church as a whole seemed to appreciate the change.

**Alive and Belonging in Abingdon.**
This was the name given to the second Church in Abingdon mission. Held in 1991 and with the intention of continuing the momentum built up by 'Abingdon Alive' as well as being a response to the national call to make the 90's a Decade of Evangelism, eighty members of the Abingdon churches visited 600 homes, making a survey of people's needs, as they saw them. This formed the basis of a report which in turn, it was intended, should be a basis for future action. One outcome would be the opening, with combined County Council and CiA support and staff, of the 'Abingdon Bridge', an advice and support centre for young people which would grow to meet the needs of over 700 young people a year.

**The influence of members on the staff at Baptist House.**
In the early '90's the church was still coming to terms with the welcome influx of members from Baptist House, following the move of the BU and BMS from London to Didcot.[147] Most of the staff joined the Didcot church but about eighteen staff members, spouses and children chose Abingdon. For two or more years the church saw its ministry to these as supportive to their national ministry and there seems to have been an unwritten rule not to include them in leadership roles at Abingdon. Gradually, as they became known for themselves, they took their natural place and their talents enriched the fellowship. At one point both the Joint Secretaries were Baptist House staff.

**Plans to extend the church hall.**
With a growing number of children and young people, due to the work

[147] The Baptist Union and the Baptist Missionary Society formerly had headquarters in Southampton Row and Gloucester Place respectively. They made the move from London, to bring the two organisations under one roof at Baptist House, Didcot, in 1989.

of the 'Searchlight' youth programme, Family Church and the uniformed organisations, the church was very short of space, especially on Sunday mornings. With groups meeting in the kitchen and, for a while in the Youth and Community Centre in Stratton Way, the Fabric Group employed an architect to draw up plans for the extension of the Hall both outwards to the north boundary and upwards. But this was put on hold when, unexpectedly, the return to the church of the lease of 35 Ock Street became a possibility. With the recession biting ever harder, the development company, under some pressure at least to keep the elements out of the crumbling property, was open to the suggestion of selling back, and finally of giving back, the lease to the church.

**Action Plan.**

In March 1993 the church adopted the Action Plan. This covered five years and listed the priorities for action by the church. Under William Carey's great words:

> 'Expect great things from God; attempt great things for God'

the plan set out its goals under two headings: 'Living the Christian Life within the Church' and Living the Christian Life beyond the Church'. Under the second heading we were able to put: 'Reconstruct 35 Ock Street for the use of the church', and added, rather hopefully, 'completion by December 1994'.

**The 35 Ock Street project.**

This was not so much the minister's vision as the church's vision. For when the possibility of regaining the old manse became reality, the church meeting reviewed the various options and unanimously agreed to develop it for church related community work and to provide the extra rooms needed for our youth and children's work. There were many hard decisions to be made, especially as the enormous cost, approaching half a million pounds, became clearer. (Half a million was the cost of four houses at that time). There were moments when the minister had to help the church to hold its nerve. Still in the depth of recession, with loss of job security and negative equity rife, the church needed to exercise great faith. But throughout the whole process decisions were practically unanimous. And when faced with the choice of three possible schemes, the church settled for the most ambitious of the three. From the start we saw the refurbishment as the responsibility of the Baptist church who owned it, but we wanted it to be a town-centre resource for the whole Church in Abingdon and hoped to draw voluntary staff from all its member churches. That autumn of 1993, the minister was due his sabbatical leave and part of this was spent visiting existing church community projects in Cambridge, Exeter and Bath, together with the Spurgeon's Child Care Centre in Bedford, to draw upon their experience as we sought the best use of our old manse.

*Figure 56 Rear of 35 Ock St. before renovation of 1996.*

*Figure 57 Front of 35 Ock St. before renovation of 1996.*

*Figure 58 Rear of 35 Ock St. after renovation of 1996.*

*Figure 59 Front of 35 Ock St. after renovation of 1996.*

**Church in Abingdon grows.**

February and March 1993 saw the drawing up of a 'mission statement' by the Church in Abingdon. About forty people drawn from the nine churches met on two Saturdays in February to agree the essential task of the CiA. The outcome was ratified at the March Assembly and was as follows

- to bring a fresh global vision of hope through God's love to the people of Abingdon, offering them good news of forgiveness, reconciliation and new life through Christ.
- to rediscover, live out and present the gospel through our fellowship and worship, unity and diversity.
- to express this message through relevant words and actions in the community, and by co-operating with others to identify and meet specific needs so that lives are changed, the Church grows and our local community increasingly reflects the values of the Kingdom of God.

St. Mary's Church, Shippon, applied for membership and was added to the other nine churches early in the 1990's. This was followed by applications from The Religious Society of Friends (Quakers) and The Salvation Army. Then in 1997 the Community Church came into membership, making 13 churches in all.

In 1994 the monthly staff meeting of all the clergy, ministers and leaders decided, as a team building exercise, to spend two days together. The retreat was held at the Carmelite Priory on Boars Hill. Its value was such that a similar two days were booked for March the following year and it became a regular annual event.

Also in 1994 the two major projects of the CiA, the Youth Drop-in Centre and the Christian Training Scheme, were put on a better financial basis by the churches committing themselves to a three year budget, and a third project, the provision of a Schools Worker for part-time work in John Mason School, was taken up. Trained for unstructured, relational work by Oxford Youth Works, a succession of excellent youth workers have come to be appreciated by students and staff alike.

1994 also saw the third major mission of the CiA. 'Abingdon Alive 94' is remembered in the churches and town chiefly on account of the local radio station which the churches set up, with expert guidance of Michael Strang, in a vestry of Trinity Church - the aerial mounted high in its spire. The cost of this and a fortnight's transmission of 15 hours a day etc. was £4,500 and was contributed by the churches. For the Baptists, the highlight was the broadcast of a Sunday morning baptismal service. Katie Hudson, Barry Wildsmith, Becca Dadswell and Stephen Hudson had been baptised on 17$^{th}$ April and the recorded service was broadcast on 8$^{th}$ May. It inspired a member of Christ Church to compose the poem, printed as appendix G. As a footnote to this mission, a local play-write is said to have drawn upon Abingdon's use of local radio for the storyline of one episode of his successful T.V. serial 'The Vicar of Dibley'.

To complete the story, mention must be made of two other developments in the Church in Abingdon in the second half of the decade. Largely under the leadership of the rector of St. Helens, Revd. Michael Goode, fellowship was engendered between the CiA and the churches in the towns with which Abingdon had a twinning arrangement. So a succession of visits were exchanged with Argentan, Lucca, Schongau, Colmar and St. Niklass. Then in 1996 the Development Group recommended to the Assembly that a comprehensive survey should be made of the Town 'to build up an accurate overview of our community, so that we can better serve and evangelise in the name of the gospel, and clarify our priorities for the start of the new millennium'. Known as 'Mapping Abingdon', the project involved well over a hundred people from all the churches and resulted in four action groups to work in the four areas of ministry - welcoming new-comers to Abingdon, ministry to the young, ministry in the world of daily work, and to develop ministry in the south of the town.

The importance of the development and life of this Church of thirteen churches cannot be over emphasised. There is still much to achieve in the movement towards Christian unity, but seeds which were being sown in the mid eighteenth century were at last producing their potential. The Baptist Church was deeply committed to the formation of this Church and has worked well with its fellow churches throughout its first twelve years. May it long continue. (Almost twelve further years have passed as I write this revision. The church in Abingdon does continue, but we should note the assessment of my successor, recorded in the next chapter, and try to hold on to the initial vision which the word 'covenant ' expressed.)

**Closer Baptist links.**

The Oxford and Abingdon District of the Baptist Association was also concerned to make its fellowship more real and, in 1995, established what they called 'Pastoral Groups' within the District. This linked Abingdon with the Bayworth and South Oxford churches and resulted in deepening and valuable fellowship. South Oxford and Abingdon were able to work with the Bayworth leadership to provide preachers and musicians for Bayworth. Joint meetings were held in the three churches and Abingdon was blessed with the occasional visit of the Bayworth church, en masse, and with musical input from two talented singers from that village church. Meanwhile good relations continued with the Drayton and Marcham churches.

**Completion of 35 Ock Street.**

Throughout 1994 and into 1995 planning and money raising continued for the refurbishment of the old manse. David Holt, of Adkins, was appointed surveyor, Kingerlee Ltd. of Oxford's tender was accepted. Oxford Archaeological Unit investigated the site and the house. Their report will be placed in the church's archive. I have difficulty in accepting their dating of what they term *Phase III* of the building's history.[148] This was the reconstruction of the front roof, 'converting the front attic to a full second floor by extending the front wall (now rebuilt in brick) and replacing the existing roof with a low-pitched gable'. This work is dated 'late 18th or early 19th century'[149]. I would argue that the brick façade must date from before 1774, which was the date of an act of parliament designed to reduce fire risk. This stipulated that the frames of all future sash windows must be rebutted into the brickwork. The two upper storeys of no. 35 are not rebutted, but those of the ground floor frontage are. I would read this to imply that the façade and the altered roof must predate 1774 and that the ground floor windows, and perhaps the fan-light over the front door, were modernised sometime after that date. The façade could therefore have been constructed by the wealthy William Fuller (the first minister to occupy the house) while the modernisation of the front rooms may have been done by the church for Daniel Turner, in the last quarter of the 18th century.

Building work began in the autumn of 1995. Throughout the whole process the church was especially indebted to David Hudson, one of our Deacons and chair of the Fabric Committee, who liaised with the builders and surveyor and whose practical advice to the church was invaluable.

The entire forecourt of the church was enclosed by the builders, leaving only a dropping-off point for about four cars and a path to the church along the east boundary. Money-raising events were held and people began to contribute from their savings. At a crucial point, when the cost of the project had to be increased to cover unforeseen work on the roof structure, to nearly half a million pounds, grants amounting to £50,000 were received or promised from the Norwood and Newton Settlements. Loans were made available by the Association and the Baptist Union Corporation. But most of the giving came from the members of the church and congregation in the form of covenants and Gift Aid. The work was completed in just over a year and the debts were virtually repaid by the year 2000.

---

[148] *35 Ock Street, Abingdon, Oxon. - Archaeological Recording Prior to Refurbishment.* Oxford Archaeological Unit Jan. 1997.
[149] op cit p 2.

Meanwhile the purchase of furniture and equipment for the meeting rooms, church office, servery and hospitality area was organised and a Management Committee appointed under the leadership of David Lovegrove. Terms of Reference were clarified, ensuring that 35 Ock Street would be part of the mission of the Baptist Church within the Church in Abingdon. It would be answerable to the Baptist Church Meeting. Isabel Bridges accepted the church's invitation to be honorary administrator. She had several assistant administrators. Four people were appointed to be responsible for the four areas of volunteer help - caterers, pastoral workers, cleaners and secretarial workers. The churches of the Church in Abingdon responded to the request for volunteers and by the year 2000 seventy people were on the rotas, made up of about forty Baptists and thirty from the other churches.

*Figure 60 The rear roof and wall timbers of 35 Ock Street. Exposed during the renovation.*

*Figure 61 The crowd at the opening of 35 Ock Street.*

35 Ock Street was officially opened by Revd. David Coffey, the General Secretary of the Baptist Union, on Sunday 15 September 1996. Guests from the Town and Vale Councils, the builders and the Church in Abingdon joined the church for the tape-cutting ceremony. Balloons were released. The newly landscaped forecourt, in warm sunshine, was the setting for the tea. David Coffey preached at the evening service which followed.

The premises were open every weekday from 10.30 a.m. to 2.00 p.m. (10.00 to 12.00 on Saturdays) for coffee and light lunches. A pastoral worker was available each day to welcome people and be ready to listen to anyone who wanted to share their problems. This team was supervised for many years by the Revd. Bernard Green, retired General Secretary of the Baptist Union. The church office was staffed and the premises cleaned. In addition a room on the top floor was rented as the regional office of 'Tear Fund' and shared by the Abingdon Volunteer Services, while an increasing number of local organisations booked the rooms for meetings, training and conferences. By 1999, thirty four organisations were using the premises, in addition to Baptist use. On Sundays the children's groups of the church met in the rooms. And on the top floor a two bed-roomed flat had been created, soon to be occupied by a second minister.

**Evangelism.**

Although all this occupied much time and energy, the more usual life of the church continued to function. 35 Ock Street attempted to serve the community in the name of Christ, but it was not primarily evangelistic. Neither could it promote the Baptist Church in exclusion to the other churches which were all involved. But its work was seen to be balanced by more overt evangelism in the form of the first 'Alpha Course' - a course in basic Christianity centred upon a meal, which was run in the autumn of 1995 for thirteen students. A special children's club on one or two Saturdays before Christmas, started by Lyn Green when placed at Abingdon for ministerial training and continued under the leadership of Alison Swift, was also becoming established as an annual activity which added children to the Sunday groups. The Family Church and those working in the Searchlight youth programme, the uniformed organisations and the music group all drew for leadership upon a generation of volunteers including Gilbert Payne, Pam and Geoff Pratt, Joy Dadswell, Judith Keymer, Gill North, Brian Collins, Stella Hambleton, Tony Valente, Pat Hudson, Alan Wood, Stephen Bodey , Margaret Bradshaw, Ruth Chown, Susan Costar, Helen Edwards, Chris and Delyth Hallion, Iain and Valerie Hoskins, Rosalie Lorrison, Lisa Sparkes, Alec and Alison Swift, Hazel Telling, Joyce and Paul Wilson, and these were supported by so many others.

**Further generosity.**

While money was being raised for 35 Ock Street, a plot of land to the west of the premises came on the market. Two church members were moved to add this to their giving and the plot was purchased for £30,000.

**Men @ ABC.**

During the last decade of this century the church took up various activities encouraged by the Baptist Men's Movement. Leading figures in the church were Bill White, Gilbert Payne, Geoff Pratt and Bob Pengelly-Phillips, who was also national president for a year. Tools with a Mission collected and renovated tools of every kind to be sent abroad to developing countries. Men were brought together and money raised by the Big, and later Bigger, Breakfasts. The Bigger Balti similarly formed and deepened friendships. Another valuable ministry pioneered by Bill White and continued after Bill's death by Gilbert and Geoff was Tapes for the Blind, later Baptist Voice. This is a monthly audio magazine, on CD or tape cassette, for blind or visually impaired people. It contains news from a selection of Baptist and other Christian material. Produced by a team of readers in the Abingdon Church, it includes prayers and hymns and by 2011 was being sent to 120 listeners throughout the UK with one in Ireland and one in the USA.

*Figure 62 Baptist Voice recording session. Gilbert Payne (L) and Geoff Pratt (R).*

**The Associate Minister.**

The new work in 35 Ock Street quickly generated pastoral opportunities and demands which were increasingly difficult for one minister to cover. At this stage another couple in the membership offered to donate the standard stipend for a second worker for a three year period. It was debated whether this person should be a qualified community development worker or a minister and people of both skills were interviewed. Finally it was agreed to look for a second minister and Andrew Hall, approaching the end of his training at Spurgeon's College was called. Andrew was ordained at Warwick on 19th July 1997 and inducted as Associate Minister at Abingdon on

13th September (just one year after the opening of 35 Ock Street). At the Induction Service Andrew announced his engagement to Roslyn Peffer of Sydney. They married the following April and the flat in the attics of 35 Ock Street became a real home and a centre for much hospitality.

*Figure 63 Deacons welcoming party for Andrew and Ros. after their wedding.*

*Kneeling (L-R) Maureen White*, Jean Clarke*, Kathleen Cook*, Rosalind Hall, Andrew Hall, Charles Orland, Alison Swift.*

*Standing (L-R) Jon Spiller*, Bill White, Mary Beackon*, Mary England, Stella Hambleton, Judith Spiller, Geoffrey England*, Dorothy Field*, Gerald Field, Nigel Chown*, Michael Hambleton, Alec Swift*, Ruth Chown, Valerie Hoskins, Ian Hoskins* photographer. (* indicates Deacons)*

Some in the church could remember the disastrous situation when the church last had two ministers, in the 1950's, and expressed concern. But, with the church's guidance, Michael and Andrew defined their respective areas of responsibility and agreed to meet weekly for pastoral sharing and prayer. Michael would continue the traditional ministry of the church while Andrew would concentrate on encouraging and developing the work of 35 Ock Street and seek to establish areas of ministry in the town. Both would share in the worship and preaching and Andrew would be given time for his probationary studies. The two ministers appeared to complement each other - age and experience was balanced by youth and energy; a more liberal, older man by a personal member of the Evangelical Alliance. There was give and take and we soon became good friends and trusted colleagues in the work. Andrew helped to streamline the administration of 35 Ock Street and developed an excellent rapport with the Primary Schools in the town - much in demand as a leader of school assemblies. He related well to the Church in Abingdon for whom he became schools representative, forging links between the clergy and the head teachers. He accepted the chair of both the Christian Aid Committee and The Bridge. Andrew was also elected chairman of ADMM - Abingdon's millennium initiative to raise money to provide drinking water for third world communities. Over £32,000 had been raised by the time his ministry in Abingdon ended.

**A Missionary Congregation.**[150]

A feature of Abingdon Baptist Church as it approached the end of the twentieth century was its busyness. Its members, numbering around 145, were heavily committed either in 35 Ock Street or in the youth work or in the administration. Every evening saw one and sometimes several activities - uniformed groups, house groups, committees, band practice, Church and Deacons meetings. Then, added to these were the two other tiers of activity - the Church in Abingdon and the Oxon. and E. Glos. Association meetings. And all this activity took place in the evenings after many of the participants had spent an exhausting day at work. This problem was not unique to Abingdon and the church began to take note of writings on the subject under the general heading of 'A Missionary Congregation'. These suggested that Christian witness should be the task of every Christian, and the place for that witness is where Christians work or live or spend their leisure time. The Abingdon church took seriously the call to nurture its members to be such witnesses and to free them for such work. This may be one of the great challenges of the coming decade or more. But a small start has been made. House Groups have studied the ideas, sermons have been preached, people have been regularly interviewed at evening services to tell us of their work and needs expressed have been the subject of prayer. The Deacons have spent a year or more gradually tightening up the committee structures, to increase democracy but also to cut down the number of people involved and meetings to be attended. At the same time the Baptist Union has challenged us to re-organise the way we associate with other churches - that when we do meet together it may be as meaningful as possible.

---

[150] I have kept the text of the original book, more or less, from here to the end of this chapter as it best expresses my thoughts of eleven years ago, as I came to the end of my ministry and the church reached its 350th anniversary. M.G.H.

This has led to the exploration of 'clustering' with the Baptists of Wallingford and Didcot and their satellite village churches.

350 years ago the Abingdon church was at the heart of such a wide fellowship, and it appears that today it is being challenged to return to its roots - to give strength to and draw strength from the Baptist churches of Berkshire and beyond. Within that cluster are many leading figures of the denomination who work at Baptist House. But unlike 350 years ago the church can no longer relate to Baptists alone. It is now part of a Church of thirteen churches representing most of the traditions of the universal Church. From this position the Abingdon Baptist Church has much to offer and much to learn. Its success or failure will be written in the history yet to be lived and recorded.

**Footnote.**
The 350th anniversary year began with the lighting of a candle which will be lit for each service of the year - a silent call to remember and give thanks for the way God has led the church through all its years. One of Michael's last activities was to act as secretary to the Church in Abingdon committee charged with the task of mounting a major exhibition in the County Hall museum. The Millennium Exhibition opened on the 1st April 2000 and ran for three months. Other celebrations have been planned - the Summer Birthday Festival in July, an event in the autumn of a more historical nature when this booklet will be launched. There will be short dramas tied into the history performed in worship through the year. Interviews on the theme 'I have a memory; I have a dream' will keep the future in focus. And as a thanksgiving, the church will raise a sum of money to set up a scholarship at the International Baptist Seminary in Prague to assist the training of ministers for eastern European countries. This same year saw the end of the ministry at Abingdon of both its ministers - Michael going into retirement in April and Andrew reaching the end of his three year contract and moving on to ministry in Thatcham. The church stands poised for a new minister or ministers and a new millennium.

# Chapter 5
# The Twenty First Century.

‘ The church stands poised for a new minister or ministers and a new millennium.’ And I have been privileged, in the eleven years since concluding my book with those words, to live in Abingdon, though a member of New Road Baptist Church in Oxford, and observe the church during the ongoing ministry of my successor.

**Ministry of Revd. David Fleming, B.A., M. St. (Oxon).**

*Figure 64 The Revd. David Fleming.*

Following his studies at Sheffield University, where he read biblical studies and archaeology, and Regent’s Park College, Oxford, David Fleming served as minister at Frindsbury Baptist Church in Kent. He now accepted the call to Abingdon and was inducted in September 2001. A Londoner, he is married to Elizabeth whom he met at Cemetery Road Baptist Church, Sheffield. By the time they moved into the Abingdon manse they had three children, Sarah, James and Callum. Andrew was born shortly after.

David recalls that his first impression of the church was that it held together a broad spectrum of Christian outlook but enjoyed a strong bond of fellowship which was greater than the views which might have divided them. He also sensed a degree of tiredness. This has already been referred to under the heading 'A Missionary Congregation' at the end of the previous chapter. Six years into the 35 Ock Street project, the church did not want its new minister to launch a further new building scheme or time-consuming programme. New initiatives were to come. But for a time the church needed a sabbatical period and would approach a new ministry with caution.

The work of 35 Ock Street was developing and the numbers using its facilities continue to increase. Over fifty local or national organisations now use its rooms and it is in use for around 80% of the time available. I interviewed David, for the purposes of this book, in March 2011, sitting at a table in the café area, which would most likely once have been Daniel Turner's dining room, and the place was buzzing with life. The monthly ministers' meeting of the Church in Abingdon was gathering upstairs. The café staff, only one of whom that morning was a Baptist, were serving and busy with the dish-washer machine. Customers filled most of the tables. A pastoral volunteer was available for anyone to chat with. Behind the reception desk Jan Hughes, the administrator, had a word for everyone coming in or leaving. David assured me that its ecumenical vision continued and it had more customers than ever. Over the years the facilities had been improved and the decorations, inside and out, kept in good order.

The Church in Abingdon obviously continued, but he felt its character had changed. It was, perhaps, less a covenanted community and more a normal 'Churches Together'. He spoke of a shift in the centre of gravity towards working together in task groups, away from large united events - suggesting that an event like 'Abingdon Alive' would be unthinkable today. Nevertheless a new church, the Abingdon Vineyard church, had joined and initiatives in joint youth ministry with a schools focus, Town Centre Chaplaincy, Street Pastors and help for the homeless, linked with the Oxford based Food Bank and Gateway had all come about in the past ten years. Furthermore, the CiA has taken its message into public spaces with Good Friday events in the Market Place and Pentecost Family Days in the Abbey Meadow. The Alpha Course has also been organised on an inter-church basis for several years.

The outward focus of the Baptist Church had led to the appointment, in September 2007, of Colin Pattenden as Community Missioner.

*Figure 65 Colin Pattenden, Community Missioner.*

Colin's training and experience were in community development rather than the ordained ministry. During his three year contract he worked in partnership with Age UK to set up and run 'Back to 35' which brought together about thirty elderly people for a meal twice a month. Working with the Church in Abingdon, Colin encouraged the formation of a Street Pastors' scheme and the establishment in the town of a branch of the Oxford charity Archway, which creates meeting places for lonely adults. RISE was started as an alternative, or adjunct to the 10.30 a.m. Sunday morning worship for people drawn to 35 Ock Street but not yet willing to commit to the worshipping church. Colin's wife, Carole, an artist, encouraged a group from the fellowship to develop their artistic skills. 'More than Pretty Pictures' was a series which helped the group to express their faith and Christian experience through art-work. After their ministry of over three years, Colin and Carole moved on, in March 2011 to take up a post as wardens at Westwood Christian Centre near Huddersfield.

The denominational initiative, The Men's Movement, taken up in the Abingdon Church in the '90's, continued to be strongly led and developed through the first decade of the new century by Gilbert Payne and Geoffrey Pratt.

From the days when Abingdon Baptist Church and its four daughter churches in the villages worked as one fellowship of churches, there had always been a good number of lay-preachers working in the area.

This remains the case today. David Fleming said it was a rare Sunday when at least one member was not away leading worship elsewhere. But there is now also a ministry team which prepares and leads worship as a group in other places as well as their home church. To encourage this, David leads a Ministry Matters Course - five sessions, repeated as required.

Prayer has continued to be an important aspect of the new decade. The old minister's vestry, to the south of the church lounge, has been refurbished as The Orland Prayer Room and is always available for prayer. There is a monthly prayer breakfast when the one topic is the programme for the coming month. For the last five years June has been set apart as a month of prayer. This is a time for experimenting in various forms of prayer. It was during such a month of prayer, in June 2008, that the minister who, he assures us, 'is not much given to flights of fancy' was praying about the church: 'I pictured the church in my mind. As I looked at the façade of the church, it was as if there was a sign over the door which read THE WELL OF ISAAC.' This led to the publication of the pamphlet *The Well of Isaac, Genesis 26,*[151] in which he sets out his vision for the church - to draw upon the rich inheritance of the past, but also to be less cautious in facing and tackling new challenges and possibilities of worship and service

**The Development Project.**

About six years into David Fleming's ministry he sensed a general groundswell among the membership for the development of the church halls. As mentioned in the last chapter, a start had been made back in the mid 90's for a new and enlarged church hall. This came to nothing as the opportunity to develop 35 Ock Street took precedence. In 2000-2001 the rear entrance to the east of the chapel was improved to give new women's toilets. But now, possibly prompted by the renovation of the neo-classical façade of the chapel in 2007, a total re-development of the chapel and halls began to be considered. The architects JBKS were appointed and consultation began. The question facing the church was, How can our present buildings be developed so as best to serve the needs of both church and community? It is felt by many that buildings which were built over a century and a half ago for a lecture style of worship, were no longer suitable for the flexible worship of today. A more welcoming lay-out was called for with larger circulation areas and halls large enough for the entire church to

[151] Copy in the Angus Library, Regent's Park College, Oxford.

meet and dine together.

Plans are being refined. The architects' impression included in this book indicates how the church was thinking early in the current year of 2011, the final plans may be very different. Permission to alter a listed building is being sought. Money is already being raised, though major appeals have to await the finalisation of the plans.

*Figure 66 Architect's impression. March 2011*

**Public Office.**
A feature of the past ten years has been the involvement of the minister and his wife in the public affairs of the town and district. They have not been alone in this. Samantha Bowering has been a district and town councillor for the Ock Meadows' ward for several years. David has been appointed chaplain to the mayor on three occasions, the first non-conformist to hold this office since records began. Elizabeth Fleming was elected to the Vale of White Horse District Council, as a Liberal Democrat and in 2011 was Chair to that council.

**Continuation.**
This book ends in the full flow of David Fleming's ministry. The church membership numbers ca.125 with weekly attendance ca.150. The leadership is strong and its organisations flourish. The Annual

Report for 2011 contains reports from the minister, Community Missioner and Secretary, from the Mission Committee, Fabric Committee, Development Project, 35 Ock Street Management Committee, House Groups, Safe to Grow, Family Church, ABC Tots, Youth Group, Beavers, Scouts, Brownies, Rainbows, Midweek Fellowship, Men at ABC, More than Pretty Pictures, Back to 35, BMS Birthday Scheme and Operation Christmas Child. Prayer is deep and large plans for growth will involve new buildings and on-going mission in the areas of evangelism, community care, ecumenism and local, district, national and international responsibility. The future life of the church has potential as limitless as the kingdom of God and the mysteries of divine being. So I have chosen to end this account with a prayer contained within the farewell article, titled 'Moving on...' written by Colin and Carole for the February edition of *Contact* in 2011:

> Our prayer is that the mission life will continue to grow and develop, meeting the needs of those on the margins and demonstrating the love of Jesus in new and exciting ways. We pray that you will continue to be a church that takes risks for the sake of the gospel, moving under the direction of the Holy Spirit, as you continue to make the necessary changes to be a relevant church in the 21$^{st}$ C.

-------------------

**Postscript:**
On the morning of the 17th July 2011, I was invited to contribute a short assessment of the Revd. Daniel Turner's ministry, prior to unveiling the Blue Plaque bearing his name and mounted on the façade of the old minister's house. This honours the memory of one, at present the most famous, of the thirty five or so who have ministered to the church during five centuries. I trust that their lives, and equally those of the thousands of church members, most of whom remain anonymous, will continue to inspire the coming generations which will make up this church and its particular understanding of the gospel of Christ.

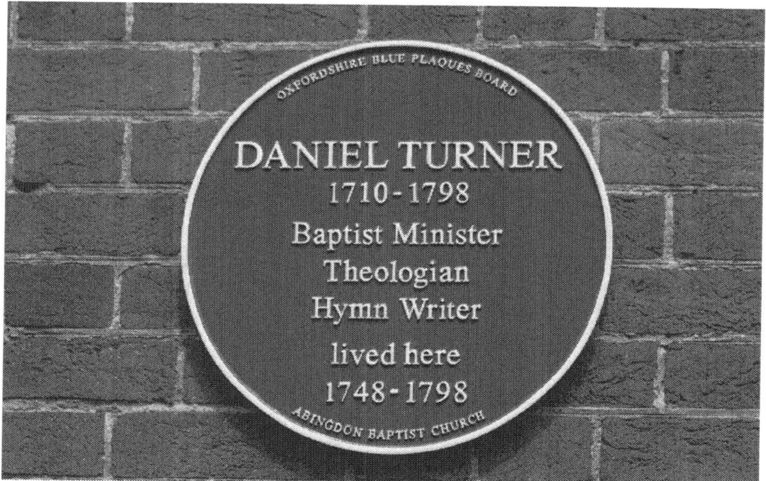


*Figure 67 Blue Plaque on exterior wall of 35 Ock Street.*

# Appendices

## Appendix A

This Appendix seeks to compile a list of those people who were known as Baptists or Anabaptists and linked to the Baptist Church in Abingdon in the almost 100 years from the first mention of the Church in 1649 to the year 1748 when the first surviving Membership Roll was compiled.

The sources from which these names have been extracted are set out at the head of each section below. Particularly in the earlier years, the church affiliation of dissenting people is not always clear. I have only included names of those specifically mentioned as being Baptist in at least one source. This does not necessarily mean that they were formal 'members' of the church.

I have arranged these names in three lists, which are more or less in chronological order:

List 1 has been preserved by the Longworth/Coate Church from 1656 and gives us the 99 names of those who had been part of the Abingdon Baptist fellowship during John Pendarves' ministry, but, with the approval of the Abingdon Church, left to form the Longworth Church. Sadly, there was no reason for a similar list to be made of those they left behind in Abingdon.

List 2 is a compilation of all Baptists I have as yet identified as forming the Baptist Church in the 17$^{th}$ century, in addition to the Longworth group. There is some duplication with the third list, which is that already printed in the first edition of this book and which records the names of those members of the Abingdon Church who lived in the first half of the 18$^{th}$ century.

This appendix continues on the following page ……

**List 1**
**Transcription from the Longworth Church Book**
**(From the Angus Library):**

At a meeting ye 12th of ye 10th month 1656 when the Church at Longworth did first stand upp as a Church of Christ distinct from Abingdon Church

That those members in & neare Longworth together with our brother Combes being first so persuaded & will most tend to the Glory of God that we stand upp as a distinct Church of Christ our Bro: Combes being with us ['with us' deleted] to walk with us soe long as himself the Church at Longworth & the Church at Abingdon shall be persuaded that his Call from ye Lord is to be amongst us to be at present ? ? to see how the Lord will own his labour amongst us,

This being resolved uppon by us whose names are under written doe in the presence of the Lord give upp our selves to the Lord and to each other to walk together as members of a Church of Christ watching over each other for good to walk in all the ordinances of Christ as the Lord shall give us Light strength and opportunity,

John Jones
Thomas Jones
Richard Leake
Thomas Haycraft
John Willmott
William Miller
Charles Ambrose
Laurence
Ambrose
Robert Patient
Thomas Wace
Thomas James
Richard Clinch
William Boon
William Baker
Moses Arkett

Bridgett
Tuckwell
Ann Newbury
Mary Tuckwell
??? Rawlins
Robert Hounton
Henry Wyatt
Thomas Wyatt
Mary Hill
Elizabeth Wyatt
Richard Fowler
Nicholas Mayow
Breget Mayow
Richard Church
John Carpenter
John Williams

John Carter
John Burdon
Mary ???
Quartermain
[above name
deleted]
John Combes
Magory Goodall
Ann Gouge
Jane Austin
Elizabeth
Dunston
Mary Thomas
Kathren Adams
Thomsin
Ambrose

Elizabeth
Livham
Elnor Dior
Heanrus Ellis
Ann Mills
Jane Butler
Ruby O'higgory
[?]
Elizabeth Patient
Heanrie
Newbury
Simon Leeke
Edward Painton
Thomas
Tuckwell
Ann Tuckwell
Heanrie Shipery
Joane Austin
Ann Ponery?
Kathren Lourd
[above name
deleted]
Ann Rawlins

Heanrie Downe
Mary Adams
Thomas Lister
Robert Kempster
Ann Morris
Elizabeth
Kempster
Elizabeth Isome?
Elizabeth James
John Burdon
John Thomas
Henrie Wall
Jane Hiide
Elizabeth Burdon
Alice Tull
Margaret Ellis
William Thomas
Martha Dolton
Mary Wace
Ambrose Tull
Usly? Wilmot
John Turner
Elizabeth Turner

Elizabeth Smith
Ann Butler
Robert Smith
Robert Williams
Mary Tuckwell
Edward Worden
Elizabeth
Worden
Anne Carter
Alice Dyer
John Mouldon
Mary Trahearn
Robert Smith
Thomas Angell
??? Hill ye elder
Jane Huchwell
Elizabeth
Moblye
Henry? Clarke
John Austin
Robert Morris

**List 2.**
**List of 17th Century Abingdon Baptists:**

Abbreviations of sources

| | |
|---|---|
| AC | *Archbishop's Cruelty,* Thomason collection, 1641 |
| PtP | *The Pastor turn'd Pope,* 1654 |
| AR | *Association Records,* 1652ff |
| CT | *The Complaining Testimony,* 1656 |
| TT | *A Testimony for Truth,* 1659 |
| IV | *Inocency Vindicated,* 1689 |
| GA | General Assembly |
| St.H | St. Helen's registers |
| AEP | Arthur E. Preston, *St. Nicolas & Other Papers* |
| MC | Mieneke Cox, *The Story of Abingdon, Pt.III* |
| *BQ* | Baptist Quarterly |
| MB | Manfred Brod |
| LK | L. Kreitzer, *Seditious Sectaryes* |

| Name | Biographical Details | Source |
|---|---|---|
| Adams, Ambrose | Millwright | AEP |
| Aldworth | | St. Helen's Birth List (St.H) |
| Allen, John | | St.H |
| Ambrose Laurence | | PtP |
| Barnes | | St.H |
| Batten, | Woolen-draper | AEP |
| Belcher, John | | BQ April '95 |
| Blackman, Thomas | Haircloth weaver | AEP |
| Buttler | 'Will. son of Will. Butler & Mary' | St.H |
| Castle, William | Linen-draper. Mayor of Ab. | AEP. AC. MC |
| Consett, William | | AR |
| Coombes, John (Combes, Comes) | Cordwainer | AR. CT. TT |
| Dickens | | |
| Dyer, William | Yeoman | AEP TT |
| Emerson, Anne | wife of Giles E. | AEP |

| Forty, Henry | pastor 1675-87 | MC. GA |
|---|---|---|
| Fox, Consolation | Captain, yeoman, maltster | MC. AEP. AR. BQ Ap.95 |
| Fox, Samuel | Scriptor | AEP |
| Garbrand, Dr. Tobias | Prin. of Gloucester Hall, Oxford, from 1660 a doctor in Abingdon | AEP |
| Garbrand Susannah | 1[st] w. of TG. d. of W. Bury, lofm Culham | AEP |
| Garbrand Anna | 2[nd] w. of TG | AEP |
| Garbrand Ann | daugh. of TG - m Thomas Danson, Abingdon Presbyterian minister | AEP |
| Garbrand John | son of TG. Lawyer in London | AEP |
| Garbrand Joshua | son of TG evicted Ab. School 1671 | AEP |
| Glover Richard | Baker | AEP |
| Green, Richard | Captain, maltster | St.H. AEP. CT |
| Hall, John | Grocer, s. of Samuel, d. 1695 | St.H , A.E.P. |
| Hagar, George | Yeoman | AEP |
| Harman | Widow | AEP |
| Hearne, Arthur & Margaret | Ironmonger | MC. TT |
| Heath, Robert | Labourer | AEP. |
| Hicks, Richard | Son of Samuel, d.1695 | MC |
| Hockton Philip | | GA |
| Hopkins, Robert & Mary | daughter, Mary, d.1697 | St.H |
| Hutt, Hanah | | AEP |
| Hutt, Robert | Basket-maker | AEP |
| Jones, John | Taylor | AR. AEP. TT |
| Kates, William | dau. d. Mch 1717 | MC |
| Lane | | St.H |
| Lathe | widow | PtP |
| Lendor, G | son, Arthur, d. 1697 | St.H |
| Lewis, Mrs. Eliza | d. 1696 | St.H |
| Loader, Ed. | son David d. 1696 | St.H |

| | | |
|---|---|---|
| Lockton, Philip & Frances | Grocer; daughter Mary d. 1656 | St.H, AEP. CT. TT |
| Lockton, Philip junr | Mercer | AEP. |
| Lovegrove, Elizabeth | spinster | AEP |
| Lovegrove, Richard | Labourer, baker | AEP |
| Lovegrove, Robert | Yeoman | AEP |
| Lyword Richard | | PtP |
| Mann, John | Schoolmaster, preacher | MC |
| Mans, Dorkis | Spinster, d. 1698 | St.H |
| May | | St.H |
| Mayo Simon | | CT |
| Mitchell, Edward & Mary | | AEP |
| Newbury, Francis | Labourer | AEP |
| Nobbs, Thomas | Taylor | AEP |
| Payne, Robert & Margery | Woolen-draper, both d. 1697. lived at 'The Bell on the Bury'. Margery became a Quaker c. 1682. | St.H, AEP. TT |
| Peck, Simon and Katharine | Maltster, house used Bapt. worship | M. Cox, AEP. CT |
| Pendarves, John & Thomasine | Pastor 1652-6, d. 1656 | AR. MC, AEP |
| Penner, Edward | | AR |
| Phipps, Thomas | Ironmonger - with A. Hearn provided material for weathervane on new Market House 1681 | MC. AEP |
| Playdell | | St.H |
| Rigden, John & Sarah | Miller | St.H |
| Roberts, Edward & Alice | Draper | AEP |
| Roberts, John | Servant to John Coombe | AEP |
| Robinson, John | Blacksmith | AEP |
| Rusen | | St.H |

| Selwood, Richard | Baker | AEP |
|---|---|---|
| Skinner, John | Physician, preacher | St.H |
| Starre, Edward | Maltster, d. 1671 | AEP |
| Steed, Willian & Dorothy | Yeoman, Wilm. d 1698 | St.H, AEP |
| Steede Robert | preacher | PtP |
| Stennett, Edward | Brazier, leading 7th day Baptist. d. 1691 | B.Q. Ap.'95. CT. MB |
| Stevenson, William | Maltster | AEP |
| Stibbs, John | Maltster | AEP |
| Stibbs, Thomas | Labourer | A.E.P. |
| Taylor, William | | St.H, AEP |
| Terrell Richard | Mercer | CT |
| Tesdale, Jane | Widow 1662 | AEP |
| Tesdale, Josiah | Yeoman, maltster | AEP |
| Tesdale, Richard | Woolen-draper | AEP. TT. PtP |
| Tesdale, Thomas | Mercer. Family tree in LK vol.I p.402 | AR. LK. TT. PtP |
| Tesdale, William & Eilzabeth | | AEP |
| Thorneton, Henry & Mary | Tobacco-pipe-maker | AEP |
| Tomkins, Benjamin | Maltster | AEP |
| Tomkins, Edward | Broom-maker | AEP |
| Tomkins, Henry | Glover, Preacher | MC. PtP |
| Tomkins, John & Martha | Pastor d. 1708, Trunk-maker, Maltster | BQ Ap.95 etc |
| Trapham, Mary | | AEP |
| Truloch, John | Barber | AEP |
| Tuckwell, Thomas & Hanah | Maltster d. 1696 | St.H |
| Turrall, Jane | Widow in 1686 | AE. |
| Turrold, Jonathan (also) | Yeoman | AEP |
| Turrold, Richard (Tyrold) | Linen-draper. Took letter To Atherton | AEP |
| Weston, William | Maltster | AEP |
| Wiblin | | St.H |

| Wickens | | St.H |
|---|---|---|
| Whitby, Nicholas | Gentleman | MC. AEP |
| White Francis | Cutler and preacher. 'they had at Stool of repentance' | PtP |
| White, William | Clockmaker | AEP. CT. PtP |
| Wise, John | Cutler, maltster | AEP. TT |
| Wise, Margaret | Widow in 1686 | AEP |
| Wolton | Cordwainer | AEP |
| Wyatt, John | | AEP |

The ten sons of Baptist parents, ejected from Roysse's School in 1671 were: Samuell Herne, John Hall, John Lockton, William Turrold, Joseph Hall, Benjamin Greene, Joshua Garbrand, Richard Teasdale, [blank] Teasdale, Jasper Teasdale.

## List 3.

The following list of members has been extracted, in the order their names appear, by Michael G. Hambleton from a reading of the earliest Church Book of Abingdon Baptist Church, which covers the years 1720 - 1746 and which is in the Angus Library of Regents Park College, Oxford. The dates of membership can only be given for those who joined the church after 1720. Of those in membership at the year 1720, only those mentioned in the Church Book are known as certainly in membership before 1720, although it is very likely that those men and women whose names are on the earliest membership roll of 1748, and whose baptism and membership is not recorded in the Church Book, were in fact in membership before 1720. These are listed after H. Grovening in the men's list and after Hester Crofts in the women's list. There will be members whose names are not included in this list, namely those in membership before 1720, who were not mentioned in the minutes and who died before the compiling of the 1748 Membership List. In the spirit of the 18th century Church Book, though contrary to my own inclinations, I list the Brothers and the Sisters separately. Only where mentioned in the Church Book are relationships between the members recorded. The date of baptism usually follows a week or so after the candidate has testified to their faith before the church (sometimes privately), some baptisms are described as 'private' also. Reception into membership usually follows about a week after the baptism, though sometimes on the day itself.

BROTHERS

| Name | Baptised | Remarks |
|---|---|---|
| William Fuller | pre 1720 | Pastor 1700-174 |
| Benjamin Tomkins senr. | pre 1720 | d. Jan. 1737 |
| Thomas Fowler | pre 1720 | moved to London 1721 |
| Leadox | pre 1720 | |
| Edward Robarts | pre 1720 | |
| Thomas Rawlings | pre 1720 | |
| Benjamin Tomkins junr. | pre 1720 | |

| | | |
|---|---|---|
| Anthony Pisly | pre 1720 | |
| Thomas Winsmore | pre 1720 | |
| William Mills | pre 1720 | |
| Charles Rawlings | pre 1720 | |
| Benjamin Jefferys | pre 1720 | |
| Joseph Hopkins | pre 1720 | |
| Richard Buttler | pre 1720 | |
| Stibbs | pre 1720 | |
| William Hutt | pre 1720 | |
| Waite (possibly John) | pre 1720 | |
| Robert Poulter | pre 1720 | |
| Avery Aldworth | pre 1720 | |
| John Tomkins | pre 1720 | |
| James Jobson | pre 1720 | |
| William Buttler | pre 1720 | |
| John Burham | pre 1720 | |
| Daniel Turrall | pre 1720 | |
| Gregory Peck | pre 1720 | |
| Robert Hopkins | pre 1720 | |
| William Wallis | pre 1720 | |
| John Hutt | pre 1720 | |
| William Wallis junr. | pre 1720 | |
| John ? (surname illegible ? Waite) | pre 1720 | |
| Josiah Buttler | pre 1720 | |
| Joseph Dicker | pre 1720 | |
| H. Grovening | pre 1720 | |
| Peter Stevens senr. | pre 1720 | |
| Thomas Panting | pre 1720 | |
| William Petty | pre 1720 | |
| John Jackson | pre 1720 | |
| William Home | pre 1720 | |
| Thomas Freeman | pre 1720 | |
| George Lewindon | pre 1720 | |
| Lovelock | pre 1720 | |
| George Giles | pre 1720 | |
| James Rawlings | Sept. 1721 | |
| Walter Tannor | transferred from Gwiggleton | May 1723 |

| | | |
|---|---|---|
| John Clanville | Dec. 1723 | |
| Thomas Fuller | Dec. 1723 | son of Thomas Fuller |
| James Collins | March 1725 | |
| Carter | transferred from Princes Risborough 1725 | |
| John Hall | Jan. 1727 | |
| Greening | Jan. 1727 | |
| Mark Holliday | Mch. 1728 | |
| Ebenezer Fuller | Jne.1728 son of Pastor."being recommended by Mr. Ed.Wallon" | |
| Joseph Harris | Sept. 1734 | |
| Benjamin Harris | May 1735 | |
| William Rawlings | Nov. 1736 | son of Thomas |
| John Burly | Nov. 1736 | |
| Gregory Peck | Nov. 1736 | son of Gregory |
| John Rooke | Jan. 1737 | |
| George Hinton | Apr. 1737 | 'excluded immoral' post 1750 |
| Kempster Greenhill | Apr. 1737 | |
| Edward Grant Tuckwell | Apr. 1737 | 'removed to London' |
| John Hinton | | trans. from Bourton/ Stow 1746. Dism. to Upton 1748. |

## SISTERS

| Name | Baptised | Remarks |
|---|---|---|
| Cowslade | pre 1720 | dismissed to Newbury, May 1730 |
| Slight | pre 1720 | dismissed to Reading, 1724 |
| Mary Mills | pre 1720 | dismissed to Southwark, 1725 |
| Jane Robarts | pre 1720 | dismissed to? 1725 |
| Elisa Southy | pre 1720 | dismissed to London |

| | | 1726 |
|---|---|---|
| Mary Wallis | pre 1720 | |
| Rebecca Feyer - spelling uncertain | pre 1720 | |
| Emarson junr. | pre 1720 | |
| Tomkins | pre 1720 | wife of John |
| Elizabeth Tyrrall | pre 1720 | |
| Plaister | pre 1720 | |
| Barbara Buttler | pre 1720 | wife of Jos. |
| Hester Crofts | pre 1720 | |
| Mary Beenham | pre 1720 | |
| Elizabeth Holmes | pre 1720 | |
| Sarah Fuller junr. | pre 1720 | daughter of Elizabeth |
| Kath Talbot | pre 1720 | |
| Martha Rawlings | pre 1720 | wife of Thomas |
| Martha Ward | pre 1720 | |
| Mary Rawlings | pre 1720 | |
| Clanville | pre 1720 | |
| Elizabeth Leader | pre 1720 | |
| Elizabeth Carefoot | pre 1720 | |
| Mary Onion | pre 1720 | 'disordered in mind' |
| Sarah Doe | pre 1720 | |
| Ann Beasley | pre 1720 | |
| Hutt senr. | pre 1720 | |
| Hannah Hutt | pre 1720 | wife of John |
| Martha Hall | pre 1720 | |
| Hester Rooke | pre 1720 | wife of John |
| Webb | pre 1720 | |
| Sweet | pre 1720 | |
| Martha Midwinter | pre 1720 | |
| Martha Merry | pre 1720 | |
| Elizabeth Windsmore | pre 1720 | |
| Mary Giles | pre 1720 | wife of George |
| Hannah Peck | pre 1720 | |
| Sarah Hinton ("then Shank") | pre 1720 | |
| Sarah Keats (mother) | pre 1720 | |
| Sarah Keats (daughter) | pre 1720 | |
| Mary Poulter | pre 1720 | wife of Robert |

| Mary Platter ("then Collett") | pre 1720 | |
|---|---|---|
| Sarah Plater (her mother) | pre 1720 | |
| Mary Parsons (Drayton) | pre 1720 | |
| Mary Parsons (Aston) | pre 1720 | |
| Johanna Green | pre 1720 | |
| Ann Costard | pre 1720 | |
| Mary Beasley ('then Jackson') | pre 1720 | |
| Sarah Kempster | pre 1720 | |
| Mary Dearlove | pre 1720 | |
| Sarah Crofts | pre 1720 | |
| Sarah Dicker | pre 1720 | |
| Beth Robarts | pre 1720 | wife of Joseph |
| Greenhill | pre 1720 | died Nov. 1750 |
| Mary Clanville | Nov. 1721 | |
| Deborah Mills | Nov. 1721 | dismissed to Southwark 1725 |
| Jane Fuller | Nov. 1721 | |
| Mary Lindsy | | transferred from London, May 1723 |
| Sheene | Feb. 1724 | |
| Hannah Winsmore | Feb. 1724 | |
| Mary Robarts | Mch. 1725 | wife of Edward |
| Sarah Hutt | Mch. 1725 | |
| Mary Dickers | Mch. 1725 | |
| "The wife of Tho: Fuller" | Mch. 1725 | |
| Elisabeth Bulky | Apr. 1725 | |
| Elizabeth Tomkins | Apr. 1725 | wife of Benj. Tomkins junr. |
| Ann Tomkins | July 1725 | wife of John Tomkins |
| Martha Hibborne | July 1725 | |
| Sarah Hutt | Oct. 1726 | dau. of T. Hutt. dism. to Mr. Wallon's, |

| | | |
|---|---|---|
| | | Southwark 1729 |
| Ann Robarts | Mch. 1727 | daughter of Edward Robarts |
| Susannah Panting | Apr. 1727 | excommunicated 1735 |
| Esther Stibbs | Oct. 1727 | |
| Ann Dowsett | Oct. 1727 | |
| Sarah Robarts | Oct. 1727 | |
| Elisa Aldworth | Feb. 1728 | daughter of Avery |
| Jane Fuller | Oct. 1728 | 'daughter of widow Fuller' |
| Hannah Dinnon | Oct. 1728 | |
| Mary Dinnon | Dec. 1729 | |
| Frances Fuller | Dec. 1729 | dismissed to Southwark, 1736 |
| Mary Browne | Feb. 1731 | 'alias Holliday' |
| Clanwell | May 1734 | wife of Francis Canwell |
| Martha Cox | | re-admitted by trans. fr. Mr Noble's, London 1734 |
| Mary Lovelocke | Sept. 1736 | |
| Sarah Freeman | Sept. 1736 | |
| "Mr. Book's maid" | 10th Oct. 1736 | 'was this day received into the church' |
| Bothian (or Bothya) Robarts | Dec. 1736 | daughter of Edward Robarts |
| Sarah Carter | Dec. 1736 | 'servant of William Fuller', 'then Fuller' |
| Elisa Kerxfoot - spelling uncertain | Dec. 1736 | |
| Elisa Rawlings | May 1737 | wife of William |
| Mary Shippory | May 4$^{th}$ 1746 | on a torn fragment of a page of the Church Book, Mary Shippory and the two below are mentioned as being baptised together |

| | | |
|---|---|---|
| Mrs. Sarah........... | | |
| plus a third woman | | |

Appendix B.

**Introduction.**
The following is a transcription, made by Michael Hambleton, of the older of the two Church Covenants preserved in the Angus Library of Regent's Park College, Oxford under the catalogue reference E23B. The document has 12 sheets of which sheets 2 to 9 are numbered 1 to 8 in the bottom left hand corner. There is one pair of square brackets in the original text, on sheet 2. The few other such brackets are my insertions and are used principally to mark the end of each sheet. Sheet 10 it is dated 16 November 1728 and signed with the initials J. H. From list 3 in appendix A, four members (all male) have these initials. The most prominent of these would be John Hutt.

My method has been to transcribe this very legible script, copying the original spelling and layout as closely as my computer will allow. I have kept the original abbreviations including the symbol '&' together with the rendering of 'the', 'them' and 'that' as 'ye', 'ym' and 'y$^{t}$'. I have not attempted to replicate the long 's'.

I have argued the case, in the main text (chap. 2, Baptism, membership and the Church Covenant) that this document could have been the text from which the fair copy, 'engrossed on parchment for all members to sign', was made. The Church Book refers to it both as 'The Covenant' and 'The Terms of Communion'.

In either case what we have here is not so much a Statement of Faith as an understanding of how the church fellowship expects its membership to live together. It is a pact which sets out the basis upon which the members bind themselves to each other and, collectively, to God. To read through this agreement and the long piece of verse which is based upon it, is to sense the heartbeat of early eighteenth century devotion. That is why I have felt it right to include the whole of this document in this book.

Much more of a Statement of Faith would have been the Catechism which is referred to on sheet 2 (page 1). If this catechism was in wider use among the churches, it may be possible to track down a copy, of which the first question is 'who is ye 1$^{st}$ & cheifest being'? This is the only reference to the catechism that I have found in the Abingdon archive.

The Church refers to itself in this document as 'a Congregational Church of Jesus Christ'. In 1729 this would have been the usual way of describing a church which was governed by its congregation, as opposed to the Presbyterians who were led by Elders. The title page of this document makes it clear that this is the covenant of a Baptist Church and not an Independent Church, like the one in the Square, which would later be known as the Congregational Church.

The somewhat amazing thirty-one verse poem or, more likely, hymn, which follows this covenant, brings to mind one of the Wesley's statements to the effect that hymns should be sung creeds. The standard of most of these verses can only be described as doggerel (including two uses of the double negative). This suggests to me that it was probably a local composition and may be unique to the Abingdon Baptist Church. If it was sung, it is in LM and a likely contender for the tune would be *The Old 100$^{th}$*, a melody from the Geneva Psalter of 1551. It occupies sheets 5 to 9 and singing it would take about fifteen minutes at the speed we sing today.

The Abingdon archive also contains a later copy or version of the above eleven paragraph covenant, This is dated March 31$^{st}$ 1739 and signed 'By J. G.', who could be John Garbrand, the London lawyer, or perhaps more likely Joshua, his younger brother. This document differs from the 1729 covenant only in two short insertions. Both insertions stress the importance of the Scriptures, upon which the whole covenant depends for its authority. The second, inserted into the final sentence, makes the important point that the Scriptures have yet more truths to reveal and it will be our duty to respond to them with similar obedience. This second document also varies slightly from the 1728 version in the biblical texts it calls upon to back up its clauses, but is otherwise an exact copy. It does not include the thirty-one verse hymn.

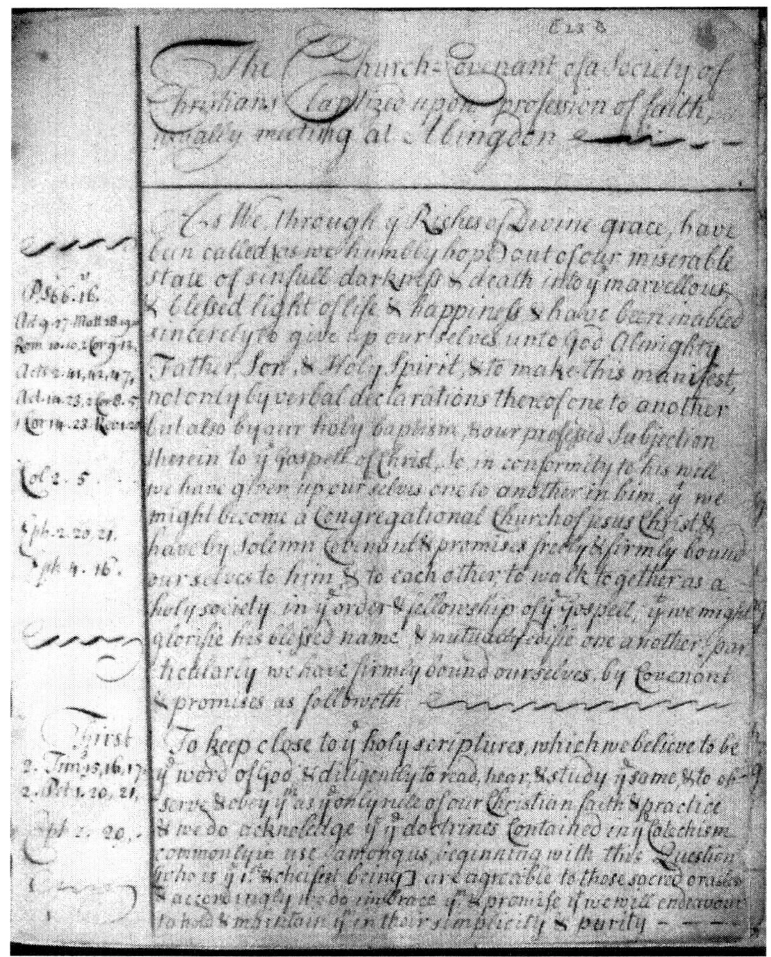
The Church-Covenant of a Society of
Christians Baptized upon profession of faith,
usually meeting at Abingdon

As We, through ye Riches of Divine grace, have
been called (as we humbly hope) out of our miserable
Ps 66.16. state of sinfull darkness & death into ye marvellous
Act 9.17 Matt 28.19 & blessed light of life & happiness & have been enabled
Rom 10.10 2 Cor 9.13 sincerely to give up our selves unto God Almighty
Acts 2.41,42,47, Father, Son, & Holy Spirit, & to make this manifest,
Act 18.23 ... 8.5 not only by verbal declarations thereof one to another
1 Cor 14.23 ... but also by our holy baptism, & our professed Subjection
therein to ye gospell of Christ, & in conformity to his will
Col 2.5 we have given up our selves one to another in him, yt we
might become a Congregational Church of Jesus Christ &
Eph. 2.20,21. have by solemn Covenant & promises freely & firmly bound
Eph 4.16. our selves to him & to each other, to walk together as a
holy society in ye order & fellowship of ye gospell, yt we might
glorifie his blessed name & mutually edifie one another, particularly we have firmly bound ourselves, by Covenant
& promises as followeth

First To keep close to ye holy scriptures, which we believe to be
2 Tim 3.15,16,17 ye word of God & diligently to read, hear, & study ye same, & to ob-
2 Pet 1.20,21, serve & obey ym as ye only rule of our Christian faith & practice
Eph 2.20, & we do acknowledge yt ye doctrines Contained in ye Catechism
commonly in use amongst us, beginning with this Question
(who is ye 1st & cheifest being) are agreable to those sacred oracles
& accordingly we do embrace ym & promise yt we will endeavour
to hold & maintain ym in their simplicity & purity

Figure 68 A Sample of the original pages transcribed here.

## Pactum Eclesiae Societatis Christianorum baptizatiunt in professionem fidei, usitale Congresi Abindoniae

---

[end of sheet 1]

## The Church Covenant of a Society of Christians baptised upon profession of faith, usually meeting at Abingdon

---

| | |
|---|---|
| c v<br>Ps 66.16.<br>Act 9.27 Matt 28.1920<br>Rom10. 10 2Cor 9.13<br>Acts 2.41,42,47,<br>Act 4.23, 2Cor 8.5<br>1Cor 14.23. Rev 1.20<br>Col 2.5,<br><br>Eph 2.20,21<br>Eph4.16 | As We through ye Riches of Divine grace, have been called (as we humbly hope) out of our miserable state of sinfull darkness & death into ye marvelous & blessed light of life & happiness & have been enabled sincerely to give up ourselves unto God Almighty Father, Son and Holy Spirit, and to make this manifest, not only by verbal declarations thereof one to another but also by our holy baptism, and our professed subjection therein to ye Gospell of Christ, so in conformity to his will, we have given up ourselves one to another in him, y[t] we might become a Congregational Church of Jesus Christ, have by solemn Covenant & promises freely and firmly bound ourselves to him, and to each other, to walk together as a holy society, in ye order and fellowship of ye Gospell, y[t] we might glorifie his blessed name, & mutually edifie one another , par-ticularly we have firmly bound ourselves by Covenant promises as followeth |
| First<br>2.Tim 3.15, 16, 17,<br>2.Pet 1 20, 21,<br><br>Eph 2.20,<br><br><br>1<br>[end of sheet 2] | To keep close to ye holy scriptures which we believe to be ye word of God,& diligently to read, hear & study ye same& to ob-serve & obey ym as ye only rule of our Christian faith & practice & we do acknowledge y[t] ye doctrines contained in ye Catechism commonly in use among us, Beginning with this Question<br>(who is ye1[st] & cheifest being] are agreeable to those sacred oracles<br>& accordingly we do embrace ym & promise y[t] we will endeavour to hold & maintain ym in their simplicity and purity |

| | |
|---|---|
| Secondly<br>1Pet 2.5,<br>Act 2. 42, 46.<br>Act 20.7 Joh 4.23,24<br>Jer. 30.31, Phil. 3,3,<br>heb 10.25, 1Cor 14.23,<br>Ps. 122.1,2,<br>Mat 6.33, heb 12.1<br>Eph 5.21, Ps 112.5,<br>1Cor.14.40, heb 12.25<br>Rom 12.1,11<br>1Pet 2.5<br>2Cor 8. 13 14, | To use our faithful endeavours to maintain and pro-<br>mote ye publick & pure worship of God in Christ Jesus<br>as he hath required of all his churches , & for these ends we<br>have promised these 4 things. 1$^{st}$. Religiously to endeavour<br>by proper means if our hearts may be only prepared<br>for ye spirituall part of divine worship, or y$^{t}$ we may worship<br>ye Father in Spirit & in truth. 2$^{nd}$. y$^{t}$ we will use all lawfull<br>en-<br>devours personally to attend upon ye publick worship<br>of God at all such times and places, as shall be agreed upon<br>& appointed by ye Church or ye greater part thereof, & to<br>endeavour so to order all our other affairs, as y$^{t}$ nothing<br>may hinder such our attendance, & y$^{t}$ in dew time &<br>order. 3$^{d}$. y$^{t}$ we will behave ourselves decently & reverently<br>in the house of God, & attend upon every part of his worship<br>in ye most pious Serious & devout manner we can. & 4$^{th}$<br>y$^{t}$ we will contribute according to our abilities respectively<br>towards defraying ye necessary charges thereof. |
| Thirdly<br>1COr 11.2,<br>Col 2.5, Col 1.18<br>Eph 5.23 . . .<br>Isa 33.22, Jam 4.12<br>Heb 13.7, 16, 1 Thes.5(<br>12, 13. 1Cor 16.16 (<br>Eph 5.21, Mat 18.17<br>2Thes. 3.6,<br>1Pet 5.5.<br>[end of sheet 3] | To endeavour to maintain & conform unto ye Discipline<br>& good government of this church, in all things according<br>to ye laws of Christ, our only head and lawgiver, & to submit<br>as is fit in ye Lord, to such as he has, or shall set over us<br>in ruling or guiding ye Church, & to such Authority<br>or power as he has been pleased to give to ye whole Church,<br>or ye major part thereof, for maintaining & preserving<br>due order & regularity in ye affairs of ye house of God.<br>& we have promised to be very Careful not to expose to<br>any others ye private affairs of ye Church |
| Fourthly<br>Eph. 4.1, 2, 3,<br>Col 3.14, 1Pet 1.22,<br>Jam 3.17, 1Cor 13.5<br>1Tim 6.4, 1Cor 13.4,5<br>Pro 14.17,49<br>Rom 14. 15,16,17<br>1Cor 10.32, Phil 2.14<br>2Cor 12.20<br>Pro 16.18, Pro 26.20<br>Eph 4.31<br>1Pet 2.1 | To be very careful and industrious to keep ye unity of ye<br>Spirit in ye bond of peace, & love, & in order thereto. 1$^{st}$<br>to watch carefully against all uncharitable jealousies,<br>or evil surmising in each of ourselves in particular.<br>2$^{d}$ . to beware of and guard against a peevish & pettish tem-<br>per, or of being touchy, or soon angry. 3$^{d}$ . not to grieve<br>or needlessly to provoke any. 4$^{th}$. to avoid those per-<br>pernicious practices of Whispering & backbiting & irregular<br>exposing each others weaknesses. & 5$^{th}$. to forebear all ye<br>evil speaking which tends to create misunderstandings<br>& disturbances. & to beget ill will or hard thoughts &<br>to lessen ye love & esteem of ye members one towards<br>another. |
| Fifthly<br>Ps. 22.6<br>Eph 6.18,19, Jer 5.16 | To pray not only for Zyon in general, but for this<br>Church in particular, & for officers,& for all ye particular<br>members thereof |
| Sixthly<br>Eph 4.16, heb 10.24,25<br>1Thes 4.18 | To Endeavour mutually to Comfort & edifie one<br>another in faith & holiness, by religious instruction<br>& councells as we have abilitys & opportunitys. |

| | |
|---|---|
| Seventhly<br>heb 3.13-19,24,25<br>1Cor 12.25,26<br>Rom 12.15, heb 13.16 | To sympathize with each other in afflictions of each kind & to be ready to relieve & comfort each other, as need may require & as we may have abilitys. |
| Eighthly<br>heb 3.13-10,24,25<br>1Cor 12.26<br>Gal 6.1, Lam 1.20<br>Lev 19.17, heb 8.13<br>2Tim 2.24,25<br>Mat 18.15,16,17 3<br>Rom 15.14<br>2Tim 5.11 to 14<br>[end of sheet 4] | To watch over one another after a Godly sort, & with meek-love and tenderness to reprove & admonish one another in case of any sin y[t] any of us is known to fall into or to be in imminent danger of, & in all private affairs offences to proceed carefully & conscientiously according to those rules which are prescribed in y[t] behalf by our blessed Lord himself in Matt 18. 15, 16, 17. |
| Ninthly<br>Ps 141.5, pro 9. 8,9,<br>Pro 19 25, 25.12<br>1Pet 5.5, Mat 16.17,<br>Jos 27.21 to 29, Jam 5.10<br>Jos 20.30 to ye end<br>2Cor 7.7, Mat 18.15<br>Lk 17.3,4. Eph 4.22<br>Col 3.13, 1Cor 13.6,7, | To hearken with patience & humility to instructions & Counsells. & to accept with all meekness, love & thankfull-ness any reproof or admonition which may be given by ye whole church or by any particular member or members thereof. & to be ready to give just and reasonable satisfaction to any y[t] may be grieved.& to be willing at all times, to receive such satisfaction from at whom we have taken any real or supposed offence, & readily to remitt ye same, & to make it manifest y[t] we have so done by pleasant & friendly carriages & deportment towards ym. |
| Tenthly<br>Tit 2.10'<br>1Pet 2.9, .<br>Rev 1.20, Phil 4.8,<br>1Pet 3.1, gen 18.19<br>Deu 6. 6,7, Jos 24. 18<br>Act 10. 2,30<br>Rom 16.5, Col 4.15<br>Phil 2.4,<br>Eph 6.11<br>Eph 5.21,22,25,33,<br>Eph 6.1, to 9th<br>[end of sheet 5] | To Endeavour to promote ye honour of our Dear Redeemer, ye Credit of his gospel, & ye increase of his Church by a holy, prudent, & exemplary conversation before ym y[t] are without & those of us who have ye Charge & government of families have solemnly obliged ourselves respectively to main-tain ye devout worship of God therein, & to Endeavour to train ym up religiously in ye good ways of ye Lord. & each of us in particular have likewise obliged ourselves to observe & perform with becoming faithfulness all those relative dutys which are incumbent upon us ___________ respectively in our several callings, stations, & relations: |
| Lastly<br>Joh 15.5, 2Cor 3.5,<br>2Cor 12.9, Phil 4.13,<br>1Cor 15.10,11, Joh14.16[?]<br>1Thes 5. 17<br>Col 4.2,3, Jam 5.16<br>Eph 6. 18<br>Gal 6. 18<br>1Cor 1.29,30,<br>Eph 1.6, | As we know y[t] we are not able to do any good thing, as of ourselves So we Covenant & bind ourselves to an humble dependance upon ye all sufficient grace of our Lord Jesus Christ & constantly to seek ye same, each one for himself, & one for another, by fervent prayer & other ____ Christian dutys for ye religious & faithful _______ performances of all these things trusting solely to his merits & divine favour for our ___________ acceptance therein. ____________________ |
| | |

| | |
|---|---|
| c v<br>1 1Joh 3. 1<br>Eph 1. 4,5,<br>Pet 2. 9<br>Rom 8. 21 | Lord I adore, that matchless Grace,<br>Most rich, most soveraigne, & most free<br>That call'd me out from sin & death,<br>That brought me into liberty. |
| Jam 1.18 2 Jam 1.18<br>Ps 27.8<br><br>1 Joh. 5.7 | That Grace, that made me willing to<br>Give up myself, my all to thee; Mark. 10. 25<br>To Father, Son, & Holy Ghost,<br>One only God, but persons three. |
| 3<br>1Joh 3. 18 to<br>ye end of ye Chap [?]<br>5.<br>[end of sheet 6] | 'Tis not in word alone, I shew<br>Profess'd subjection, Lord to thee.<br>But by baptism, Heart & life<br>This manifests sincerity |
| 4.<br>1Cor 8.5<br>Eph 2.19<br>Eph 4.16<br>Matt 5.16 | Lord, I have freely bound myself<br>To thee, & to thy Church in thee<br>that I may walk with them in love<br>thy blessed name to glorifie. |
| 5.<br>Luk 13.6<br><br>Luk 22. 32 | Oh! grant I may not, be a shrub<br>a dead & fruitless branch in thee<br>oh! give me Lord, Triumphant grace:<br>that I thy saints may edifie |
| 6.<br>Joh 5. 29<br>Luk 12. 28<br>Ps 19. 11 | Oh! may I keep, close to thy word First<br>thy word it 'tis, I do believe<br>oh! may I read, hear, study it<br>And in my heart, thy word receive |
| 7.<br>Heb 8.10<br>Ps 119. 66<br>2Cor 1.12 | Help me: to hold & to maintain<br>thy sacred word in purity<br>Inform my judgement, rule my life<br>to keep it in simplicity |
| 8.<br>Heb 10. 25<br>Ps 50. 23<br><br>Joh 5. 23 | Publick worship, may promote Secondly<br>thy namr to praise, &glorifie<br>such as is offered up in Christ<br>Worship as will, thee magnifie |
| 9.<br>Pro 16. 1<br><br>Joh 4. 23,24<br>1Cor 10. 31<br><br>[end of sheet 7] | Prepare my heart to wait on thee<br>in worship sacred & divine<br>oh! may I worship thee in truth<br>oh! may thy Glory be my aim<br>6 |
| 10. | |

| | |
|---|---|
| Heb 10. 1<br>Ps 42. 4<br>1Cor 14. 40<br>Matt 22. 11 | oh! may I use all lawful means<br>on publick worship to attend<br>in time & order my I go<br>Least I should thee, O Lord offend |
| 11.<br>Pro 6. 15<br>Heb 12. 28<br>{<br>John 14. 23 { | When I am there, keep eyes from Sleep<br>& Heart in awe, & reverence<br>then I shall find, sweet comfort Lord<br>Divine quickenings from thy presence |
| 12<br>1Pet 1. 3<br>{<br>1Cor 16. 2 {<br>{ | As thou hast blest, me with good things<br>may I of it, Contribute to.<br>defray ye Charges of ye Church<br>necessary for me to do |
| 13.<br>Eph 1. 22<br>Heb 13. 7,17<br>Matt 18. 17<br>1Tim 3.12,13 [?]<br>1Pet 5. 5 | May I conform to Christ my head Thirdly<br>& such as he ordains to rule<br>& guide ye Church, in peace & love<br>may I submit without Control - y[t] is willingly |
| 14.<br>1Tim 5.18,19[?]<br>1Cor 11. 2<br>Pro 11. 13<br>Ps 78.1,2,3,4 [?]<br><br>to keep me from evil<br>speaking Ps 39.1 | Let me not Church affairs expose<br>but retain it close & private Pro 25.9<br>direct my tongue to speack thy praise<br>not y[t] which tends to make debates |
| 15.<br>Eph 4. 3 }<br><br>Ps [?]<br>Eph 4. 11,12<br>7<br>[end of sheet 8] | Oh! may I keep ye unity Fourthly<br>of ye Spirit, in bonds of peace<br>this I desire, & this I love<br>'tis love that makes all jarrings cease |
| 16.<br>1Cor 13. 4,5 }<br><br>Ps 119.43<br>Ps 119. 165 | Lord, keep me from Cherishing thoughts<br>that evil jealousies surmise<br>Such thoughts as these, I do abhor<br>but thoughts of love & peace, I prize |
| 17.<br>1Tim 6. 4 }<br>Pro 15. 18 | Lord keep me from a pettish or<br>an agry mind which tends to strife<br>oh! let my mind be meek & calm |

| | |
|---|---|
| Jam 3. 17 } | that I to none mat not cause grief |
| 18.<br>1Pet 4. 8<br>Pro 8. 9<br><br>2Cor 12. 20 } | <br>oh! give me love , which covers faults<br>which will prevent backbiting talk<br>& not expose friends weaknesse's<br>such evil practise tends to hurt |
| 19.<br>1Pet 2. 1 }<br>}<br>Pro 25. 11 | oh! keep my tongue, within dew bounds<br>from evil talk which tends to make<br>disturbances, begets ill will.<br>oh! give me wisdom when to speak |
| 20.<br>Ps 122. 6<br>Eph 6. 18<br>Col 4. 3<br>Jam 5. 16 | <br>I pray for Zion thy delight 5.thly Ps 87. 2<br>& all thy Saints where e're they be<br>& also for my minister<br>& members particularly. |
| 21st<br>1Thes 5. 11 }<br>Rom 14.1 Sol 8.6<br>Mal. 3.16<br>8<br>[end of sheet 9] | my fellow members, I delight Sixthly<br>to * chear infaith & holiness. * Comfort<br>tho small my gift, yet strong my Love<br>with ym I love much to Converse |
| 22.<br>1Cor 12.25,26<br>Rom 12. 15<br>Heb 13. 16 }<br>} | <br>I do desire to bear a part 7tly,<br>with them in their great afflictions<br>ready to help & relieve them<br>according to my relation |
| 23.<br>Rom 14.19<br>Heb 3. 13<br>Lev 19. 17<br>Gal 6. 1 | <br>Oh! may I watch, o're ym & they 8thly<br>o're me, & faithfully reprove<br>each other when fallen into sin<br>& that with tenderness & love |
| 24.<br>Mat 18. 15,18,17 }<br>}<br>}<br>} | <br>And if they will not it receive<br>oh! may I carefully proceed<br>according to thy precept Lord<br>as in thy word thou dost prescribe |
| 25.<br>Ps 141.5<br>Pro 25.12<br>Pro 1. 5<br>Pro 9. 8 | <br>oh! may I kindly take reproofe . 9thly<br>& Hearken to wise instruction<br>with love & meekness accept it<br>& Listen to admonition |
| 26. | |

| | |
|---|---|
| }<br>Mat 18.21,22 }<br>}<br>Col 3.12,13,14 } | If any grieve me, I forgive<br>tho: they should often me offend<br>this will I manifest by love<br>& own tm as beloved friends |
| 27.<br>Ps 50.23<br>Tit 2.9<br>Pet 3.1<br>2Cor 1.12 | Lord grant I may thy honour seek 10thly<br>& my redeemer glorifie<br>oh! let my conversation be<br>both holy & exemplary |
| 28.<br>Act 10.2,30<br>Mat 6.6<br>Ps 55.17<br>Rev 1.18 | thy worship Lord I will maintain<br>in private, public, & family<br>morning & evening I will pray<br>to God who lives eternally |
| 29.<br>Joh 15.5<br>2Cor 3.5<br>2Cor 12.9<br>Pro 3.6 | Lord, as of myself I can't do Lastly<br>nothing good in thy most pure sight<br>I do depend on grace divine<br>to aid me in these things aright |
| 30. | Lord assist me always to pray<br>& seek for all sufficient grace<br>which is in Christ my dearest Lord<br>Help me. to run my Christian race |
| 31. | 'twas grace o Lord before all works<br>I humbly hope in Christ chose me<br>Grace caus'd me to believe in time<br>Grace keeps me, grace crowns in glory |
| | Finis |
| [end of sheet 10] | Nov ye 16th 1728<br><br>J. H. |
| 1Thes. 5. 17<br><br>Eph 14.14.<br>Col 1.19. Col 2. 9.<br>Heb 12. 1. | |
| | |

| c v<br>Eph 1. 4. 2Tim 1. 9 Jer.31. 3.<br>Habb. 1. 12.<br>John 1. 12, Rom 8. 30. 1Pet 1.<br>5. 1Thess. 2. 13.<br>Rev 5 - 9 10 11 12 13 &c<br>____________________________<br><br>[end of sheet 11] | |
|---|---|

[sheet 12 has two short lines of very faint text in the top right hand corner which may read:

Joh 9.30th chap 10
Joh 14.5 2Cor 8.5

only the 2Cor. text is legible]

# Appendix C.
# Tomkins Family Tree

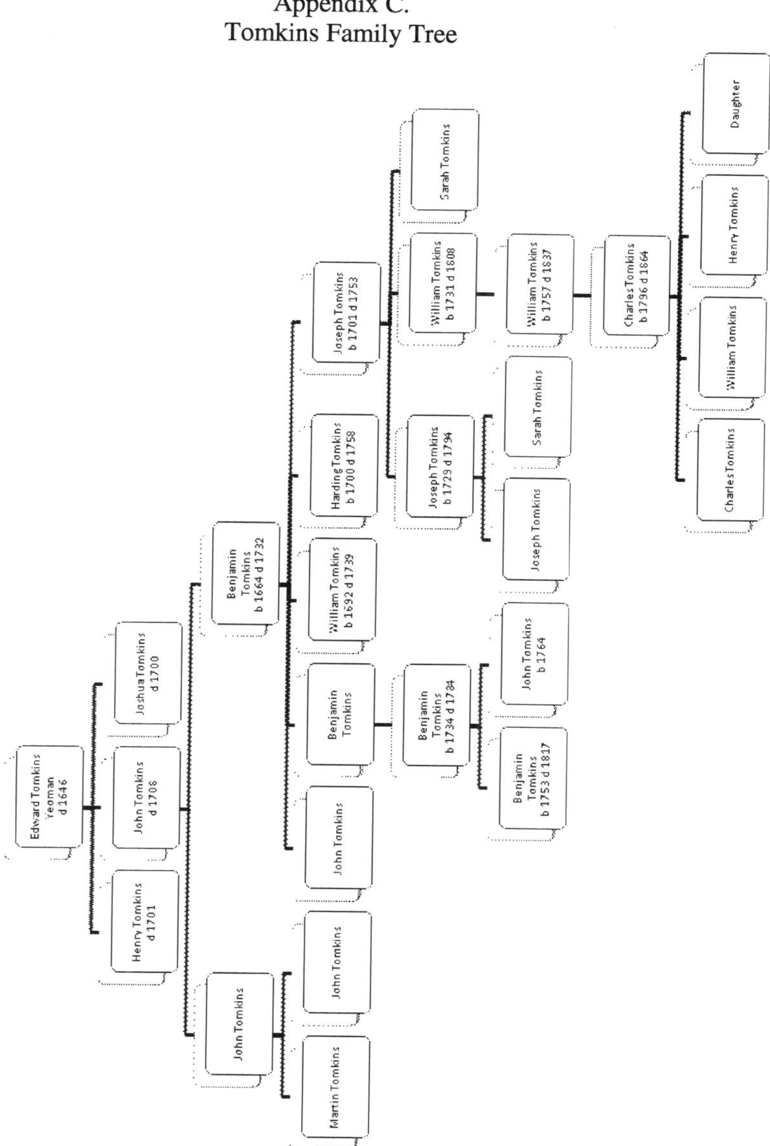

## Appendix D

The Tomkins' and Buswell's Charities.

For over three hundred years the Abingdon Baptist Church has provided trustees to administer the following trusts and endowments:

1. The Almshouse Trust. Established by the Will of Benjamin Tomkins the Elder in 1731, this gave property and money for the building of almshouses in Ock Street and for the care of "four old men and four old women" chosen by the Trustees from the poor of the town. Benjamin's grandson, also Benjamin, added to this in his Will dated 1751 to provide clothing for the inhabitants - "cloth of light Brown color, cuffed with White Plush exactly to match the patterns herein left". They were to receive a new gown each year. In 1896 Mr. William Finch Smith added to this Trust and donations to the Trust were made by various other persons including bequests from Mr. G. Salisbury and Miss I.M. Sedgefield. Responsibility for the administration of this Trust was transferred by the Baptist Trustees to the Governors of Christ's Hospital in 1986, who then undertook a major refurbishment programme of the properties, completed in 1989.

2. The Bread Charity. Established by the Will of Benjamin Tomkins in 1731 to provide £20 yearly for distribution among "the common poor people of Abingdon".

3. Poor Dissenters of Abingdon and Poor Baptist Ministers. This was also established by the Will of Benjamin Tomkins the Elder in 1731 confirming an arrangement made in 1725 whereby a sum of £1000 was entrusted to Wilm. Fuller (minister), Edward Robarts and Benjamin Tomkins (son of Benjamin the Elder) the interest to be used for poor Abingdon dissenters and poor Baptist ministers generally.

4. Charity for Baptist Churches. Established by the Will of D. Joseph Tomkins in 1753 for "the support of the Baptist Church in Abingdon or any other Baptist Church he should think proper to pay the same to". Further monies were left for the Baptist Churches of Stratton, Wilts, and Newbury, Berks.

5. Buswell's Charities. Established by the Will of William Buswell in 1829. Various endowments were made for the education

of poor children, "without distinction of sex", in Abingdon, Cirencester, Gloucester and Oxford. Grants were also available for poor people of Abingdon, for poor Baptist ministers and for village schools in Berkshire.

Since 1989 the Trustees, under the guidance of their Chairman, Gilbert Payne, and with the approval of the Charity Commissioners, have amalgamated and simplified these Charities and their many sub-clauses, enabling more efficient distribution of the accumulated interest to people in need, some of whom are Baptist ministers, to Baptist churches, and to individual young people and schools for educational purposes.

For further information see Denise Mulvey, *A Financial History of the Tomkins' and Buswell's Charities, 1986 to 2008.* This, with other archive material of the Charities, can be sourced in the Angus Library, Oxford.

Appendix E.

**Letter from Mr. Roland Caudwell to the Revd. Cox c. 1970's.**

OX14 2DX

52 Thesiger Road
Abingdon
Berks [deleted]
Oxfordshire

Dear Mr. Cox,

Many thanks for your letter, & as requested I saw Mr. Carslaw, & no doubt you have received the notice for the 7th which I hope you will find convenient. I will have a word with Mr. Cullen to see if travelling expenses can be met, out of the funds.
I have tried to answer your queries about the Primitive Methodist cause based on Wallingford. I believe that Church is now closed but am not sure. I will give you on the back a list of the Chapels in the Circuit, but the Open Air Preaching Stations at one time numbered 70. Village Greens & Trees & Barns.

[page 2]
Wallingford Circuit.
Cholsey
Park Corner (near Nettlebed)
Blewbury
South Moreton
East Hagbourne
Didcot (there was sometimes an Assistant Minister there)
Long Wittenham
Milton
Chilton
Brightwell.
Job Hall (a grocer) built an extension to his cottage to form a Chapel. I preached there many times. (Chilton)
Charles Hall of Blewbury (Grocer) gave a site in his Orchard for the Chapel there.
Job Hall had a pony and cart for business but refused to use the pony on Sunday & would walk to Wallingford to preach, of course he knew all the field paths. I was on the Primitive Plan & the Wantage Wesleyan Plan for many years & then on the Trinity (Abingdon) Plan.

[page3]
With regard to the East Ilsley Sheep Market these were held fortnightly, but I think were suspended in Dec. & January. My Great Uncle Trewin was a Farmer & Sheep Dealer & lived at Goring Heath. My Father lived there & helped him for several years as a young man, & he told me that Uncle always went to the Weyhill Sheep Fairs on Salisbury Plain, & would buy a flock of sheep & tell his Drover to meet him at Ilsley perhaps in a fortnight or three weeks, the Drover knew all the green drove roads along the plain to Hackpen Hill then the Ridgeway to Ilsley. They knew where the dew ponds were & planned to get to one at night fall, the sheep would rest there & the man slept in his rough coat, his dogs saw to it that the sheep did not wander.

[page 4]
The sheep fed on the downs as they slowly went along & when they got there Uncle was waiting, he knew the seasons for buying & selling profitably. The sheep were not sold by Auction but by dealing between the Dealer & the Farmer who needed sheep.
Henry Wilson who I knew quite well lived at Cheveley & did the same.
John Lay of Harwell brother to Will Lay at Fyfield was another man who dealt extensively in sheep.
I hope this is the information you wanted.
I hope you are now quite fit & I shall be pleased to see you on Oct 7th.

Yours sincerely
Roland Caudwell

# Appendix F.

## Preaching Plan for Abingdon Fellowship of Baptist Churches

Mr Orland

ABINGDON FELLOWSHIP OF BAPTIST CHURCHES

Minister Rev. G.Relfe

| | JANUARY | | | | | FEBRUARY | | | | MARCH | | | |
|---|---|---|---|---|---|---|---|---|---|---|---|---|---|
| | 3 | 10 | 17 | 24 | 31 | 7 | 14 | 21 | 28 | 7 | 14 | 21 | 28 |
| **ABINGDON** | | | | | | | | | | | | | |
| Morning 11.0 a.m. | 6 | 1 | 1 | 1 | 5 | 1 | 1 | D | 1 | 6 | 1 | 1 | 1 |
| Evening 6.30 p.m. | 1C | 2 | 1 | 2 | 1 | 3C | 1 | 1 | 18 | 1C | 7 | 2 | 1 |
| **COTHILL** | | | | | | | | | | | | | |
| Evening 6.0 p.m. | 4 | 5 | 7C | 3 | 2 | 7 | 9 | 4C | 5 | 3 | 11 | 1C | 9 |
| **FYFIELD** | | | | | | | | | | | | | |
| Morning 11.0 a.m. | 12 | 6 | 3 | 19 | 4 | 5 | 3 | 1 | 2 | 12 | 19 | 7 | 5 |
| Evening 6.0 p.m. | 5 | 1C | 5 | 9 | 3 | 9 | 7C | 5 | 8 | 5 | 1C | 9 | 3 |
| **MARCHAM** | | | | | | | | | | | | | |
| Morning 11.0 a.m. | 1C | 19 | 2 | 10 | 6 | 12 | 20 | 10 | 3 | 1C | 6 | 19 | 20 |
| Evening 6.30 p.m. | 3 | 13 | 9 | 5 | 7 | 1C | 19 | 9 | 13 | 7 | 3 | 5 | 2 |
| **DRAYTON** | | | | | | | | | | | | | |
| Evening 6.15 p.m. | 17 | 10 | 20 | 1C | 19 | 17 | S | 2 | 1C | 17 | 5 | 10 | 6 |

**PREACHERS**

1. Rev. Relfe
2. Mrs. Relfe
3. Mr. Caudwell
4. Mr. Edgington
5. Mr. Gosling
6. Mr. Orland
7. Mr. Bowden
8. Mrs. Gosling
9. Mr. Keay
10. Miss Rouse
11. Miss Kinchin
12. Mr. Clack
13. Miss Bailey
14. Mr. Hooke
15. Mr. Hughes
16. Mr. Redhead
17. Miss Whitehead
18. Oxford L. P.
19. Mr. Clifton
20. Mr. Pressler

C. Communion
S. Supply
D. Mr. Dangerfield

Any Preacher unable to fulfil his appointment kindly inform Mr.A.Gosling 9 North Street, Marcham as soon as possible.

Appendix G.

## Living Waves

Radio Abingdon Alive, a community radio station, which broadcast for 15 hours a day, from 7-22 May, 1994, was manned entirely by volunteers from the Churches in Abingdon.

A perfect morning greeted me
That Sunday as I drove the car
Across the country to the motorway.
And quiet Abingdon stood soaked in soothing sun,
Asleep, but shielded and umbrella'd by the waves
Transmitted from a tall church spire
Then mingling with the glorious flood that bathed
And kissed the fields.
Thus borne on silent rays, the silent message spread,
And probed in every corner, every crevice fed.

My radio's listening ear lapped up
The light-fast waves that made them sound
Of morning worship from the Baptist Church.
And as I crossed the Thames and left the stone-hewn town
The singing lifted me, for though no engineer
Of sound had tweaked it with his art,
Unpolished praises spoke of real folk
With real faith.
Although I heard no bright or strident chorus strive,
This muted morning hymn brought Abingdon alive.

At sixty, down the Causeway, four
Young people seemed to pull me back.
Plucked from the band where they had sung and played
They spoke, some nervous (one from notes) of altered ways.
I thought how low-slung sunlight makes the green grass glow
Or mustard-dusted fields
Infect the atmosphere with shimmering gold
Of new-sprung life,
For each of them had picked today to be baptised

*A Sweet And Hopeful People*

And each one told how Jesus Christ had changed their lives.

Enthralled, I knew the signal's strength
Would fall and fade with my fast flight
But as I heard each person's tale unfold
I willed it not to vanish as the fields flashed by
With distant Didcot's curving chimneys blurting steam.
In road-cleft Clifton Hampden still
It stirred the circuits, stayed as I went past
A car-boot sale.
Though far from home the waves with undiminished might
Were still advancing, blended with the beauteous light.

It now became a game to see
How far the light-enhancing light
Would shoot before its swooping circle sank.
I swung round roads and crossed a roundabout but still
Heard ringing praises and their love-songs to their God
And then the minister explained
The special meaning of the love-lined hymn
That they had sung.
His voice was calm like starlit waters and it brought
The sense of Christ within him guiding every thought.

At last, the stabbing static struck
The signal south of Stadhampton.
The wafted waves no longer rolled along
But crashed and fractured on the hedges and the trees.
Yet intermittently the voice returned serene;
Rebuked the storm and calmed the air
Repeatedly until the final phrase
At Little Milton.
Briefly I mourned its death, but then discerned a tower;
Another church arose and shone with sun-flung power.

# General Index

This index does not contain all the names of Baptists listed in the Appendices.

## A



## B

## C

# D



# E

## F



## G



## H

## M



## N



## O



## P

## Q



## R



## S

# T

## U



## V



## W

## Y



## Z